Faithful Volunteers

Faithful Volunteers

THE HISTORY OF RELIGION IN
TENNESSEE

Stephen Mansfield
and George Grant

CUMBERLAND HOUSE
NASHVILLE, TENNESSEE

Published by Cumberland House Publishing, Inc., 2200 Abbott Martin
Road, Suite 102, Nashville, Tennessee, 37215.

Distributed to the trade by Andrews & McMeel, 4520 Main Street, Kansas
City, Missouri, 64111.

Scripture quotations noted NKJV are taken from the NEW KING JAMES
version. Copyright © 1979, 1980, 1982 by Thomas Nelson, Inc. Used by
permission. All rights reserved.

Scriptures noted NIV are from The Holy Bible: NEW INTERNATIONAL
VERSION. Copyright © by the New York International Bible Society.
Used by permission of Zondervan Bible Publishers.

Jacket and interior design by Harriet Bateman.

Library of Congress Cataloging-in-Publication Data

Mansfield, Stephen.
        Faithful volunteers : the history of religion in Tenneessee /
Stephen Mansfield and George Grant.
        p cm.
        Includes bibliographical references and index.
        ISBN 1-888952-14-8 (pbk. : alk. paper) 978-1-684423-98-9
        1. Tennessee—Church history. 2. Tennessee—Religion.
3. Tenneessee—History. I. Grant, George, 1954- . II. Title.
BR555.T2M36 1997
200'.9768—dc21   97-2287
                                                                              CIP

1 2 3 4 5 6 7—02 03 01 00 99 98 97

To

Governor Don Sundquist,

Pastor Don Finto,

and

to the faithful volunteers

who have carried the banner of faith

all across the ages

Contents

$\mathcal{I}$llustrations[1]

$\mathscr{A}$cknowledgments

Ultimately a man is not judged by what he has done or what he has written but who he has influenced—and who has influenced him.

Andrew Nelson Lytle

$\mathscr{T}$o enumerate all those who have helped us in the development and execution of this project would be as prodigious a task as taking the census of the tribes of Israel. Nevertheless, our gratitude for the faithful labors of friends and colleagues demands that we make the attempt.

Stephen Mansfield would like to thank:

Jackie Lusk for her covenant faithfulness, her gifts, and her vision for Nashville and the state of Tennessee; Elizabeth DeBeasi for the research skills and servant heart that made much of this book possible; Phil Bennett for his craziness, his friendship, and for "surf and turfs" past and future; Dawn Ruff for listening, for standing watch, and for Caitlin and Hannah; George Grant for teaching me what history is and showing me how to write it; Alice S. Creighton at the Nimitz Library of the U.S. Naval Academy; Mary Glenn Hearne at the Nashville Room of the Nashville Public Library; Don Finto, Bill Ruff, Tim Jones, David Hooper, Joseph DeBeasi, Sandra Elkins, Jim Davis, Wanda King, Mick Antanaitis, Charlie Newman, Rob McDonald, Brad Watson, Brian Wade, and Casey Baluss for their many gifts and sacrifices; and, of course, my beloved wife and children for their forbearance and selfless love.

George Grant would like to thank:

Ron and Julia Pitkin at Cumberland House for their vision and support for this project from the moment it was first suggested; David Drye, Joe Costello, and Dean Stein for their commitment to a wise remembrance of the past; Scott Roley, Chris Williamson, Paige Overton, Damon Cathey, Terry Hancock, Box

Hawkins, Ruth Johnson, and Tricia Arnold for their commitment to substantial cross-cultural urban ministry here in Tennessee; Jim and Gwen Smith, Jerry and Cindy Walton, Bill and Robin Amos, Tom and Sylvia Singleton, Tom and Jody Clark, Bill and Sharon Taylor, Darrow and Marilyn Miller, Jeff and Karla Kessler, Ron and Jean Nash, Rich and Liz Mays, Steve and Marijean Green, and Steve and Annie Chapman for their constant encouragement and support for the King's Meadow Study Center; Dale and Ann Smith, Stephen and Trish Mansfield, Steve and Wendy Wilkins, Gene and Susan Hunt, Tom and Yo Clark, and David and Diane Vaughan for their pastoral watchcare; the always helpful librarians at the University of Tennessee in Knoxville, Middle Tennessee State University in Murfreesboro, and Covenant College in Chattanooga for their time, energy, and bibliographic expertise; the staffs of my favorite antiquarian haunts—Elder's Books in Nashville and Argosy Books in New York—for their enthusiastic encouragement and professional support; and, of course, my own wife and children for their long-suffering, which continues to be an inexplicable marvel of God's grace and providence in my life.

Together we gratefully acknowledge the mentoring encouragement of Don Finto and the inspiring leadership of Governor Don Sundquist. And last, but by no means least, we are thankful for the members of the numerous historical committees, community associations, study groups, and anniversary commissions charged with celebrating Tennessee's bicentennial with what has turned out to be something substantially more than just a cursory nod to our state's men and women of faith. It has been our distinct privilege to serve at your side and to share in your labors.

To these faithful volunteers—and to all those who preceded them and all those who are sure to follow them—we dedicate this glancing portrait:

> Grace to you and peace from God our Father and the Lord Jesus Christ. I thank my God upon every remembrance of you, always in every prayer of mine making request for you all with joy, for your fellowship in the Gospel from the first day until now, being confident of this very thing, that He who has begun a good work in you will complete it until the day of Jesus Christ.[1]

$\mathscr{I}$ntroduction

*If you really want to hear a good story surely you ought to listen to
the tale the history of faith has to tell.*

John Crowe Ransom

$\mathscr{H}$istory. Henry Ford called it "bunk."[1] Augustine Birrell called
it "a dust heap,"[2] Guy de Maupassant dubbed it "that excitable
and lying old lady,"[3] and even Shakespeare wrote "it is a tale told
by an idiot, full of sound and fury, signifying nothing."[4]

Not surprisingly, many Americans share these opinions of
history. They not only live in a nation and at a time when things
shiny and new are prized far above things old and timeworn, but
the tortures they endured in history classes have convinced them
that the past is both boring and meaningless. History is nothing
but dates and dead people, they believe; the droning, monotonous
succession of the "Age of This" and the "Period of That." Sound
and fury, signifying nothing.

This situation rightly has historians and educators up in
arms. Studies show that most of the history Americans know, they
learned from dubious television miniseries and Hollywood block-
busters. Not surprisingly, newspapers are filled with reports of
high school students who cannot identify our current national
leaders, much less those of the distant past, and thus are unable to
construct even the most rudimentary chronology of their great historical legacy. College graduates seem to fare little better—their
absurd *faux pas* are the brunt of many a joke. But the situation is
hardly humorous. If Karl Marx was right when he said that "a people without a heritage are easily persuaded,"[5] then this appalling
national incognizance of the past helps explain the ever-shifting
sands of American fashion and fancy on most every subject.

Yet to say that Americans are ignorant of the past is not to say
they aren't interested. In fact, to the extent they hate the academic
variety of history they clearly love the kind of history that stirs the

imagination and grips the heart. Works of history regularly top the best-seller lists. Historical fiction is at an all-time high in popularity. Movies, plays, and television specials dealing with historic periods and themes command huge audiences. In addition, Americans flock by the hundreds of thousands to the nation's battlefields, living history sites, history theme parks, museums, and even amusement parks where lifelike robots portray popular heroes from the past. Combine this with an explosion of interest in local history, a nearly national obsession with genealogy, and an almost extravagant zeal for commemorating the nation's historic events and anniversaries, and it becomes obvious that Americans are seeking a connection to the past through popular history that they never found in the classroom version.

One wonders what this says about how history is taught. If Americans are repulsed by the standard textbook version of history yet feel so passionately about a past they can "walk in" and make their own, then we have to ask what it is about our classroom presentation of the past that makes it such an uninspiring caricature of the original.

The answer may be one of philosophy rather than technique. The average history course interprets history solely as a road leading to the present. In this light, what is important about the past is its contribution to the present. The focus is therefore upon mass movements, the settling of land, technology, the evolution of political ideas, innovations of every kind, and how the resolution of past conflicts shaped the future. Only what has contributed to the present is deemed important because the present is, in this view, the goal of history.

The fact is that this modern ideological approach normally fails to ask the critical question, "Why?" Why did men live as they did? Why did they take such risks and make such huge sacrifices? What moved them to greatness, stoked their inner fire, and incited an energy beyond their own to course through them? Surely these are questions that should be explored in the classroom. Surely these very human issues of heart and mind and soul ought to be addressed. Surely these are the matters of which history is actually made. Surely the importance of religion in the documentary account of any people or culture ought to be more than a little obvious.

Theologian Paul Tillich has suggested that religion should not be defined solely in the formal sense—in terms of buildings or priesthoods or creeds or ceremonies. Religion should also be defined as "ultimate concern," as that for which a man is willing to die, that which consumes his energy, his money, his thought life, and his passion.[6] However wrong he may have been in so much of the rest of his theology, surely Tillich was right in this. Using his rather commonsense definition, it is not hard to see how essential religion—the "ultimate concerns" of mankind—must be to a study of the past. Men act because of what they believe. They have certain ideas about God or eternity or morals or themselves, and they live their lives and build their civilizations accordingly. To understand men of any age means understanding the passionately held beliefs, the "ultimate concerns," that gripped their hearts. To ignore their religious faith and focus on their actions alone is to make of them cardboard cutouts rather than the three-dimensional human beings they really were.

This approach has been a particularly sticky problem in the teaching of American history. In our national preoccupation with the separation of church and state we have in fact achieved a separation of religion from reality and a resultant exorcising of religion as a motive force in history. Students learn today that men dared to sail to America for mere material gain, that those early pioneers were simply fleeing from hardship and persecution at home, that they celebrated the first Thanksgiving to give thanks to their Indian friends, and that what religion was espoused by them, and by their progeny in the succeeding centuries, was little more than a cynical camouflage for the evils of slavery, nationalism, and imperialism.

The modern history teacher, confident that religion is merely the opiate of the people, does his students the "favor" of stripping the "religious veneer" off the past so they can see "what really happened." But of course, in so doing he removes many of the most important lessons the past has to teach.

The greatest tragedy of this thoroughly modern approach is that we produce heartless, insubstantial, and hollow men—or, in the telling phrase of C. S. Lewis, "men without chests." Between the seat of reason—the head—and the seat of drive and appetite—the stomach—is the chest, where Lewis believes we find faith, compassion, and character. To teach a history concerned with intellect and drive alone is to paint a past populated by men without chests: single-dimensional men without faith or feeling. The result is nothing short of disastrous. Thus, as Lewis writes: "We make men without chests and expect of them virtue and enterprise. We laugh at honor and are shocked to find traitors in our midst. We castrate and bid the geldings be fruitful."[7]

When we paint a past of faithless men, why in heaven's name are we shocked to find a faithless generation on the rise? An essential ingredient in the remedy for our current cultural malaise must therefore be to begin to understand the world of the past in terms of the religious faith that created it, to insist that the most important part of any age was that body of dearly loved truths for which men lived and gave their all.

How very important this perspective is for the study of Tennessee history, for Tennessee past and present is as much about religious faith as anything else. Tennessee is certainly not the best educated, most populous, most productive, or most prosperous of American states. It is not the largest exporter, the most *avant garde* trendsetter, or the mightiest political force. But as a religious influence Tennessee is today, and has been throughout its history, virtually unrivaled among American states. Tennessee's spiritual leaders, denominations, religious publications, revivals, movements, music, and religious industries have helped to define religion in America and the course of Christianity worldwide in an unprecedented fashion. The story of Tennessee, as much as it is about Indians and longhunters and dogtrot cabins and bitter battles and taming the wilderness and the rise of great cities, is also about the influence of the dynamic religious faith that empowered men to work and dream and live as they did.

To tell the story of religion in Tennessee does not require a retelling of the entire history of the state. That story has already been told and told well. Instead, what is needed is an overview of the religious characteristics of Tennessee history that help explain the already familiar story. We know, for example, that Cherokee Indians occupied the eastern part of the state before white men settled there. But do we know what these Indians believed, what changed about their beliefs through contact with the white man, and how it occurred that the Cherokee Nation forced to move west of the Mississippi River in the 1830s considered itself a "Christian nation"? We know the famous story of the State of Franklin, but do we know why its Constitution required that anyone who held public office had to believe in God, the truth of the Protestant religion, and the divine authority of both the Old and New Testaments?

This small volume is a portrait of how faith has shaped our state and how it will shape our future. Its eight chapters are surveys, interspersed with various sidebars, biographical notes, illustrations, maps, and highlights, and thus are not intended to exhaust the subject. Indeed, that would be nigh unto impossible. But they are intended to point the way toward a new perspective of our state—or rather, to revive an old perspective, long neglected.

To know the "what" of Tennessee history without knowing the "why," without understanding the beliefs that made men act as they did, is to leave us with an uninspired and potentially uninspiring heritage. It might tempt us to believe that we have been a state of nearsighted doers but not a state of believers and holy dreamers. Nothing could be further from the truth. And nothing could leave us less prepared for the destiny we are called to forge.

Faithful Volunteers

1
$\mathscr{T}$he $\mathscr{T}$ribes of $\mathscr{T}$ennessee

The native peoples who settled along the banks of the wild Tennessee
River left a mark upon the land—a spiritual mark that yet endures.
                                          Thomas Whitehall Jackson

$\mathcal{O}$f all who have lived in Tennessee, the people who were perhaps the most connected to the land—to its mystery and power—
were the Indians who lived here when the first European pioneers
began to settle.[1] At that time, there were primarily three tribes in
Tennessee. In the east were the Cherokee, who occupied not only
what they called *tanisi* but also a region spanning from the middle
of Kentucky to the western portions of North and South Carolina
and the northern parts of Georgia. Middle Tennessee was largely
occupied by the Shawnee, who controlled a territory that included
much of Kentucky, southern Illinois, southern Indiana, and Ohio.
And West Tennessee, from the Tennessee River to the Mississippi,
was part of a Chickasaw domain that also included portions of
Kentucky, Mississippi, and Alabama.

Though European settlers who first encountered these tribes
often wondered if they had any religion at all, the truth is that the
Indians of Tennessee were indeed a people of faith, a people who
had for centuries lived in a visible world they uniquely understood in terms of the invisible. Their beliefs, too, have a place in the
story of religion in Tennessee, for these tribes were Tennessee's
"host people," and what they believed and how they were treated
laid a kind of unseen foundation for the spiritual life of the state.
The fact is that many early whites found the Indian religions so
developed they wondered if the Indians were the lost tribes of

1

Israel. James Adair, in his *History of the American Indians*, is probably best known for this belief, but he was hardly alone—Bartolomé de Las Casas, who sailed with Columbus, held this view, as did William Penn, Roger Williams, Cotton Mather, and John Eliot.

*T*HE *C*HEROKEE

It is interesting that the word *Cherokee* has no meaning in the Cherokee language. Instead, the Cherokee called themselves the *ani yunwiya*, the "Real People," and in the same way that their true name is largely unknown today, the history of these fascinating people—their relatively rapid acceptance of white culture, the principles of their nation, and their tragic removal from the land—is also an unfamiliar tale to most Americans. This is unfortunate, for the story of the Real People is one of the most moving and revealing in all of Tennessee history.

They had lived in their land, said one of their chiefs, since "time out of mind," in some sixty towns and villages along the streams of the southern Appalachians.[2] Though their exact origins are shrouded in myth and mystery, we do know that the Real People called the Delaware tribe "grandfather," as did many other eastern tribes, and their language was a branch of the Iroquois family. Beyond this, little is known, and the Real People themselves, who were "accustomed to look forward to new things rather than to dwell upon the past," provided no real insight.[3]

Each village of the Real People and the nation itself were governed by two chiefs: a "war chief," who tended to matters of battle, and a "peace chief," who was responsible for the civil affairs of the people. The people themselves were divided among seven fiercely loyal clans: the Wolf, Deer, Bird, Paint, Blue, *kituwah*, and Long Hair People. And every town, chief, and clan of the Real People looked to one site as the most important and sacred place in their nation: *chota*, on the banks of the Little Tennessee. As Donald Davidson wrote in his masterful *The Tennessee*, "*chota* was a kind of city of refuge," not unlike the biblical judicial sanctuar-

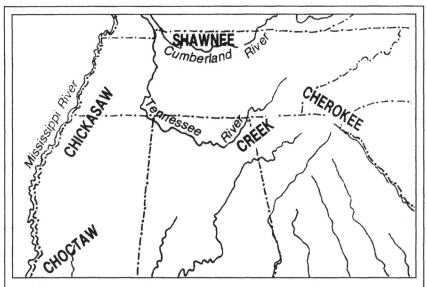

1.1 *Territory of the Indian Nations.* The Cherokee people originally controlled far and away the largest amount of territory in Tennessee. Their lands included most of the Cumberland Plateau, as well as much of the Appalachian Mountain region. The Shawnee, Creek, and Choctaw peoples had only small holdings in the state, while the Chickasaw people inhabited a portion of the southwest corner of the state.

ies, in that it furnished asylum for a manslayer or prisoner of war. No blood could be shed within its bounds. It was their "old beloved town," the place where they met to negotiate and to make treaties."[4]

Judging from the journals and letters of their earliest white visitors, the Real People were a physically impressive tribe. William Fyffe, a plantation owner from Charles Town, wrote that they were:

> Much of the color of the orange that's painted for a sign to your toy shops especially after its a little dirtied black. Have straight limbs and are generally taller than whites. They are a hardy people though their hardiness consists rather in bearing much exercise than labor. The men have no hair on their chin or lips and both sexes shave it off their privities.[5]

Lieutenant Henry Timberlake wrote that the men were:

> of middle stature, of an olive color, though generally painted, and
> their skins stained with gunpowder pricked into it in very pretty
> figures. The hair of their head is shaved . . . except a patch on the
> hinder part of the head, about twice the bigness of a crownpiece.[6]

They wore:

> a silver breastplate, and bracelets on their arms and wrists of the
> same metal, a bit of cloth over their private parts, a shirt of English
> make, a sort of cloth-boots, and moccasins, ornamented with por-
> cupine-quills; a large mantle or matchcoat thrown over all com-
> pletes their dress at home.[7]

William Bartram, a Philadelphia botanist, was similarly
impressed with the look of the women among the Real People:

> The dress of the females is somewhat different from that of the men;
> their flap or petticoat, is made after a different manner, is larger and
> longer, reaching almost to the middle of the leg, and is put on dif-
> ferently; they have no shirt or shift but a little short waistcoat, usu-
> ally made of calico, printed linen, or fine cloth decorated with lace,
> beads etc. They never wear boots or stockings, but their buskins
> reach to the middle of the leg. They never cut their hair, but plait it
> in wreathes, which is turned up, and fastened on the crown, with a
> silver broach, forming a wreathed top-knot.[8]

Beyond physical appearance, though, what often endeared
the Real People to early white visitors was their deeply poetic soul
and the way it flowed through a beautifully expressive language.
When a woman was in love with a man, she said that he "walks in
my soul." Without him, she would not just be lonely, but she had
uhi'sodi, a "supernatural melancholy," or a "desperate soul yearning." When someone told false tales he was a "singing bird," but
those who would not learn from others were *tsundige'wi*, "closed
anuses." A grandmother was called, in tones of great honor, *ulisi*,
"she carries me on her back." A greatly revered woman, one who
was permitted to speak in council about important matters and
who knew the spiritual lore of the tribe, was called *gighau*,

"beloved woman." The Real People prayed every day to be *u'da'nuh't*, a "kind person," but tried not to be a *u'ne'go'tso'duh*, a "person with blackness of soul."[9]

This is not to say, though, that the Real People were a nation of peaceful poets. Without doubt, war was their highest and most cherished pursuit, made all the more necessary by the belief that a murdered man could not go to the "darkland," the land of the departed dead, until his clan had avenged him. As William Fyffe wrote:

> War is their principal study and their greatest ambition is to distinguish themselves by military actions. . . . Even the old men who are past the trade age themselves use every method to stir up a martial ardor in the youth. Their young men are not regarded until they kill an enemy or take a prisoner. Those houses in which there is the greatest number of scalps are most honored. A scalp is as great a trophy among them as a pair of colors among us.[10]

When whites once asked the Real People not to make war on the neighboring Tuscarora tribe, the chief replied, "We cannot live without war. Should we make peace with the Tuscaroras, we must immediately look out for some other nation with whom we can be engaged in our beloved occupation." To prepare champions for their "beloved occupation," youths were forced to watch the torture of prisoners, to endure pain and hunger without complaint, and to recite from memory the military feats of their fathers. Every warrior was an orator who inspired the community with tales of greatness in battle and even the women participated, especially when there was an unfortunate prisoner to torture to death. Even the tribe's favorite game, a distant precursor to lacrosse, was called *anet'sa*, the "little brother of war."[11]

Yet to the same extent that the Real People were poetic in expression and vicious in war, so they were unorthodox in spiritual matters. Other tribes held to long-cherished religious traditions. Their myths were complex, their ceremonies intricate. By comparison, the Real People were progressives, ever striving for the new and the simple in spiritual matters, ever borrowing from the religions of other tribes rather than holding on to their own time-honored ways. Davidson says that while other tribes accumulated, the Real People "dropped off and simplified." They "forgot their own traditions and history with a facility that seems amazing in a primitive people."[12] It was not uncommon for a tribal storyteller to conclude a stirring tale from the history of the Real People by flatly stating, "But no one remembers who did that."

Perhaps the reason for this is that the Real People had long before rebelled against their priests. Apparently they had once had a priestly class called the *nicotani*, but these became domineering and demanding. Once when the young men were off to war, the *nicotani* violated their wives. When the warriors returned, they slaughtered all of the *nicotani*. From that day on, spiritual leadership amongst the Real People was provided by *adawehi*, the "conjurers," and *ghigau*, the "beloved women," who knew the tribal traditions and the secrets of healing. Though the practical lore survived, the history and great legends often suffered loss.[13]

What history and lore remained were transmitted orally from generation to generation in the form of myths and stories. A mother began such a story with, "When I was a girl, this is what the old women told me they had heard when they were girls," thereby passing the tribal lore to her children. Many of these wonderfully expressive myths have passed into modern American life through the "Uncle Remus" stories of Joel Chandler Harris—though the tales are retold in the idiom and through the characters of the southern plantation experience.[14] Everything the Real People needed to know—from their spiritual beliefs to their code of conduct to their store of knowledge about healing—were contained in these intriguing tales.

The Real People believed that at one time all was water. There were animals living then but only in *galun'lati*, the "world above." The animals wondered what was below the water and sent a water beetle to find out. The beetle searched in every direction but when it could find no firm surface it dived to the bottom and pulled up some soft mud. This mud began to grow and eventually became earth, which later was fastened to the sky with four cords. Typical of vital omissions in the myths of the Real People, no one remembers who fastened the earth to the sky.[15]

The animals in the world above were eager to go down to the earth and sent out *luuidi*, the "great buzzard" to see if it was safe. When he had flown over the entire earth, the great buzzard tired and came to rest in what became the land of the Real People. The mighty flapping wings of the great buzzard so beat upon the still-soft mud of the earth that the familiar mountains and valleys of the Smokies were created. Soon afterward, the sun was set in the sky, but those who did it placed it too low and the shell of the red crawfish was baked to a bright hue. The sun was raised again and again until it was seven handbreadths high and just under the sky arch.[16]

Fire was placed on earth when *ani hyuntikwalaski*, the "roaring thunders," sent lightning and put fire in the base of a hollow sycamore tree that grew on an island. The animals knew about the fire because they could see the smoke spiraling from the hollow tree, but they could not reach it. They sent the raven to get the fire, but he failed and was scorched black in the attempt. They sent the screech owl, the hoot owl, the little blacksnake, and the great blacksnake, but all failed. Finally, *tutsi*, the "water spider," carried fire for the animals in the bowl she carries on her back. The Real People believed it was the continuation of this same fire that burned in the council house of every town and village as the *galunkw'ti'yu*, the "sacred fire."[17]

Similar myths explained most everything in the world of the Real People: why the animals roamed free, why the buzzard was bald, why the deer's teeth are blunt, the origin of disease and medicine, what the stars really are, how berries came into existence, the origin of the Milky Way, how the Real People got tobacco, where corn came from, and hundreds of other great natural mysteries. The Real People were essentially animists, believing that there is a spirit—a force—living within everything, animate and inanimate. To be in harmony with the world around them they had to show a respect that bordered on worship for each of these spirits. The myths helped them keep this reverential awe alive.

The task of the eagle-killer is a good example of this sense of honor for the spirit in all things. In the fall, when the time for the eagle dance arrived, the eagle-killer would go alone into the mountains and fast four days. When he finished, he would lure an eagle within range, using magical songs and the carcass of a deer, and shoot him. He was careful not to celebrate his victory, though. Instead, he stood over the dead bird and begged the spirit of the eagle not to seek vengeance, explaining that it was some distant enemy and not one of the beloved Real People who had done such a thing. When the eagle-killer returned to his village, he would remark in a casual way—so that neither the eagles or the snakes would become aroused—that a little snowbird had been killed. Only after further ceremony and ritual would the feathers of the eagle be drawn from the carcass, allowing the eagle dance to begin.[18]

Ruling over all of the creation for which the Real People had such respect was *yo-he-wa*, the "master of life." He was the provider, the great one who lived in a heaven above the sun and the moon. His powers were vast. When the peace he so cherished was broken by his people, he turned them into pipes so that the smoke would remind others not to quarrel. Since the Real People called their country the "land of a thousand smokes," the smoke of the pipe stood as a stark reminder. Through his four winds *yo-he-wa* ruled the world. Each wind carried either good or evil for men. The north wind brought trouble, the east wind bravery and success, the south wind peace and happiness, and the wind of the west brought death.[19]

The Real People also believed in other spiritual beings beside *yo-he-wa*. There were *nunnehi*, the "immortals," who were a race of spirit people who lived in the high mountains. Though they could look like Indians if they chose, they were invisible most of the time. The *nunnehi* often helped those who were lost, aided the Real People in battle, and even loved to drum and dance throughout the night. Besides the *nunnehi*, the Real People believed in the *yunwi tsunsdi*, the "little people." No higher than a man's knee, these gnomes, fairies, or elves had beards that grew to their toes and multicolored caps. Often they worked for the Real People, helping them hunt, harvest corn, or even cure the sick, but they could be mischievous too. For example, if a hunter took something from the woods without asking the little people, they might actually throw stones at him as he went home.[20]

The virtue and integrity of the community was a major concern of the the Real People. They almost always thought first in terms of corporate life. Some of their most important myths and symbols stressed this preeminence of the clan. A witch was defined simply as "a selfish, self-centered person who had no respect for clan or communal harmony." Even the famous story of the origin of the bear taught the importance of harmony in the clan. According to this myth, bears were once a group of dissident humans who lived in the woods apart from the tribe. In time, they grew hair all over their bodies, forgot the Real People's language, and began to walk on all fours. They had ceased to be human, to be Real People, because they had ceased to care about the community.[21]

Only by understanding this sense of spiritual community is it possible to understand the significance of the Green Corn ceremony, the high holy rite of the Real People's religious year. This ceremony cleansed the past, made all things new, and allowed each individual to live in the new year without regret. Since the Real People believed that their survival was tied to the virtue of each member, the Green Corn ceremony assured that the community was covenantally protected. The ceremony began with a throwing out of the old that was both spiritual and physical. Old mats, bedding, furniture, and even clothing were burned. The people purged their bodies by fasting and drinking the powerful *gunega ada-ta-sti'*, the "black drink," which they consumed in large quantities to induce purging and vomiting. Then the moment came when all the fires were extinguished, including the most sacred fire of the council house. After the sacred ritual was performed, the sacred fire was lit again, and all the other fires of the town were lit from it. This signaled that the past had been consumed and extinguished. Every crime but murder was forgiven. Even secret lovers, who would have been severely punished under the strict adultery laws of the Real People, could make their affairs public and be forgiven.[22]

To sustain the cleansing of the Green Corn ceremony, the Real People maintained rigorous bathing practices. Each morning, everyone who was able made his or her way from the town to *har-*

peth, the "long water" or "river," and plunged in for a ritual bath, singing and chanting all the while:

> Listen! Now you have come to hear, O Long Man
> O helper of people, you let nothing slip from your grasp.
> Let the white staff of long life be in my hand.
> Let my soul stand erect in the seventh heaven.[23]

The bath was usually followed by prayers to the provider asking for purity, health, and long life. The Real People never forgot to ask the provider to make each of them a *u'da'nuh't*, a "compassionate, just person." In October, because the swirling rivers were reminiscent of a conjurer's boiling cauldron of healing herbs, the Real People performed the medicine ceremony. The entire tribe held hands along the banks of the river, and when a beloved woman or conjurer had prayed to *yo-he-wa*, all entered the water together to receive a cleansing they hoped would last until the next medicine time.[24]

This matter of disease was a serious concern to the Real People. They never called sickness by name, for to do so would attract its attention. Instead, it was the "important thing" or the "intruder." They believed sickness was caused by animal spirits that had invaded the body. Healing came by summoning stronger animal spirits of a friendly variety to drive off the spirits of sickness. The conjurers knew how to do this, though they also administered herbs, recommended fasts, and even insisted on time in the sweat house to cleanse the body of impurities. No matter the discomfort, the Real People were thankful for anything that brought healing, for to die sick might allow the "raven mockers" to carry the soul off to the "darkland." Nothing could be worse.[25]

By most accounts, the Real People could be a deeply affectionate and friendly people. It is tragic, then, that some of their tribal customs, when misunderstood by European settlers, had disastrous results. The Real People, for example, believed that to know a man's name was to have power over him. Often, false names were given to strangers, and true names might never be disclosed, even to close friends. Also, the Real People would only shake hands with strangers, whom they called "those one holds by the ends of the fingers." Once an acquaintance became a friend, he was greeted with a gripping of both forearms followed by a hug. To make matters even more difficult for neophyte observers, when the Real People were being formal and wished to show respect, they cast their gaze downward, so as not to offend by looking directly into the eye, and spoke in a formal third person. "This one thinks" or "This one is not sure," they would say, which often sounded insultingly distant to the unpracticed ears of the settlers. And if all this wasn't confusing enough, the Real People, as a quiet, contemplative folk, often sat in stony silence, even in the middle of conversations. Though settlers thought this rude, it was actually how the Real People showed respect for a weighty thought. The Real People didn't understand the noise and commotion of European society. Indeed, their word for Methodists meant simply "Loud Talkers."[26]

The Real People proved to be among the most fascinating of American Indian tribes. Because of their progressive ways in spiritual matters, they adopted European culture and religion faster than any other tribe, mixing these new ways with the beauties of their own culture. In fact, what they became was exactly what the settlers had always dreamed the "savages" would become.

When the Cherokee were forcibly removed from their ancestral homeland in the 1830s, the displaced nation was actually more consistently Christian than their American conquerors. The Real People came to call this tragic and ironic experience *nunna-da-ult-sun-yi*, the "trail where they cried" or more simply, the "trail of tears."[27] Alas, it was a trail well named.

THE SHAWNEE

Though the Shawnee were driven out of Tennessee by a combined Cherokee and Chickasaw force about the time that French Lick was established on the present site of Nashville, they nevertheless continued to have an influence on the state's history. Part of this influence was through their interaction with the tribes that remained in Tennessee, part of it was through the role they played in the region called *kain-tuck-ee*, and part of it was through the life of a dynamic young leader named Tecumseh.

It was the French of the Great Lakes region who first named the Shawnee. They spoke of them as the "southerners," giving them the name *chaounanons*. The English transformed this into the present "Shawnee." Like the Real People, the Shawnee were of the Iroquois language family, called the Delawares their "grandfather," celebrated a Green Corn ceremony, and were intensely interested in the martial arts. They, too, had their "black drink," their animistic beliefs, and their strict codes of clean and unclean. However, there the similarities end.

The Shawnee were, as one Mohican chief observed, a "restless people," delighting in war. They were, in fact, the nomads and the mercenaries of the Tennessee Indians. So warlike and rootless were they that other tribes often asked the Shawnee to settle near them to help them fight their enemies. Not surprisingly, the first time the tribe is mentioned in American history, in the *Journals* of Captain John Smith of Jamestown in 1607, was to note that the Shawnee were at war with the Iroquois along the Susquehanna River. Tecumseh's brother, the Prophet, speaking in the 1820s, could name only three tribes with whom the Shawnee had not been at war—and scholars believe he was wrong about two of them.[28]

It is possible that some of this warrior drive was rooted in the tribal myths of the Shawnee. Though all American Indian tribes figure prominently in their own myths and legends, few produced a systemic belief in tribal self-importance quite like the legends of the Shawnee. In 1803 a Shawnee chief, speaking in a conference at Fort Wayne, explained this sense of superiority:

> The master of life, who was himself an Indian, made the Shawnee before any other of the human race; and they sprang from his brain: he gave them all the knowledge he himself possessed, and placed them upon the great island, and all the other red people are descended from the Shawnee. After he had made the Shawnee, he made the French and English out of his breast, the Dutch out of his feet, and the long-knives out of his hands. All these inferior races of

men he made white and placed them beyond the stinking lake—the Atlantic Ocean.[29]

This sense of preeminence was also confirmed by a mythological tradition among the Shawnee that contains striking parallels to the stories of the Bible. According to this tradition, the ancestors of the Shawnee once inhabited a foreign land. When they decided to leave this land, they marched to the seashore under the guidance of a leader of the "turtle tribe." Upon stepping into the sea, the waters parted and the Shawnee walked along the bottom of the ocean until they reached the "promised world."[30] Not surprisingly, the retelling of this myth to generations of Shawnee may well have produced a sense of superiority and destiny that fueled their violent inclinations.

Yet, as violent as the Shawnee were, their myths and theology were as vibrant and intriguing as those of the Real People. The Supreme Being and ruler of the universe in the Shawnee religion was *washemoneto*, often called simply *moneto*. He was the "master of life." There also existed an evil spirit called *machemoneto*, which every Shawnee tried desperately not to offend. The "great spirit" and "ruler of destinies" was subordinate to *washemoneto* and was known as *okomthena*, the "grandmother." She sat in her home near the moon, constantly weaving a *skemotah*, a "seine" or "big basket." When she finished it she was to lower it to draw from the earth all who had been deserving. But every night when she slept, her little dog unraveled the *skemotah*, and she was forced to begin the great task again. This was perhaps fortuitous, for a terrible fate awaited all evildoers. Of course, since morality was a fixed law of the universe, every Shawnee knew from birth how he should behave:

> Do not kill or injure your neighbor, for it is not him you injure, you injure yourself; but do good to him, therefore add to his days of happiness as you add to your own. Do not wrong your neighbor, nor hate him, for it is not him that you wrong—you wrong yourself; but love him, for *moneto* loves him also, as he loves you.[31]

Like most other tribes, the Shawnee lived in an animistic world of spirits, and their religious practices were largely aimed at efforts designed to live in harmony with these spirits and draw from their power. Children were named according to an *unsoma*, a "sign" or "event" that happened at the time of birth. The name was to be carefully chosen because it would ultimately determine the fate of the child. Thus, Tecumseh's famous *unsoma* was a flashing light in the sky that gave him the name "Panther in the Sky." Each warrior carried a *pa-waw-ka*, a "personal token," which gave him power in hunt and battle. He might also have a medicine bag filled with objects of his own choosing, which the Shawnee believed gave them good fortune. Women spent their monthly time of menstruation in a special hut on the edge of the town because, as in the Levitical code, a menstruating woman was considered "unclean." Such practices were meant to keep the Shawnee in step with the pace of the universe, in harmony with the great "island of the earth."[32]

Because of their beliefs about the first settlers and their inherent inferiority, the Shawnee were not as quick to absorb European culture and religion as the Real People were. What religious changes took place through contact with their new neighbors occurred largely outside of Tennessee. There were, however, a few notable exceptions.

For instance, in 1742, Count von Zinzendorf, the famous Moravian leader, made a trip to the American colonies and became interested in spreading the gospel among the Shawnee, about whom he had heard so much. The Shawnee in turn resented his intrusion and conspired to kill him. One September evening, when Zinzendorf was busily attending his journal, a rattlesnake that slithered into his warm tent passed undetected over one of the man's legs:

> At this moment, the Indians softly approached the door of his tent, and slightly removing the curtain, contemplated the venerable man, too deeply engaged in the subject of his thoughts, to notice either their approach, or the snake which lay before him. At a sight like this, even the heart of the savages shrunk from the idea of committing so horrid an act; and, quitting the spot, they hastily returned to

the town, and informed their companions, that the great spirit protected the white man, for they had found him with no door but a blanket, and had seen a large rattlesnake crawl over his legs without attempting to injure him.[33]

$\mathscr{T}$HE $\mathscr{C}$HICKASAW

If the Shawnee were the nomads and mercenaries, the Chickasaw were certainly the spartans of Tennessee. They commanded a reputation as the fiercest of warriors, who roared after their enemies with a deadly sense of vengeance. James Adair, who lived among them, insisted that they "never forgot injuries" and were "revengeful of blood to a degree of distraction." Their feats of strength and skill were legendary. Adair claimed that in a long chase they would "stretch away, through the rough woods, by the bare track, for two or three hundred miles, in pursuit of a flying enemy, with the continued speed, and eagerness of a staunch pack of blood hounds, till they shed blood."[34]

Yet the Chickasaw could be loyal friends as well. General James Robertson, founder of Nashville, thought so highly of his Chickasaw brothers that he defied authority to arm them against the Spanish—even equipping them with a "swivel gun." Other settlers were impressed with this tribe as well. They described them as a "tall, well-built people" whose women were "beautiful and clean" and "of a mild, amiable, soft disposition: exceedingly modest in their behavior, and very seldom noisy, either in the single, or married state."[35] Both men and women had "reddish brown skin, raven black hair, and large, dark eyes, their actions exhibiting a superior and independent air."[36]

The religion of the Chickasaw, like that of the Shawnee and Real People, was closely tied to the natural forces that governed their lives. This was especially exemplified in their sense of time and history. They lived in close accordance to lunar cycles and strove to appropriately greet each new moon. Thus, they always repeated "some joyful sounds," and "stretched out their hands towards her." Years were also measured according to lunar cycles—though like so many of the neighboring tribes, they described the passing of time in terms of "winters." They were pioneers among Indians in the use of calendars, which they made from leather thongs with knots in them or with notched sticks. The tribal leaders had large numbers of these calendars made and distributed among the people so that all were agreed as to the number of winters they had survived or how many new moons had passed.[37]

The deity for the Chickasaw was one called *ababinili*. This god was a "composite force" consisting of four beloved things: sun, clouds, clear sky, and "he that lives in the clear sky." Like the Real People, the Chickasaw believed that at one time all was water until an animal—which for the Chickasaw was the crawfish—brought up mud from the bottom and formed the earth. Other animals created all the other features of the earth. Also like the Real People, the Chickasaw maintained sacred fires in each town, and every household lit its fire only from the sacred fire in honor of the sun above.[38]

The Chickasaw elders told their people that they had once dwelled in the west but that *ababinili* ordained a long and difficult search for a new home. They set out then, guided by a sacred pole that leaned every morning of the trek in the direction the people should continue. The pole moved them constantly eastward toward the rising sun until they eventually crossed the Mississippi River. When they came upon the Tennessee River, they camped and arose the next morning to discover that the pole was erect. The people took this as a sign that they had found their promised land, and this region around the Tennessee River became known as the "old fields." In time, though, the pole leaned again—this time toward the west. The people abandoned their towns on the Tennessee River and marched toward the *tombigbee* highlands of northern Mississippi, where the pole again stood erect. There the tribe settled permanently.[39]

Many of the religious rituals of the Chickasaw were primarily concerned with pleasing *ababinili* and the lesser deities of their pantheon. These lesser spirits included *hottuk ookproose* and *hottuk ish-tohoollo*, good spirits who inhabited high ground. Also of concern were the *lofas*, ten-foot-tall giants who created great mischief, and *iyaganashas*, "the little people," who imparted to the Chickasaw their special powers for healing and hunting. The rituals to placate all these spirit beings were mastered by the *hopaye*, two "beloved holy men." These priests were not only the primary advisors to the chiefs, but they also presided at the tribal ceremonies—particularly at the great *busk* festival and the *picofa* ritual.[40]

The *busk* festival was essentially the same as the Green Corn ceremony of their neighbors. Like the Real People, the Chickasaw renewed the sacred fire, consumed a purging drink for the sake of physical and spiritual purity, and forgave on this solemn occasion all wrongs except murder. The *picofa* ritual was a special fast for healing. A chosen class of the *hopaye*, the *aliktce*, adept in both the spiritual powers of healing as well as the medical lore of the tribe, were assigned the task of overseeing the *picofa* fast. While the *aliktce* administered potions and healing concoctions, the clan of the sick person conducted a dance led by one who wore the skin of the animal spirit presumed to be causing the sickness. When the right animal spirits had been summoned to drive the offender off, the dance ended with feasting and celebration.[41]

The belief that sickness was caused by the invasion of animal spirits that other more friendly animals could dislodge was really the cornerstone of the healing arts among Tennessee Indians. Adair observed, for example, that if a tribe member was beset with fever, the ceremony to bring healing involved dancing:

Two or three times round the sick person, contrary to the course of the sun. Then they invoke the raven, and mimic his croaking voice. They also place a basin of cold water with some pebbles in it on the ground, near the patient; then they invoke the fish, because of its cold element, to cool the heat of the fever. Again they invoke the eagle . . . they solicit him, as he soars in the heavens, to bring down refreshing things for their sick and not to delay them, as he can dart down upon the wing quick as a flash of lightening.[42]

Should the ill person die, though, the matters pertaining to burial would have to be carefully attended. How one was buried determined how successful the journey to judgment after death would be. Every deceased person was buried in a sitting position, facing west, "for otherwise it was thought that the soul would lose its way." The body was equipped with everything a Chickasaw might need for an earthly journey. The mourning period lasted twelve moons, with warriors shooting arrows around the grave to ward off evil spirits and the women wailing loudly to awaken the dead for their journey. The Chickasaw knew that once the journey began the deceased would either live in the sky with *ababinili* or would be sentenced to a horrid place of confinement, "that from which came witchcraft."[43]

Interestingly, both the Real People and the Chickasaw associated movement to the west with death. The Real People called the land east of the Mississippi the "sunland" and the land in the west the "darkland" or "nightland." As with Chickasaw religion, the dead moved from the east to the west—from which also came evil spirits, witches, and "raven mockers."[44] This aspect of their native religion is especially ironic in light of the fact that, ultimately, both the Real People and the Chickasaw were forcibly uprooted from their beloved land, the land *yo-he-wa* and *ababinili* had given them, and displaced across the great river to the west, the land of death.

How intensely horrible this removal was for the Indians, how agonizing this rending of heart from land, the European settlers could only guess, though one Christian minister did movingly capture the pain he saw in the experience of his Chickasaw friends:

> There was not a true Chickasaw who would not have considered it a privilege to suffer death in any form or endure torture in any degree if by such suffering he could rescue the land of his birth and his love from the grasp of the white man, and make it a sure possession of his tribe. But he knew resistance was folly. He bowed to the fiat of destiny, and turned from the land dearer to his heart than life.[45]

*E*ARLY *E*UROPEAN *E*XPLORERS

It is no surprise that Tennessee's native peoples were left confused and alarmed by their early contact with European pioneers. The Indians had never thought of themselves as these men now saw them—as primitive, heathen, and backward. They certainly did not see themselves as a servile and subject people. Nor did they have any desire to serve as pawns in a larger European conflict far removed from the concerns of their people. Yet all of this and more was thrust upon them as increasing numbers of Europeans made their way into the beloved land of the Real People, the Shawnee, and the Chickasaw.

When Hernando de Soto entered Tennessee in 1540, searching for "gold-bearing mountains," his reputation preceded him. Though many of the earliest Spanish explorers were pious men intent on the conversion of the tribes they encountered in the Americas, de Soto was apparently not among their number. Already his troops had brutalized the men, women, and children they had encountered, torturing those who resisted their authority and stealing whatever valuables they may have found. "Intent upon capturing Indian slaves," they "brought along iron neck collars attached to chains and by cruelties inflicted upon the natives spread hatred and terror as the expedition advanced."[46] The commander's own secretary, Rangel, "whose priestly soul deplored de Soto's lack of effort to convert the heathen," was grieved as well by the utter farce the venture became:

> I have often wondered at the venturesomeness, stubbornness, and persistency of firmness, to use a better word, for the way these baffled conquerors kept on from one toil to another, from one danger to many others; here losing a companion, there three, again still more; going from bad to worse without learning from experience. I wonder that they should have been so blinded and dazed by a greed so uncertain, and by vain discourse which Hernando De Soto was able to utter to these deluded soldiers. He thought that his experience in the south—in Peru—was sufficient to show him what to do in the north, and he was deceived, as history will tell.[47]

De Soto entered Tennessee near the Little Tennessee River, made his way to a Cherokee encampment near Chattanooga, where he camped for a while, and then trekked across the northern portions of Alabama and Mississippi, reentering Tennessee near another encampment called *quizquiz*. There he had the unfor-

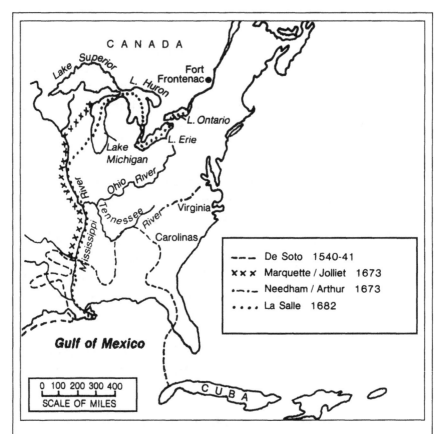

1.2 *European Exploration.* The first known European exploration of Tennessee—if the unsubstantiated Celtic and Norse expeditions are excluded—was conducted in 1540 by the Spanish adventurer Hernando de Soto. Next came the Mississippi expedition of the Frenchmen Jacques Marquette and Louis Jolliet in 1673. Following in his countrymen's footsteps, Robert Cavelier La Salle explored the region in 1682. In 1673 James Needham and Gabriel Arthur were the first Englishmen to enter the territory from the trading settlements of the Virginia colony.

tunate experience of battling the fierce Chickasaw, who almost defeated him. De Soto died in the spring of 1542, and his men buried him in the Mississippi. As Rangel movingly recorded, "So, onward to his grave in the great river which he was to discover, marched the conquistador, Hernando de Soto, until on the banks of the father of waters, finding all things against him, he sickened and died."[48] It is telling that de Soto's men probably never celebrated mass in Tennessee because the needed ritual utensils were destroyed in the struggle for conquest.

The next Spanish expedition into Tennessee arrived in 1566, a quarter of a century after de Soto's, and was led by Juan Pardo. Pardo built a fort at the Creek town *chiaha* but did not tarry long, returning to the Carolinas at the earliest opportunity. Historian Robert Corlew, in summarizing these early Spanish explorations, wrote that "Although the Spaniards were the first Europeans in Tennessee, they left no trace of their civilization, except perhaps ill will among the Indians, who told succeeding generations of their cruelties."[49]

More than a century later, in 1673, the French first laid claim to Tennessee during the travels of fur trader Louis Jolliet of Quebec and missionary Father Jacques Marquette. Marquette had proclaimed: "I want to seek toward the south sea—the Gulf of Mexico—nations new and unknown to us, in order to make them know our great God of whom they have been up to now ignorant."[50]

While exploring the Mississippi, Marquette and Jolliet stepped into Tennessee at the Chickasaw Bluffs on the present site of Memphis, dined on buffalo with their accommodating red-skinned hosts, and claimed all the surrounding region in the name of God and the King of France. As spiritually or politically significant as this claim may have been, it was not one that weighed heavily on the minds of the Indians living on the land in question.

Others came and made their slight marks as well. England claimed Tennessee in the same charter of 1606 that gave birth to the Jamestown expedition. Later, in 1673, James Needham and Gabriel Arthur became the first Englishmen to arrive in present-day Tennessee. In 1672 Robert Cavelier de La Salle built Fort

Prud'-homme while searching for one of his men; it was the very first structure built by European settlers in Tennessee. One of La Salle's men, Martin Chartier, married a Shawnee woman and settled on the present site of Nashville, which was ultimately named French Lick when Jean de Charleville built a trading post on the site in 1714. In 1739 the French built Fort Assumption on the present location of Memphis.

Though each explorer and each settler dreamed of a unique future for Tennessee, none was quite as unique as the dream of one Christian Priber for a socialist utopia called the "Kingdom of Par-

1.3 *Attakullakulla and the Cherokee Delegation.* One of the most influential and accommodating Cherokee chiefs during the period of European settlement was Attakullakulla. He personally negotiated many of the treaties that insured a relatively peaceful integration of the land. He also was among the first Native Americans to assimilate Western ways—including an acceptance of the Christian faith. In 1730 he traveled to London with a delegation of six other Cherokee chiefs to attend the court of George II, where the only likeness ever made of him was engraved by a member of the Guild of Royal Artisans.

adise." One of many idealistic communities that ultimately graced the land of Tennessee, Priber's Kingdom was intended for citizens whose only private property were to be pen, paper, and book. Ironically, he set out to establish his great literary utopia among the Real People—who could neither read nor write. Undeterred by such practical obstacles, he set to work on an essential dictionary of the Real People's language. Before he could complete this ambitious undertaking, however, Priber was exposed by neighboring English settlers as a Jesuit priest in the hire of the French. He was arrested and taken to the British prison at Fort Frederica in Georgia where he later died.[51] One can almost picture the Real People sitting around their council fires, utterly confounded by the doings of these strange white men—their religion seemed to be little more than a justification for their material and political conquests.

But before long, rugged Scots-Irish missionaries began hearing a call from over the mountains. Armed with a stout Calvinist faith and legendary courage, these soldiers of the Reformation answered the call and moved into the world of the Real People and the Chickasaw with a zeal to claim both the land and its occupants for God. Among them, at last, the native peoples were to encounter a living faith of vitality and integrity—one that would ultimately shape the destiny and ordain the fortunes of their beloved soil.

PROFILE 1  *The Land*

*The only difference between Tennessee and the rest of our beloved
South is that Tennessee really is God's country.*

Thomas Maxwell

*O*ne of the most intriguing revelations of history is how land
often comes to symbolize the spiritual dreams and aspirations of
mankind. We are told, for example, that the biblical Patriarchs
were strangers and aliens on the earth because they were looking
for a country of their own—a heavenly one. Men have climbed the
Himalayas for generations, knowing all the while they were not
just seeking the clarity of a mountaintop, but more a clarity of soul
that comes in the wake of struggle. And it is hard to tell at times in
the writings of the Crusaders whether they were speaking of the
earthly or the heavenly Jerusalem as the prize of their labors. Time
and again, earthly land has become so identified with the invisible
geography of the spirit that the one has become a virtual incarna-
tion of the other.

So it has been with the land called Tennessee. Whether we
speak of the early Cherokee and Chickasaw inhabitants, the
Spanish and French explorers, the Scots-Irish pioneers as they
flooded over the mountains, or the great diversity of mankind who
would ultimately come to dwell in Tennessee, those who came
cherished dreams of what could be if they labored "in the land."
They came to love the land, then, not only for what it was in itself—
it was, after all, a fabulously rich, dizzyingly varied, and gloriously
beautiful land—but also for what it promised to become in their
hands as they harnessed its sundry resources to their overarching
vision. The land became home, place, and belonging, and they
inevitably came to define their lives and destinies in terms of it.

The result of this near-mystic attachment to the land could
sometimes be humorous. During the lamentable War between the
States, the Confederate government issued regulations listing the

diseases that might afflict Southern troops and hinder them in battle. One of these was a particular problem for soldiers from Tennessee, for among the debilitating and sometimes life-threatening diseases on the list was "Nostalgia," from the Greek word for "a yearning to return home."[1]

Yet, to understand the essential connection between land and faith in Tennessee history we must go beyond the mere notions of nostalgia to understand the difference between "space" and "place." The hunger for space is a search for freedom, as theologian Walter Brueggemann has written, "without coercion or accountability, free of pressures and void of authority."[2] It is the drive to escape responsibility, meaningless routine, and subjection, to find an emptiness that can be filled with free choice. Many throughout the centuries have seen Tennessee merely as space. Often they were simply passing through to other destinations. Frequently they were escaping something by pursuing nothing. Tennessee was to them little more than a haven from all that dared to rein them in or place demands, an opportunity to escape history.

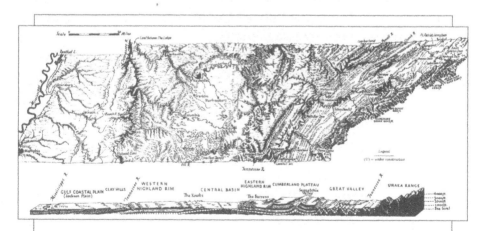

1.4 *Physiographic Map of the Land.* Tennessee is a land resplendent with a variety of natural wonders. From the Smoky Mountains in the east to the rich Mississippi Delta in the west, from the Rolling hills of the Cumberland Plateau across the central highlands to the Great Valley of the eastern lowlands, Tennessee is blessed with both great beauty and generous resources.

But place is much different. Place, Brueggemann writes, is "a protest against the unpromising pursuit of space. It is a declaration that our humanness cannot be found in escape, detachment, absence of commitment, and undefined freedom." Place is possible only where people have "established identity, defined vocation, and envisioned destiny." It comes from the sense of connection to land and people and heritage that occurs when people try to "provide continuity and identity across generations."[3] Place is costly, too, because it only happens where covenants are cut, demands are issued, and sacrifices are made. But this is precisely what people of faith expect when they enter a land of promise, and this is precisely what makes place—their place—so infinitely priceless.

The history of religion in Tennessee is the story of those who have found place in Tennessee. They have invested themselves here, lived out the dictates of their faith, and built a legacy for their children's children. Here, also, they have sinned, compromised, and lived far beneath the lofty ideals they espoused. But this is what place is about as well; the monuments to failure are as much a part of the landscape of faith as are the chapels of worship, and often more importantly remembered.

Yet all was lived in the land called Tennessee, the land which was for so many the land of promise.

$\mathscr{T}$he $\mathscr{V}$anguard of $\mathscr{C}$hrist

2

From such tender shoots grew a great and fruitful garden of faith.
James Blount

$\mathscr{I}$t is difficult to say with certainty exactly when Christianity first entered Tennessee. Though we know that men like de Soto, Pardo, Marquette and Jolliet, and even Priber made claims in the name of Christ and Crown, there is some indication that Christians may have entered the land long before. The evidence is admittedly scant, and the stories that arise are murky, shrouded in myth and mystery. Nevertheless, these stories of early Christians are part of an integral aspect of the lore of Tennessee, if not part of the catalog of fact. True or false, they are historically important because those pioneers who preceded us not only believed them but understood their heritage in terms of them. Besides, as C. S. Lewis has written:

> Myth can arouse in us sensations we have never had before, never anticipated having, as though we had broken out of our normal mode of consciousness and possessed joys not promised to our birth. It gets under our skin, hits us at a level deeper than our thoughts or even our passions, troubles oldest certainties till all questions are reopened, and in general shocks us more fully awake than we are for most of our lives.[1]

Most Americans believe that no Europeans came to the New World until the time of Columbus, who, as every school child knows, sailed the ocean blue in 1492. But this is far from certain. We now know that Vikings and Celts made their way to the shores of the Americas long before Columbus, and there is a good possibility that various Gaelic, Chinese, Phoenician, Jewish, and African expeditions may have also accomplished the feat. Some of the evidence for this is quite startling.

In Wyoming County of West Virginia, there is an inscription carved into a mountain using an ancient language called Ogam. The inscription reads:

> At the time of sunrise a ray grazes the notch on the left side on Christmas Day, a Feast-day of the Church, the first season of the Christian year, the season of the blessed Advent of the Savior, Lord Christ—*Salvatoris Domini Christi.* Behold, He is born of Mary, a woman.[2]

Indeed, researchers have found that on every December 25, the day of the Winter Solstice, a shaft of light penetrates a notch in the rock face and illuminates a picture of a sunburst next to this inscription, just as it describes. Astoundingly, Dr. Robert Meyer, professor of Celtic Studies at Catholic University, has determined that the inscription dates from early in the sixth century and was probably placed there by Irish monks.[3] That Irish monks might have been in the hills of West Virginia only five centuries after the resurrection of Jesus, probably evangelizing Indians, is certainly a challenge to the standard textbook history of the coming of Europeans to the New World.

Tennessee has similar tales to tell. A stone found at Bat Creek contains a Hebrew inscription with the words "A comet for the Jews." This was a standard phrase indicating the Bar-Kochbar revolt of the second century, which was associated with a prophecy regarding a comet. Scholars date the stone between the third and seventh centuries and again wonder if Irish monks might have ventured as far as East Tennessee.[4]

Similarly, in 1818 a coin was found near the Elk River where the town of Fayetteville now stands. The coin was engraved with the words *Antonius Augustus Pius, Princeps Pontifex Tertio Consule* on one side and *Aurelius Caesar* on the other. Scholars believe the coin was issued sometime in the middle of the second century from Roman-occupied Wales.[5] It is possible that one of de Soto's men dropped the coin at Elk River, or the coin may be part of a more intriguing story that has stirred the imaginations of Tennesseans for generations.

When European settlers first began to ask the Cherokee about their history, one of the stories they told was of a white-skinned people who preceded them. The Cherokee called these people the "Welsh tribe" and knew that they claimed descent from white forebears who had "crossed the Great Water."[6] A legend like this among the Cherokee would probably have gone unnoticed except that in Wales there are indeed tales of a local prince named Madoc ap Owen Gwynedd who sailed west and discovered land sometime after the year 1190. There is sufficient evidence for some to conclude that Madoc's company actually landed at Mobile Bay and made their way into Tennessee, thus accounting for several mysterious stone forts near Chattanooga and Manchester. According to this reconstructed account, the band continued through the Ohio Valley to Louisville, where they eventually intermarried with the Mandan Sioux and moved up the Missouri River to the Dakotas.[7]

If Cherokee legends and Welsh tales were the only support for this fantastic story, it probably would not have had the strength to survive the centuries. However, in his *Principal Navigations* of 1589, Richard Hakluyt offered the story of Madoc in support of English territorial claims to the New World. Hakluyt insisted that because of Madoc "it is manifest that that country was by Britons discovered, long before Columbus led any Spaniards thither." He offered also a few lines of the famous Madoc ballad:

Madoc I am the son of Owen Gwynedd
With stature large, and comely grace adorned:
No lands at home nor store of wealth did please,
My mind was whole to search the Ocean seas.[8]

Additional support for the legend is found in the writings of American artist George Catlin. While drawing pictures of the Mandan Sioux in northern Missouri, Catlin discovered Indians with uncommonly pale complexions and blue or gray eyes. He believed they might indeed be descendants of the legendary Welsh colony of Madoc and argued the case in his famous *North American Indians*, written in 1841.[9]

None of this proves the Madoc legend, of course. Nor are we entirely certain, for that matter, that Irish monks ever entered Tennessee before the Spanish and English explorers began coming in the fifteenth and sixteenth centuries. What we know for certain is that many throughout Tennessee history have believed these legends. Even prominent Tennesseans like John Sevier, the state's first governor, believed in the Welsh tribe,[10] and more than one Tennessean's heart has been stirred by the vision of heroic monks whose religious zeal brought them to the New World a millennium before Columbus. Perhaps the true value of these legends, though, is what they say about the faith of later generations and how very much they wanted to believe in early Christians who braved all to claim both native hearts and virgin lands for God.

THE SCOTS-IRISH PRESBYTERIANS

Yet, if it is for heroes of the faith that men put stock in dimly remembered legends, then legends are unnecessary when it comes to the story of Tennessee. We have the indisputable history of the Scots-Irish. Almost two centuries after de Soto and a century after Marquette and Jolliet, the Scots-Irish were the first Europeans to finally settle in Tennessee and plant their hearty version of Christianity amongst the "over mountain people."[11] We have them to thank not only for a rich religious heritage, but also for many of the state's early institutions of learning, for some of its finest leaders, and for more than a few of its most colorful characters. Indeed, it is possible to claim that no stream of Christianity has so shaped the history of Tennessee quite like the Presbyterianism of the Scots-Irish.

Though the Presbyterians were relatively late in coming to America, when they did come they arrived in such numbers and were armed with such an unswerving Christian worldview that they permanently changed life in the colonies. They were not typical Europeans. They were of the hardiest Celtic stock, and they were adherents of the hardiest of all Christian theologies: Calvinism. Not only were they the Highland heirs of William Wallace and Robert the Bruce, they were the sons and daughters of John Calvin, whose *Institutes of the Christian Religion* proclaimed a gracious God who sovereignly established the destinies of individuals just as surely as He providentially confirmed the course of nations. They were the children, too, of John Knox, whose prayers Mary Queen of Scots had feared, so she said, more than all the armies of Europe.[12] And they were the descendants of the Scottish Covenanters, who stubbornly bound themselves together by "sacred covenants" in fierce resistance to all manner of oppression, both religious and political.[13]

2.1 *Samuel Doak.* One of the great pioneer Presbyterian preachers, Samuel Doak seemed to have a knack for being at the right place at the right time. He was present at the Battle of King's Mountain in 1780—a significant turning point in the American Revolution. He traveled with many of the veterans of that great battle into the Watauga Settlement, ministering along the frontier, establishing churches, evangelizing among the new settlers, and offering counsel to the leaders of the fledgling State of Franklin. Perhaps his greatest legacy was that he founded the first educational institution in Tennessee—which ultimately became Washington College.

Their loyalty to this proud heritage had already been severely tested. When an imperial British law of 1703 required all who held public office to take the sacrament of communion according to the rite of the Anglican Church, Calvinists throughout Scotland and Ireland found themselves dislodged from their livelihoods and persecuted by authority of the crown. This persecution, coupled with years of drought in Ireland and exorbitant rents that left many homeless, caused huge numbers of Scots-Irish to turn their eyes toward the promise of America. In 1717, the first ships were charted, and five thousand men and women made their way to a new home in Pennsylvania. Waves of immigrants followed, landing both in Pennsylvania and further south in Charleston. Later, following the devastation of the Scottish Highland clan structure during the Great Rising of 1745, even more came. In fact, so many came that Parliament eventually set up a commission to find out why Scotland and Ireland had become so rapidly depopulated.[14]

When the Scots-Irish Presbyterians arrived in America, they eagerly pressed beyond the settled regions of the east and pushed westward to become the vanguard of the pioneer migration. True, they were hungry for land and for freedom from the restraints of the still-British colonies, but they also saw their migration in spiritual terms. They were the new Israelites, possessing a promised land by dispossessing a pagan horde—and all at the express command of a sovereign God. It was this sense of commission, of playing a role in a divine drama, that prompted an explorer like Daniel Boone to claim that he was "ordained of God to settle the wilderness." It was also what made Scots-Irish Presbyterian preachers some of the most courageous lions of faith on the frontier. As Theodore Roosevelt wrote in *The Winning of the West*:

> Their preachers . . . followed close behind the first settlers, and shared their fields rifle in hand, and fought the Indians valorously. They felt that they were dispossessing the Canaanites, and were thus working the Lord's will in preparing the land for a race which they believed were more truly his chosen people than was that nation which Joshua led across the Jordan.[15]

So determinedly faithful were the early Scots-Irish that it was said "when the crops failed and food was short, they could live off the Shorter Catechism."[16]

Not surprisingly, then, the first ministers in Tennessee were Presbyterians. In 1757, during the French and Indian War, the British established Fort Loudon, the first garrisoned fort in the history of the state. It was a lonely outpost, days of hard travel removed from the nearest towns on the other side of the mountains. Nevertheless, two Presbyterian ministers, both sent by the famous Hanover Presbytery of Virginia under the leadership of the revered Samuel Davies, made their way to the fort and so became the first Protestant clergymen ever to appear in Tennessee. The first of these, Reverend John Martin, preached to the soldiers of the fort in the summer of 1758 and was apparently accompanied by the legendary Chief Attakullakulla himself, known affectionately among whites as "Little Carpenter" for his ability to "join" the interests of the Cherokees and the Europeans the way a carpenter joins wood. Martin remained only a short while, though, before moving on to settle in the upper part of South Carolina. Apparently his impact on the Real People was quite limited. As one of his contemporaries recounted in his memoirs:

The Cherokee generally concur . . . in the belief of one superior Being, who made them, and governs all things, and are therefore never discontent at any misfortune, because they say the Man Above would have it so. They believe in a reward and punishment as may be evinced from their answer to Mr. Martin, who having preached Scripture till both he and his audience were heartily tired, was told at last that they knew well that if they were good they should go up; and bad, down; that he could tell no more; that he had long plagued them with what they no ways understood, and that they desired him to depart the country. This, perhaps, was at the instigation of their conjurers.[17]

Martin was followed in his ministry by the Reverend William Richardson, a younger man from Whitehaven, England. As Richardson traveled to Fort Loudon, he happened upon Martin at the Enoree River, where he was comforted to hear from the older man "of the disposition of the Indians to hear the gospel, which dissipated my Fears of the Indians, and Encouraged me to go ahead."[18] Given Martin's failure with the Real People, one wonders at his counsel to the aspiring young missionary. Yet, under Richardson's ministry there were not only several baptisms at the fort but renewed opportunities to teach the Scriptures to the admittedly tense Cherokee, including such honored leaders as Old Hop and Standing Turkey. Richardson's greatest contribution, though, was the Christian encouragement he gave to the soldiers at the fort. Such encouragement was surely providential given that all but one of the soldiers would lose their lives in the bloody slaughter that ultimately closed the fort in 1760.

Before much longer, though, it was not just soldiers in forts but settlers in towns who needed attention from these pioneering pastors. In 1769 William Bean and his wife, Lydia, moved into the lush Watauga valley, becoming the first permanent white settlers in the land that became Tennessee. Bean was a close friend of Daniel Boone and even named his homestead "Boone's Creek" to honor his friend. Two years later James Robertson, who would eventually play such a prominent role in the history of Tennessee, arrived in the Watauga countryside and concluded that he had reached "the promised land."[19] Within another two years more than one hundred families had joined them along the Holston and Watauga Rivers—the vast majority of Scots-Irish Presbyterian stock.

Though they were technically within the over-mountain territory claimed by North Carolina, they found themselves largely ignored by the distracted legislature of that colony. When Indian problems, land decisions, and the practical matters of government went unattended beyond the point of endurance, these early settlers formed themselves into the Watauga Association in 1772 and so launched the first distinctly American attempt at self-government. Theodore Roosevelt wrote of these vitally significant pioneers: "They outlined in advance the nation's work. They tamed the rugged and shaggy wilderness, they bid defiance to outside foes, and they successfully solved the difficult problem of self-government."[20]

The first minister to venture into the Watauga commonwealth was Charles Cummings, a passionate Irish Presbyterian who had pastored two churches on the Holston River in southwestern Virginia. Cummings was the classic frontier preacher: rugged, fearless, buckskinned, frontier-wise, fiery, and unswervingly devoted to God. He spent thirty years of his life ministering to settlers on the frontiers of Kentucky and Tennessee, and for many he was the only minister of Jesus they ever knew. A typical Sabbath required him to "put on his shot-pouch, shoulder his rifle, mount his stallion, and ride off to church."[21] He preached "two sermons with a short interval between" to men who fingered their rifles as they listened, ever prepared to repel an Indian attack.[22] Many a sermon was interrupted by the call to arms only to be resumed by an unshaken Cummings when the fighting was over, the smell of gun smoke hanging thickly in the air. Cummings and the other faithful pastors of the frontier like him are best remembered as a combination of John the Baptist and Daniel Boone, "with a Bible in one hand, a musket in the other, and a heart of gold between."[23]

In the wake of these early firebrands, the Reverend Samuel Doak came to Tennessee in 1777 and became one of the most renowned men of God in the state's history—and for good reason. His credentials were impressive. He had studied at Princeton and the school that became Washington and Lee, served on the faculty of Hampden-Sydney College, and been ordained by the energetic Hanover Presbytery of Virginia, which assumed spiritual oversight of the entire East Tennessee region. Esteeming an educated ministry, the Presbyterians of the Watauga region welcomed Reverend Doak with open arms. For several years he moved among the settlements of the Holston and Watauga rivers, caring for needy souls and passionately proclaiming the truth of his God.

Eventually he planted a church, though this came about in a rather unusual manner. While riding in the wilderness in 1780, he happened upon some settlers who were felling trees:

> Learning that he was a minister, they requested him to preach to so many of them as could be assembled immediately. He complied, using his horse for a pulpit and the shady grove for a sanctuary.

They were pleased with the sermon, and entreated the preacher to tarry long with them. He yielded to their entreaty, and this led to his permanent settlement among them.[24]

Reverend Doak became the pastor of this congregation at Salem and built there the first "regular church in this cradle-spot of Tennessee."[25] But his evangelistic zeal knew no bounds, and with astonishing energy he also established congregations at New Providence, Carter's Valley, Mount Bethel, Upper Concord, New Bethel, and Hebron.

Doak built schools with the same industry with which he pioneered churches. Colonial pastors were usually the most educated members of their communities and often served as schoolmasters in addition to their spiritual duties. Doak had already taught privately in frontier settlements for years, so it was not surprising that in 1783 he secured a charter for a classical school from the legislature of North Carolina. Named for that state's governor, Doak's school was called Martin Academy and was the first literary institution founded in the Mississippi Valley. In addition, Doak, as a member of the Constitutional Convention, championed the cause of a state-funded university and so planted the first seeds of the mighty University of Tennessee.

Yet men of this caliber are seldom remembered just because they were first. It is their exceptional character that so endears them to later generations, their great sacrifices that bring them such honor. Doak was no exception. In 1798, while he was serving in the east as a commissioner for the General Assembly, he acquired a small library. Inspired by a vision to take Christian education to the settlers of the West, he loaded the books onto packhorses and walked more than five hundred miles across the rugged mountains. Theodore Roosevelt captured the character of this man best when he wrote:

> Possessed of the vigorous energy that marks the true pioneer spirit, he determined to cast in his lot with the frontier folk. He walked through Maryland and Virginia, driving before him an old "flea-bitten grey" horse, loaded with a sackful of books; crossed the Alleghenies, and came down along blazed trails to the Holston

Settlements. The hardy people among whom he took up his abode were able to appreciate his learning and religion as much as they admired his adventurous and indomitable temper; and the stern, hard, God-fearing man became a most powerful influence for good throughout the whole formative period of the southwest.[26]

In addition to his ministry to early settlers and his groundbreaking work as an educator, Doak is also celebrated for what he did at a place called Sycamore Shoals on September 25, 1780. It was but a few days before the famous Revolutionary War battle at King's Mountain, and the Tennessee militia had gathered at Sycamore Shoals to prepare for the engagement. Before the men marched into the pages of history, Samuel Doak was asked to speak to them and say a prayer. This was not uncommon. Throughout the colonial period, "armory sermons" were often preached when militias assembled. But on this day, Samuel Doak spoke beyond the immediate occasion and captured what some have called the "American spirit," that broader sense of the divine destiny of the nation. Because of sermons and prayers like this, King George III said that he most feared the "Black Regiment" of all the forces of the colonies—the company of colonial clergymen who stoked fires of revolution in their black preaching robes. Indeed, his name for the Revolutionary War was simply the "Presbyterian Parsons' Rebellion."[27]

It is not hard to picture the faces of these buckskinned warriors, many standing with their families, hearts stirred by the power of Pastor Doak's words:

My countrymen, you are about to set out on an expedition which is full of hardships and dangers, but one in which the Almighty will attend you. The Mother country has her hands upon you, these American colonies, and takes that for which our fathers planted their homes in the wilderness—our liberty. Taxation without representation and the quartering of soldiers in the homes of our people without their consent are evidence that the Crown of England would take from its American subjects the last vestige of freedom. Your brethren across the mountains are crying unto Macedonia for your help. God forbid that you shall refuse to hear and answer their call—but the call of your brethren is not all. The enemy is marching hither to destroy your homes. Brave men, you are not unacquainted with battle. Your hands have already been taught to war and your fingers to fight. You have wrested these beautiful valleys of the Holston and Watauga from the savage hand. Will you tarry now until the other enemy carries fire and sword to your very doors? No, it shall not be. Go forth then in the strength of your manhood to the aid of your brethren, the defense of your liberty and the protection of your homes. And may the God of justice be with you and give you victory.[28]

And then, with hats removed and heads bowed, each family huddled tightly together, the men of Sycamore Shoals heard Samuel Doak pray a prayer that men destined for battle would quote for generations to come:

Almighty and gracious God! Thou has been the refuge and strength of Thy people in all ages. In time of sorest need we have learned to come to Thee—our Rock and our Fortress. Thou knowest the dangers and snares that surround us on march and in battle. Thou knowest the dangers that constantly threaten the humble, but well beloved homes, which Thy servants have left behind them. O, in Thine infinite mercy, save us from the cruel hand of the savage, and of tyrants. Save the unprotected homes while fathers and husbands and sons are far away fighting for freedom and helping the oppressed. Thou, who promised to protect the sparrow in its flight, keep ceaseless watch, by day and by night, over our loved ones. The helpless woman and little children, we commit to Thy care. Thou will not leave them or forsake them in times of loneliness and anxiety and terror. O, God of Battle, arise in Thy might. Avenge the slaughter of Thy people. Confound those who plot for our destruction. Crown this mighty effort with victory, and smite those who exalt themselves against liberty and justice and truth. Help us as good soldiers to wield the Sword of the Lord and Gideon. Amen.[29]

He then led them in lustily singing an old Celtic battle song— drawn from the great imprecatory repertoire of Psalm 91.

With "The Sword of the Lord and Gideon" as their battle cry and the lilt of the Psalter pacing their hearts, the "over-mountain militia" defeated the forces of British Colonel Patrick Ferguson in sixty-five minutes. Ferguson himself was killed and 225 of his men lay dead with another eight hundred captured. The militia suffered only twenty-eight dead and sixty-two wounded, an astounding victory that not only gave rise to the reputation of the famed "Tennessee Volunteers" but also caused the over-mountain men to throw off King George's restrictions and claim the land from the Appalachians to the Mississippi for their own.[30]

As for Reverend Doak, his labors for the good of his land continued until his death on December 12, 1830. He saw Martin Academy become Washington College in 1795. He helped his son, the Reverend Samuel Doak, found Tusculum Academy in Greeneville and spent the rest of his life there, giving "a good and practical education" to some seventy students.[31] He organized the Abingdon Presbytery of East Tennessee and southwest Virginia, which eventually extended to thirty-six congregations and dozens of ministers. His was one of the earliest voices to rise in opposition to slavery, then spreading so rapidly in the over-mountain region. The influence of this passionate orator led directly to the strong abolition sentiment that took such firm root in East Tennessee. When Samuel Doak died at the age of eighty, men counted not only dozens of fiery preachers as his spiritual and intellectual sons, but also congressmen, governors, educators, and scholars.

More than one author has concluded that "This man of learning and religion probably did more for Christianity on the American frontier than any other living soul."[32] As the original marker on his tomb at the Salem Cemetery of Washington College read, "The name of the mighty have perished but the righteous shall be held in remembrance forever. Let his dust then rest in peace until the Chariot wheels roll in fire."[33]

The measure of this man may perhaps best be taken in the quality of those who followed him. Soon there were dozens of mighty Presbyterian giants in the land, many of whom had graduated from the schools Doak founded. One of the most powerful was Gideon Blackburn. A graduate of Tusculum Academy, Blackburn's unique gifts well prepared him to help shape the frontier for God. He possessed a commanding physical presence, oratorial skills, and a deep compassion the early settlers rarely saw among the more hard-bitten frontier preachers of their day. Blackburn pastored the New Providence and Eusebia congregations in the Maryville area but quickly turned his attention to educating and evangelizing the Cherokee. In 1803 Blackburn established a mission school near Jellico. Others may have seen the children of the Cherokee as "nits that make lice," but Blackburn believed that "if Christianized and educated they would grow up to be a blessing to the world."[34]

Blackburn's success was astounding. The Cherokee children learned their three R's with amazing speed, mastered simplified forms of Presbyterian doctrine, and revealed a unique affection for the poetry and hymns of the settlers. Blackburn delighted in showing off his "promising geniuses" and was most delighted when Governor John Sevier himself was in attendance at one ceremony in 1805. Sevier was reduced to tears by what he saw. "I have often stood," he told Blackburn, "unmoved amidst showers of bullets from the Indian rifles, but this effectually unmans me. I see civilization taking the ground of barbarism, and the praises of Jesus succeeding the war whoop of the savage."[35]

In time, Blackburn moved over the Cumberland Mountains and became a pioneer of Presbyterianism in Middle Tennessee. Throughout the region his sermons were printed and discussed as

2.2 *Gideon Blackburn.* The first missionary to the Cherokees, Gideon Blackburn was a Scots-Irish Presbyterian intent on fulfilling the Great Commission along the frontier. He found the neglect of the Native American people a travesty of Christian principle and in 1804 opened a school for Cherokee children at Oothcaloga. His work inspired the first attempts at the development of a written record of Cherokee traditions and legends.

much as those of any preacher. This is all the more intriguing since Blackburn always prepared his sermons while engaged in some form of manual labor.

> For example, while he ploughed, Blackburn would often have a piece of paper and an inkhorn on a stump at the end of the field. When he came to the end of a row, he would record on the paper the main headings of a sermon. While continuing to work, he would review the skeleton speech, periodically stopping to write down the ideas that had come to him, until he had filled out each major part. Many a discourse that reeked of fire and brimstone was prepared as he tilled the soil.[36]

There were others who followed in the footsteps of Doak and Blackburn. Samuel Carrick organized a congregation in Knoxville and, typical of the Presbyterian passion for education, founded a school called Blount College that eventually became East Tennessee University and later the University of Tennessee. Carrick was appointed by the legislature as the president of Blount College, a post he held while pastoring the congregation in Knoxville until his death. There was also Thomas Craighead, who mounted a stump on a Saturday afternoon in 1785 and preached the first Presbyterian sermon ever heard in Middle Tennessee. A Princeton classmate of Samuel Doak's, Craighead established Davidson Academy the same year he entered the region, a school which later became the University of Nashville. Hezekiah Balch, also a Princeton classmate of Doak's, assumed the leadership of the Mount Bethel congregation that Doak had organized and, in what had become standard Presbyterian pattern, soon after obtained a charter for Greeneville College in 1794. Balch also brought the first religious controversy to Tennessee when he accepted the ideas of Samuel Hopkins, a New England clergyman who taught a minor modification of Calvinism. The resulting debates and church splits prefigured many like them later in the state's history.

It is not without reason that King George III feared the impact of the "Black Regiment" of the American colonies, that his Prime Minister complained "I hear that our American cousin has run away with a Scots-Irish parson."[37] The Scots-Irish Presbyterians possessed a theology perfectly suited to their rugged character. They believed in a sovereign God who ruled in the affairs of men. They knew they were chosen, that their mission was divinely ordained, and that they were immortal until their work was done. They believed the Bible was the charter for a new kind of society, a society to be won by hard labor but with victory divinely assured. Thus, by the time Tennessee became a state in 1796:

> with twenty-seven congregations stretching from East Tennessee to the Nashville area . . . John Calvin's spiritual descendants had become the state's most powerful religious force. And Presbyterians in those early days were associated so closely with education that they virtually monopolized it.[38]

In fact, so all-pervasive was the Reformed influence in the early history of Tennessee that even the charters of government reflected it. During the American Revolution, the Watauga Association submitted itself to the colonial administration of North Carolina in order to join itself with the independence movement. The entire over-mountain area became known as Washington County. After the war, however, there was a good deal of confusion and conflict over the jurisdictional authority in the region. In 1784, the frustrated citizens of Washington County, and the adjoining Greene and Sullivan magistratical jurisdictions formed themselves into the "free and independent sovereign state" of Franklin, named for the revered Benjamin Franklin.[39]

The citizens of this fledgling—and as yet, unrecognized—state were largely of Scots-Irish descent and largely Reformed. They held the Calvinist view that church and state should be like in faith—that is, built on the same thoroughly biblical principles—but entirely separate in function. The constitution of the new state, therefore, required that anyone entrusted with civil power had to hold the same view of God and Scripture that its founders believed could assure liberty and righteousness in the new state:

> That no person shall deny the being of a God or the truth of the Protestant religion or the divine authority either of the Old or New

Testament, or who shall hold religious principles incompatible with the freedom and safety of the State, shall be capable of holding any office or place of trust or profit in the civil government within this State.[40]

Amazingly, this requirement was much stricter than the one in the North Carolina constitution, the model for the Franklin document; indeed, it was much stricter than the Tennessee constitution of 1796. The citizens of Franklin clearly wanted a Christian state, and the Reformed faith of its Scots-Irish Presbyterians provided the model.

Clearly, with their devotion to bringing all of human society into submission to Jesus, with a character shaped by struggle and hardship, and with a passion for liberty virtually unsurpassed in American history, the Scots-Irish Presbyterians laid a foundation for spiritual greatness in Tennessee that later generations built upon with gratitude.

𝒯HE 𝒝APTISTS

The movement of the Baptists into Tennessee was quite different from the path of the Presbyterians. Though the Baptists were also mostly Calvinists, they did not demand an educated ministry, and they avoided church hierarchies. This makes Baptist history in Tennessee less about clergymen and organizations and more about congregations and Christian community. Often entire bodies of believers crossed the mountains to become the nucleus of new churches in Tennessee—and all without a pastor at the lead. In fact, the history of the early Baptists in Tennessee is a bit unclear only because there were probably functioning congregations of believers long before any official body took note of them or any pastor was in place whose journal might provide some clue about the church's origins.

Typical of the Baptist experience, the first congregation was probably started at Sinking Creek in 1775 and sprang from a revival in the home of the Charles Robertson family. It was four years later, in 1779, that the first church building was begun. Established at Buffalo Ridge in Washington County, the church was pastored by Tidence Lane, one of the most powerful spiritual leaders in the state. Lane was born in Maryland and later moved with his family to North Carolina, where he encountered the ministry of Shubal Stearns, a visionary frontier preacher who had been converted under the preaching of George Whitefield. When Lane, who held the most "hateful feelings toward the Baptists," heard that Stearns was preaching nearby, curiosity drove him to attend a meeting.

> Upon my arrival I saw a venerable old man sitting under a peach tree with a book in his hand and the people gathering about him. He fixed his eyes upon me immediately, which made me feel in such a manner as I had never felt before. I turned to quit the place, but could not proceed far. I walked about, sometimes catching his eyes as I walked. My uneasiness increased and became intolerable. I went up to him, thinking that a salutation and shaking of hands would relieve me, but it happened otherwise. I began to think that he had an evil eye and ought to be shunned, but shunning him I could no more effect than a bird can shun the rattlesnake when it fixes its eyes upon it. When he began to preach my perturbations increased, so that nature could no longer support them, and I sank to the ground.[41]

In time Lane became a powerful influence among Baptists in Tennessee, a model of the godly "farmer-preacher" who did so much to keep faith alive in the remote stations and towns of the wilderness. During his ministry he served as a tax assessor, surveyor, supervisor of road construction, farmer, and custodian of orphans, but he nevertheless left "a deeper impression upon early Tennessee Baptist life than any other pioneer Baptist minister."[42]

Like the story of Tidence Lane's conversion, the lives of early Baptists were often dramatic and inspiring. There is the tale of Garner McConnico, who ran like Jonah from his calling to ministry and found himself in Davidson County. When an elderly preacher sensed his gifts and challenged him to again take up his destiny,

McConnico repented and gave himself wholly to the cause of his Lord. He was described as having a "trumpet-like" voice and it was not uncommon for those who attended his church near Franklin in Williamson County to see people cured when this bold man of God shouted, "In the name of the Lord, I command all unclean spirits to leave this place."[43]

There is also the story of Jonathan Mulkey, who some Baptist historians believe was the first Baptist minister in Tennessee, preceding even Tidence Lane. Mulkey was the true frontier Baptist preacher, a man who came to Tennessee in 1775, hunted buffalo for his food, fought the Cherokee, and repeatedly lost his home only to rebuild it again and again. So fiery a preacher and evangelist was he that some called East Tennessee the "Mulkey Dominion." One deacon traveled ten miles every Sunday to hear "Father Mulkey" preach, and when the beloved minister was "too old and too feeble to preach standing, the church, it is said, made him a suitable and easy pulpit-chair, that he might sit down and pour out

2.3 *The Methodist Circuit Rider.* Methodism was spread throughout the frontier lands by itinerant preachers on horseback known as circuit riders. Typically, they were former tradesmen or artisans who had undergone a dramatic conversion and thereafter dedicated themselves to the spreading of the gospel. They were generally responsible for a predominantly rural circuit 200 to 500 miles in circumference. Their relentless commitment was so widely acknowledged that on stormy days there was a proverbial saying: "There is nothing out today but crows and Methodist preachers."

his soul in melting exhortations to a devoted people who would listen to his every word."[44]

Like Mulkey, aging ministers on the frontier were held in the highest esteem. If he remained faithful to his call, if he managed to escape early death in the wilderness, and if he loyally served his people, such a pastor was regarded as a saint by his grateful congregation, his death a major loss to the entire community. The story of James Whitsitt illustrates this fact all too well. He was the beloved pastor of four churches in the Cumberland Valley. After nearly sixty years of ministry, he suddenly closed his sermon one Sunday with, "And now, brethren and sisters, farewell. This is our last interview. I am old and rapidly failing. The winter is almost upon us, and I can not be with you. Before the spring comes I shall be gone. Farewell." The tearful congregation was utterly undone.

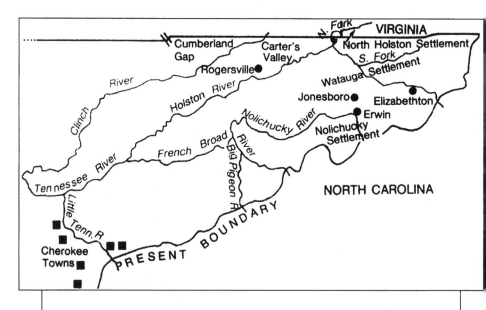

2.4 *Early European Settlements.* Most of the earliest settlements in Tennessee were clustered along the narrow Appalachian wedge between the Cumberland Gap and the Pigeon River. Several towns were established; the largest—Jonesboro—eventually became the capital of first the Watauga Settlement and then the State of Franklin.

Shortly afterward Reverend Whitsitt did indeed pass away, a man who "left a broader mark upon his generation than almost any of his associates in the ministry."[45]

By the time Tennessee achieved statehood there were two "associations" of Baptists: the Holston in East Tennessee and the Mero in Middle Tennessee. Yet the story of the early Baptists is not a tale of organization but of organism. It is the story of the triumph of community, of bearing one another's burdens, of knowing that each part made the whole possible. If a godly pastor was available, fine, but life and mission never waited for the blessings of official-dom. The early Baptist congregations were communities in the truest sense, and a pastor was profitable only as a single con-stituent part of that community—and even then only if he had a clear "call" from God and if he refused to rise above his people in any way other than in character and godliness. These unique val-ues caused the Baptists to grow far more rapidly than their Presbyterian brethren, whose learned "divines" and insistence on structure were rather difficult for the rough new breed of frontier settlers flooding into the region to understand. The community of early Tennessee Baptists was like a hardy creature, ever adapting and growing, yet ever faithful to the "faith once for all delivered to the saints" that was its characteristic lifeblood.

𝒯HE ℳETHODISTS

Of the three Christian denominations shaping Tennessee life at the end of the eighteenth century, the Methodists were the lat-est, the smallest, and on the surface, the least promising. They had much against them. Anti-British sentiment was so strong that the citizens of Nashborough decided to change their settlement's name to the more continental-sounding Nashville in the very year the Methodist church was formed in America. This no doubt hin-dered their ministry. Independence-minded Americans did not forget, either, that Methodism's patriarch, John Wesley, had opposed the American Revolution. Besides, Methodism was essentially a lay movement—its "preachers" were little more than devoted laymen armed with Bible, hymnbook, and John Wesley's sermons. What could one expect from such "a day of small beginnings?"[46]

Yet the skeptics who asked such questions failed to understand the indomitable impulse and impetus behind the movement. Indeed, the very name "Methodist" was originally a term of derision, used by the Oxford students of the early eighteenth century to ridicule the silliness of a group who called themselves the "Holy Club." Men such as John Wesley, George Whitefield, Charles Wesley, and George Oglethorpe had founded this Holy Club to "perfect holiness in the fear of God." In their meetings they hammered Christlikeness into their lives, daily searching their souls for any offending way. They read books like *The Imitation of Christ* by Thomas a Kempis, *A Serious Call to a Devout and Holy Life* by William Law, and *The Life of God in the Soul of Man* by Henry Scougal. They visited prisoners and cared for the poor because their Lord commanded it, they humbled themselves publicly in ways shocking to the customs of the time, and they preached their high call to holiness throughout England, even from tree stumps and wagons when the pulpits of the churches were closed to them. From their meetings, revival spread through England. And that remarkable revival fomented a good deal of dramatic cultural change—a transformation that was desperately needed if William Hogarth's engravings depicting the moral life of the day are any indication. Indeed, many scholars attribute the great Wesleyan revivals with saving England from the anarchy of a French-style revolution of its own.[47]

The Methodists who first entered Tennessee were the spiritual sons and daughters of a people who had withstood every kind of opposition in order to see nations and cultures transformed for Christ. To find themselves a bit late on the scene, a bit opposed, and a bit few in number was hardly cause to quench the revival fire that burned in their souls. They were ready to pay any price to see the lost saved and the new land tamed for Jesus. Who could know that they would be aided in their task by a fresh wave of revival that exceeded the "outpouring" their forefathers knew? When that wave of revival washed over America in the early nineteenth century, the Methodist societies were like ships waiting to catch the tide.

Yet, until that revival began, the sailing was more than a little difficult indeed for the early Tennessee Methodists. In 1783, one year before the famous Christmas Conference in Baltimore that officially launched the Methodist Episcopal Church in America, the Holston Conference of Methodists was formed, which included congregations along the Nolichucky, Watauga, and Holston Rivers. The first minister into that region was Jeremiah Lambert, a selfless, hardworking servant. When he arrived, there were but sixty Methodists on his "circuit," as the series of settlements a preacher tended was called, and he was able to add only sixteen more in his years of service. He was followed by Henry Wills in 1784, who apparently fared no better. But Methodists were nothing if not persistent, and in 1786 Acuff's Chapel, the first Methodist building in Tennessee, was erected near Blountville to house the 250 converts of three other circuit riders. The tide was beginning to turn.

In the Cumberland region, a Revolutionary War veteran named Benjamin Ogden preached a circuit that included Nashville, Clarksville, and Gallatin. Through long hours in the saddle and longer hours in prayer, Ogden eventually saw the growth of Methodist societies in the Middle Tennessee area and the building of a stone meeting house in Nashville in 1790. How thrilled Ogden must have been when even the founder of Nashville, the heroic James Robertson, together with his amazing pioneer wife, joined the Methodist movement. The Robertsons became part of a small but growing band which at the time of statehood numbered about 550 members and were pastored by four circuit riders. Small by human standards, perhaps, but they were holy and devoted, ready for everything their God brought their way as the revivals of the early 1800s would soon show.

*T*HE *S*CENE AT THE *E*ND
OF THE *C*ENTURY

Yet, as thrilling as it is to remember the sacrifices and victories of the early pioneers of Christianity in Tennessee, the fact remains that much of the population was largely adrift spiritually. Methodist Bishop Francis Asbury thought he knew why:

> I am of the opinion it is as hard, or harder, for the people of the west to gain religion as any other. When I consider where they came from, where they are, and how they are called to go further, their being unsettled, and with so many objects to take their attention, with the health and good air they enjoy, and when I reflect that not one in a hundred came here to get religion; but rather to get plenty of good land, I think it will be well if some or many do not eventually lose their souls.[48]

Historian Henry Adams agreed with Asbury that the weak influence of religion on so much of the American frontier grew largely from the reasons men crossed the mountains in the first place.

> The Pilgrims of Plymouth, the Puritans of Boston, the Quakers of Pennsylvania, all avowed a moral purpose, and began by making institutions that consciously reflected a moral idea. No such character belonged to the colonization of 1800. From Lake Erie to Florida, in a long, unbroken line, pioneers were at work, cutting into the forests with the energy of so many beavers, and with no more express moral purpose than the beavers they drove away.[49]

Neither of these men exaggerated. The wide-open spaces and opportunities for wealth brought men of every type over the mountains, some for reasons of faith, most for escape and profit. The result was that entire populations arose who were completely disconnected from the ardent faith of their fathers. A visiting minister who prayed over his food at dinner was not surprised to be asked why he was talking to his plate.

As late as 1796, no more than one in twenty identified with any of the three denominations. Out of a population approaching 100,000, fewer than 5,000 held church membership. The Baptists had attracted the largest following with approximately 2,500 members; the Presbyterians had 1,500; and the Methodists fewer than 600.[50]

Yet, as is so often the case in Church history, desperate times drove believers to their knees with one cry: "Revive us again, O Lord." In the next century, many found that cry answered—and the spiritual life of Tennessee, as well as that of the nation, was forever transformed.

2.5 *Samuel Austin Worchester.* A Presbyterian missionary who devoted his entire adult life to translating the Bible and various Christian hymns into the Cherokee language, Samuel Austin Worchester was also one of the founders of the Brainerd Mission near Chatanooga. He moved with his wife and family to New Echota—the capital of the Cherokee Nation—and there helped to establish *The Cherokee Phoenix* newspaper. During the removal of the Cherokee people, he traveled with his adopted people along the Trail of Tears, ministering among them as he always had.

PROFILE 2   *Lost Americas*

There are yet many Americas with which our destiny must deal.
Benjamin Franklin

Few today realize that the late eighteenth and early nineteenth centuries saw the establishment of several independent republics in and around the original American colonies. It was by no means a foregone conclusion that all of these would eventually give way to the continental hegemony of the United States—at least not to the pioneers who founded them.

Vermont was a region long disputed by the colonial governments of both New York and New Hampshire, but its residents always saw themselves as a breed apart. When the thirteen colonies issued their united Declaration of Independence, a small group of Vermont's leading citizens likewise issued a manifesto of secession. In the days that followed, they established a functioning republican form of government, elected representatives, and raised a militia. Under the judicious magistratical supervision of President Thomas Crittenden and the brash military prowess of Ethan Allen and his Green Mountain Boys, Vermont successfully confirmed its sovereign and free national status. Over the next fifteen years it operated as an entirely independent nation, even exchanging diplomatic delegations with the thirteen American states to the south and east. It was not until 1791 that the fiercely autonomous republic was enticed to join its fortunes with that of its neighbors under the newly ratified federal Constitution.[1]

Likewise, the settlers along the Gulf Coast from Mobile Bay to the Mississippi River were disinclined to give up their sovereign status to join the American federal union. Under the presidency of Fulwar Skipwith—a distant relative of Thomas Jefferson—the residents of that isolated West Florida land established an independent republic and elected legislators to represent them at their capital, Baton Rouge. Though the land was disputed by the Spanish and the English crowns, the settlers declared their sovereign intent and set about the task of governance. It was not until 1810, when President James Madison dispatched troops from Louisiana to take possession of these Florida parishes and forcibly annex

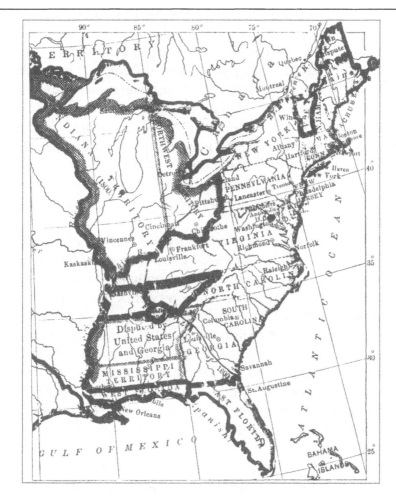

2.6 *Lost Americas.* This unique surveyor's map—dating from sometime just before 1791—shows the boundaries of many of the early American republics, including the Republic of Vermont, the Republic of West Florida, the State of Franklin, the Cherokee Nation, and the disputed territories of Scotia Maine, Spanish East Florida, the Alabama Range, and the Northwest Indian Lands.

them to the new American possessions nearby, that the "Bonnie Blue Flag" of the little nation was lowered and replaced by the Stars and Stripes.[2]

And of course Franklin, the over-mountain settlement that had grown out of the Watauga Association, engaged in its own struggle for independence. When the North Carolina legislature failed to make appropriate accommodations for the over-mountain communities, the residents called upon their leaders to interpose a magistratical jurisdiction that would truly represent them. As a result, a legislature was elected and John Sevier assumed the office of the presidency. Though their first choice was to obtain admission to the American union as a new state, when their appeals seemed to fall on deaf ears, they asserted their sovereign national autonomy. Eventually, the residents were persuaded to merge their fledgling nation with the newly formed Tennessee territory, but their rugged individualism would forever set them apart.[3]

What is striking about each of these early national experiments is that they were all driven by a fierce commitment to political freedom and liberty that grew naturally out of the Scots-Irish Presbyterianism of their respective residents. Though each was ultimately absorbed into the larger union, and though their distinctively Reformed character was gradually diluted by successive waves of new immigrants and new religious movements and traditions, their overall effect was lasting. Indeed, the impress of their worldview and the impact of their convictions are still felt today. The renowned streak of proud independence, the tough-minded regionalism, and the unbending cultural autonomy of Tennessee's political institutions are evidence of that. Visit the Deep South of Mississippi and Alabama or the villages of taciturn Vermont and you'll see that the same thing is true there as well. Though their unique American republics are no longer sovereign and independent, their impact upon us all is by no means lost. Likewise, though the Scots-Irish Presbyterians no longer dominate the cultural, theological, and educational scene, their rich legacy is everywhere evident.[4]

3
$\mathcal{D}$ays of $\mathcal{G}$lory, $\mathcal{D}$ays of $\mathcal{F}$ire

To discern the difference betwixt and between true revival and mere revivalism may well be the cornerstone of wisdom in these difficult days.

Francis Asbury

$\mathcal{A}$s the eighteenth century came to an end and the dawn of a new era began, Americans who took stock of their nation's spiritual state found much that was troubling. It fell to the General Assembly of the Presbyterian Church to sound the alarm.

We perceive, with pain and fearful apprehension, a general dereliction of religious principle and practice among our fellow citizens, a visible and prevailing impiety and contempt for the laws and institutions of religion, and an abounding infidelity which in many instances tends to Atheism itself. . . . The profligacy and corruption of the public morals have advanced with a progress proportionate to our declension in religion. Profaneness, pride, luxury, injustice, intemperance, lewdness, and every species of debauchery and loose indulgence greatly abound.[1]

The Presbyterians were certainly not alone in their concerns. The Baptists, too, had "suffered a very wintry season. The love of many waxed cold. Some of the watchmen fell, others stumbled, and many slumbered at their posts."[2] One protestant Episcopal bishop thought his church "too far gone ever to be revived." This trend pervaded all the denominations, and as the churches declined, their schools followed. Lyman Beecher later recalled that at Yale College in those years:

3.1 *Bishop Francis Asbury.*
English-born Francis Asbury was converted as a youth under the ministry of John Wesley. In 1771 he sailed to the American colonies for the express purpose of ministering among the burgeoning frontier communities in the West. He quickly organized vast Methodist Districts all across the frontier and recruited circuit riders to care for each district. During his long and productive career, he established dozens of churches, five schools, two publishing houses, and twelve missionary societies.

The College was in a most ungodly state. The college church was almost extinct. Most of the students were skeptical, and rowdies were plenty. Wine and liquors were kept in many rooms; intemperance, profanity, gambling, and licentiousness were common.[3]

Students at schools founded to advance the gospel of Christ calmly debated "whether Christianity had been beneficial or injurious to mankind."[4] With sadness, many throughout the nation concluded with the Presbyterians that "The eternal God has a controversy with this nation."[5]

But what a shock this must have been for many Americans. After all, they had just won a war for independence against a king many colonists believed was "the Antichrist."[6] A new Constitution and Bill of Rights promised both political stability and complete religious freedom. And most Americans thought of themselves as Christians in a Christian nation. The reality, though, was quite different. The sad truth was that the churches and religious institutions had not yet recovered from the devastation of the Revolutionary War. Knowing the power of colonial Christianity, the British had routinely burned Bibles, murdered rebel clergy, and converted what churches they captured into riding stables or houses of prostitution.[7] Regaining their prewar momentum had taken time, and the churches were simply not yet ready for the spiritual demands of their growing society.

To make matters worse, after the war several of its greatest heroes launched vicious and unrelenting attacks on orthodox Christianity. In 1784 Ethan Allen, Vermont's hero of Ticonderoga, published a book called *Reason: The Only Oracle of Man*, in which he flatly stated, "There could be no justice or goodness in one being's suffering for another, nor is it at all compatible with reason to suppose that God was the contriver of such a propitiation."[8] Joining Allen was Thomas Paine, whose pamphlet of 1776, *Common Sense*, tipped the scales in favor of independence from England when many were yet uncertain. Following the war, however, Paine published *The Age of Reason*, in which he asserted that "The Christian mythologists, calling themselves the Christian Church, have erected their fable which, for absurdity and extravagance, is not exceeded by anything that is to be found in the mythology of the ancients." Paine also referred to the gospel as "the fable of Jesus Christ" and the Virgin Birth as "blasphemously obscene."[9] When revered men like Allen and Paine maliciously attacked the established doctrines of Christianity, it moved others to first question and then discard their own faith.

What filled the vacuum for many thousands was a religion of the new American republic itself. If revealed religion was found wanting, then perhaps a religion of the state would do, a religion of democracy and freedom, a religion of "Americanism." It was an easy doctrine to sell in those early days of heady national optimism, but it was powerless to stem the tide of lawlessness and immorality in the land. Many a preacher reminded his congregation that "Where there is no revelation, the people cast off restraint."[10]

In Tennessee matters were no better. One Methodist preacher probably captured the spirit of the land best when he declared the state "a sink of iniquity, a Black Pit of irreligion."[11] Though early Christian leaders had labored valiantly to establish the state on a solidly Christian foundation, the tide of unrighteousness that poured over the mountains after the Revolution was simply too overwhelming for the already weakened churches to battle. Beginning in 1787, church affiliation declined and continued to do so unchecked for another ten years. Criminals escaping authorities in the east moved into Tennessee and Kentucky, formed gangs, took over entire towns, and dared authorities to stop them. Drunkenness, prostitution, corruption, and murder ruled the day on the frontier, and it looked to many as though the over-mountain regions were doomed to become America's outland cesspool. Even when the good citizens formed vigilante bands of "Regulators" to clean up their towns, the resulting bloodshed and backlash only made matters worse. In utter desperation and alarm, Tennessee Christians turned to their ultimate weapon—fervent seasons of prayer and fasting.

ℱIRE IN THE 𝒲EST

The deliverance the faithful prayed for began on a warm day in 1796 when James McCready rode into the bedeviled territory of Logan County, Kentucky. McCready was a Scots-Irish Presbyterian, though not at all of the traditional variety. He wore buckskin breeches and spoke with a rough pioneer's plainness that other frontiersmen found appealing. McCready himself claimed that he did not swear, drink, or break the Sabbath and that he had made private prayer a daily habit since the age of seven. Though born in Pennsylvania, McCready moved to North Carolina while a young child, and it was there, at the age of thirty, that he began his ministry in Guilford County.[12]

When McCready arrived in the Carolinas, he found the state of Christianity there desperate. Before long, though, his stirring preaching about the wrath of God led to many conversions. One of McCready's converts was Barton W. Stone, who later led the famous Cain Ridge Revival in Bourbon County, Kentucky. Stone wrote of McCready:

His person was not prepossessing, nor his appearance interesting, except his remarkable gravity, and small, piercing eyes. His coarse, tremulous voice excited in me the idea of something unearthly. His gestures were *sui generis*, the perfect reverse of elegance. Everything appeared by him forgotten but the salvation of souls. Such earnestness, such zeal, such powerful persuasion . . . I had never before witnessed.[13]

McCready's successes made him controversial and quickly generated opposition. He was accused of "running people distracted" and of keeping people from their labors and duties. At one point protesters tore out his pulpit and burned it. When a letter written in blood warned McCready of a foreboding future, he decided to accept the invitation of several friends to move west into the southern part of Kentucky.[14]

In January of 1797 McCready became the pastor of three churches in Logan County—Red River, Gasper River, and Muddy River. The tall, muscular preacher quickly got about the business of bringing revival to the county. People were astounded, for many who attempted similar success in this violent region called Rogue's Harbor were driven out or killed. McCready, however, had walked this road before, and he was not about to be intimidated or deterred.

McCready immediately launched into the fiery preaching and diligent pastoral efforts that had brought him success before. Though "universal deadness and stupidity" prevailed for a season, the darkness began to lift a bit, with eight or nine hard-won conversions among his rugged neighbors.[15] By the next winter, the old deadness seemed to return, and many fell away. McCready was undaunted, though, for he had a secret weapon—a solemn "Covenant of Prayer." He gathered the few remaining faithful believers and asked them to give themselves to it wholeheartedly. It was the kind of clarion that drew the battle lines clearly.

When we consider the word and promises of a compassionate God, to the poor lost family of Adam, we find the strongest encouragement for Christians to pray in faith—to ask in the name of Jesus for the conversion of their fellow-men. None ever went to Christ, when on earth, with the case of their friends that were denied, and although the days of his humiliation are ended, yet for the encouragement of his people, he has left it on record, that when two or three agree upon earth, to ask in prayer, believing it shall be done. Again, whatsoever ye shall ask the Father in my name that will I do, that the Father may be glorified in the son. With these promises before us we feel encouraged to unite our supplications to a prayer-hearing God, for the out-pouring of his Spirit, that his people may be quickened and comforted, and that our children, and sinners generally, may be converted. Therefore we bind ourselves to observe the third Saturday of each month, for one year, as a day of fasting and prayer, for the conversion of sinners in Logan County, and throughout the world. We also engage to spend one-half hour every Saturday evening, beginning at the setting of the sun, and one-half hour every Sabbath morning, at the rising of the sun, in pleading with God to revive his work.[16]

For more than six months, nothing happened. In fact, it seemed that things just got worse. The valiant band of prayer warriors searched their hearts, repented of their own sins, and continued to pray. And then it happened. On the fourth Sunday of July 1798, during a "sacramental meeting" of the Gasper River congregation, "the Lord poured out His Spirit in a very remarkable manner." Many were "gloriously awakened," and the fires began to spread. By the first Sunday of September the people of Muddy River were similarly moved, and then it hit the Red River congregation. It seemed that the grip of evil on Logan County was about to be broken as increasing numbers reported marvelous "proofs of God's Spirit."[17]

Critics of the revival quickly emerged. They so violently attacked the work that McCready's three congregations reverted to "a dismal state of deadness and darkness." Their pastor was resolute, however, and devoted himself even more faithfully to prayer and fasting. Eventually, the tide turned for good. One congregation after another experienced the "moving of God's Spirit." There was even a new church founded at Clay-lick, and revival swept that congregation as well. At Muddy River, in late September of 1799, "the greatest and most solemn and powerful time of any that had been before" occurred. The congregations swelled, and many were convinced that the long-sought revival had begun.[18]

The promise of a greater work during the sacramental meetings of the next summer kept the covenanted intercessors praying throughout the winter, though some of the converted lapsed into complacency. McCready was confident that the first breakings of a mighty work of God had taken place. Of what would happen that next summer, he later wrote:

> All the blessed displays of Almighty power and grace, all the sweet gales of the divine Spirit, and soul-reviving showers of the blessings of Heaven which we enjoyed before, and which we considered wonderful beyond conception; were but like a few scattering drops before a mighty rain, when compared with the overflowing floods of salvation, which the eternal, gracious Jehovah has poured out like a mighty river, upon this our guilty, unworthy country. The Lord has indeed shewed himself a prayer-hearing God: he has given his people a praying spirit and a lively faith, and then he has answered their prayers far beyond their highest expectations.[19]

In June of 1800 four or five hundred members of the three congregations met at the Red River meeting house for a series of services scheduled to last from Friday to Monday. Some among them had been praying for revival for more than three years. Expectation ran high. For the first few days of the meetings, people were touched repeatedly. But on the last service of the last day, it seemed the dam broke.

William Hodge, a minister who had joined McCready, preached a long and powerful sermon. People began to weep, and one woman in the east end of the building began to cry and shout. When Hodge was through, Methodist preacher John McGee of the Cumberland Valley strode to the pulpit. McGee began to sense the power of what was happening and later reported, "there was one greater than I preaching." As he continued his sermon:

> I exhorted them to let the Lord Omnipotent reign in their hearts and submit to Him, and their souls should live. Many broke silence. The woman in the east end of the house shouted tremendously. I left the pulpit to go to her. . . . Several spoke to me: "You know these peo-

ple. Presbyterians are much for order, they will not bear this confusion." I turned to go back—and was near falling, the power of God was strong upon me. I turned again and losing sight of fear of man, I went through the house exhorting with all possible ecstasy and energy.[20]

The pandemonium that ensued was overwhelming. Worshipers were overcome by what they thought to be the power of God and fell unconscious to the floor, a condition those in attendance called "slain" because of its deathlike appearance. McCready remembered that the floor was "covered with the slain; their screams for mercy pierced the heavens." One could see "profane swearers and Sabbath-breakers pricked to the heart and crying out 'What shall we do to be saved?'"[21]

When the meeting was over, the ministers were dumbfounded and made plans immediately to hold another sacramental service at the Gasper River church the last weekend in July. McCready knew the crowds might be huge, and he put out the word that people should bring their wagons and come prepared to camp for the duration. A large clearing was cut in the woods, and preaching stands and simple benches were built. Many historians identify this as the first "camp meeting,"[22] though the term was not used until 1802.

In spite of all the preparations, no one was quite ready for the size of the crowd. More than ten thousand people attended. This was at a time when the largest town in Kentucky was Lexington, which had only eighteen hundred people. The crowd at Gasper River was so huge that several of the ministers could preach at the same time and, as at Red River, "the power of God seemed to shake the whole assembly." McCready exulted:

No person seemed to wish to go home—hunger and sleep seemed to affect nobody—eternal things were the vast concern. Here awakening and converting work was to be found in every part of the multitude; and even some things strangely and wonderfully new to me.[23]

McCready was not alone in his amazement at the strange things taking place. Even Barton Stone, who had traveled for a week to take part in the revival, was astonished.

> The scene was new to me and passing strange. Many, very many, fell down as men slain in battle and continued for hours in an apparently breathless and motionless state. . . . After lying there for hours, they obtained deliverance. They would rise, shouting deliverance, and then would address the surrounding multitude in language truly eloquent and impressive. With astonishment did I hear men, women, and children declaring the wonderful works of God, and the glorious mysteries of the Gospel.[24]

John McGee said that "the mighty power and mercy of God was manifested. The people fell before the word, like corn before a storm of wind, and many rose from the dust with a divine glory" upon their faces.[25] This experience of people "falling" under the Spirit or the Word of God seems to be one of the most remarkable signs attending these revivals. Since so many of the leaders referred to the fallen as being "slain," the phrase "slain in the Spirit" began to circulate—a term still widely in use today.

The experience of being "slain" was not the only evidence of an overwhelming work of God. Barton Stone, who called "being slain" the "falling exercise," also spoke of "the jerks," the "dancing exercise," the "barking exercise," the "laughing exercise," and the "running exercise." Apparently this last was performed by onlookers who began to feel their own bodies affected. There was even what he called the "singing exercise." This latter occurred when some began to "sing most melodiously, not from the mouth or nose, but entirely from the breast. It was most heavenly. None could ever be tired of hearing it."[26]

The meeting came to an end, but the fervor of revivalism continued. The attendees returned to their towns and churches and immediately began to organize camp meetings. Throughout Tennessee, Kentucky, Ohio, and even into Virginia, revival fires roared. The most famous of all of these was the celebrated Cain Ridge revival led by Barton Stone. Inconceivably, more than twenty thousand people attended the meeting in 1801, and the extraordinary reports of supernatural "signs and wonders" exceeded even those of Red River.[27]

Throughout the history of revivalism, controversy was as much in attendance as were the throngs of the faithful—and the Red River meeting was no exception. When some sought to surpass the relative restraint of the early "exercises," extreme emotional and behavioral excesses set in, and the meetings became even more wild and unruly. At the same time, division set in. Doctrinal disputes began to divide the very denominations that had only lately experienced fresh unity. Some with overheated imaginations added to the confusion by preaching bizarre and unbiblical ideas. Barton Stone's sad summary of these troubled times might well be used to describe similar periods of disruption throughout church history: "These blessed effects would have continued, had not men put forth their hallowed hands to hold up their tottering ark, mistaking it for the ark of God."[28]

Despite these troubles, it would be difficult to overestimate the impact of the revival movement launched in Logan County. It certainly gave birth to thousands of smaller revivals like it, and even some larger like Cain Ridge. But it also contributed a number of "new measures" and innovative methodologies that quickly became distinctive of broad American evangelicalism—like "the anxious bench,"[29] the protracted evangelistic crusade, and the camp meeting. Popular evangelists like Charles Finney, Dwight Moody, and Billy Sunday would use each of these with great impact in the decades that followed. Frontier religion as a whole was shaped by revivalism, too, particularly as waves of pioneers drank in the revivalistic spirit while passing from the east through Tennessee and Kentucky to the west. Even the idea of revivalism as an agent of social change became a part of American religion through the experience at Logan County, as did the themes of individual conversion, denominational unity, miracles, and the priority of preaching. Revivalism even affected the course of American music. As historian Bill Malone explains in *Country Music USA*:

> Camp meeting songs or songs inspired by them began to appear in books soon after the earliest Kentucky revivals, and both their the-

ology and their structure have endured as part of the fabric of southern religious music and country music. Simple, singable melodies and song texts characterized by choruses, refrains, and repetitive phrases have always been obvious characteristics of country music.[30]

Interestingly, one of revivalism's most ardent critics, Dr. George Baxter of Washington Academy in Virginia, was most disturbed by the reports of the Red River meetings and was eager to discredit the movement. In November 1801 he traveled to Kentucky to produce a report for the famous Presbyterian leader, Archibald Alexander, which both men expected would expose the folly and deception of the revivalistic phenomenon. But the report that later circulated in the *Connecticut Evangelical Magazine* was far from what either man expected, for what Dr. Baxter saw convinced him that the revival was in fact genuine:

> The power with which this revival has spread, and its influence in moralizing the people, are difficult for you to conceive, and more so for me to describe. . . . I found Kentucky, to appearance, the most moral place I had ever seen. A profane expression was hardly ever heard. A religious awe seemed to pervade the country. . . . Never in my life have I seen more genuine marks of the humility which . . . looks to the Lord Jesus Christ as the only way of acceptance with God. I was indeed highly pleased to find that Christ was all and in all in their religion . . . and it was truly affecting to hear with what agonizing anxiety awakened sinners inquired for Christ, as the only physician who could give them any help.[31]

ℱIRE IN 𝒯ENNESSEE

Reports of the Red River revival reached Tennessee even before the meetings were over. There was tremendous excitement and hope that similar "outpourings" might take place in Tennessee. In September 1800 that hope was fulfilled. During a "sacramental service" at Desha Creek near Shiloh, a huge crowd appeared under the direction of William and John McGee, James McCready, and numerous other Methodist and Presbyterian pastors. When at the preaching of the Word the people "fell like corn before a storm of wind" and many of the same wonders occurred as witnessed at Red River, the leaders believed that Tennessee was destined for a "transforming work of God."[32]

With mounting expectation, William McGee began a five-day meeting at Drake's Creek in Sumner County. Revival manifestations again began to occur among the one thousand people in attendance, and their excitement reached fever pitch when on the last day of the meeting Bishop Francis Asbury, Bishop Richard Whatcoat, and revered elder William McKendree rode onto the site. All three were asked to preach, to the delight of the crowd, as Asbury later recorded in his journal:

> The ministers of God, Methodists and Presbyterians, united their labors, and mingled with the childlike simplicity of primitive times. Fires blazing here and there dispelled the darkness, and the shouts of the redeemed captives, and the cries of precious souls struggling into life, broke the silence of midnight.[33]

The aged Bishop always remembered Drake's Creek as the place where "heaven smiled."[34] And that was just the beginning.

Revival continued to blaze throughout Tennessee. Soon the Baptists joined the Presbyterians and Methodists in meetings that ranged to over five thousand people. Stories circulated of hardened sinners, town drunks, and even brutal killers who were transformed by the power of the revival and commissioned by God to preach the good news to others. The tales the faithful most enjoyed were of those who came to heckle and ridicule the meetings only to get the "jerks" or the "laughs" themselves. How terrifying this must have been to the uninitiated we can only guess, but it was as difficult then as it is now to explain to those not actually in the meetings how truly "acrobatic" they were. Methodist circuit rider Peter Cartwright claimed that he had seen more than five thousand persons jerking at one time and some "were hurled through the air by the jerking of the head." It was not uncommon to see the affected rolling, running, dancing, and even barking. In fact, those who were given to this barking often gathered around trees on all fours and claimed they were "treeing the devil." When a Presbyterian minister from East Tennessee got the jerks and in desperation clung to a tree to gain control of himself, albeit unsuccessfully, those watching jokingly shouted that he was "barking up a tree."[35]

But the revivals were not all physical and emotional. Preaching played a prominent role, and so did biblical doctrine. To preserve the interdenominational unity of the meetings, preachers carefully downplayed doctrinal differences and focused on radical commitment to Jesus Christ and "yielding to the Spirit." Nevertheless, what might be called a "revival theology" arose, which emphasized the availability of salvation to all men and the priority of personal religious experience over doctrine or organization. In addition, the revivals themselves were increasingly seen as less a matter of the sovereignty of God and more the result of "measures," that is, techniques like protracted meetings, fiery preaching, "anxious benches," exciting testimonies, and unrelenting emphasis on holiness and religious zeal.[36]

The old guard Scots-Irish were more than a little astonished by the seemingly odd antics and doctrinal drift of revivalism. They were concerned that the leaders of the movement had encouraged a shift from an emphasis on the gracious work of a sovereign God to an emphasis on sheer personal experience. But many of their more recently arrived frontier neighbors had no such compunctions.

Since for the rugged Methodists such Arminian views were already part of their theology, the revivals only helped to spread their theological distinctives over and against those of their more Reformed brethren. The revivals clearly presaged a changing of the guard. Thus the once marginally significant Methodists benefited greatly from the revival in both numbers and influence. Already stressing free will in their preaching, already pressing their hearers for radical holiness and dedication, and already prepared by the itinerant ministry of Wesley for "excitements" to break out in public meetings, the Methodists were perfectly positioned to let the fresh waves of revival carry them to new evangelistic and institutional success.

In addition, the Methodist circuit riders appeared to be the perfect messengers of revivalism. Once called "God's shock troops," these unlettered but passionate men carried the message of the new birth to remote regions along circuits that were often five thousand miles in length. So faithful were they that people often joked when bad weather hit that "there is nothing out today but crows and Methodist preachers."[37] In a fitting tribute, Methodist historian John McFerrin described these stalwart pioneers:

> They were instant in season and out of season. No change of weather or climate, no swollen streams or lofty mountains, hindered them; on they pressed, preaching day and night, and praying sinners everywhere to be reconciled to God. Poverty was no barrier; hard fare was not in the way; they slept in cabins, or camped in the open air; lived on wild meat and bread of pounded meal; wore threadbare garments, and suffered privations of every sort; yet on and on they pressed, counting not their lives dear to them, so that they might finish their work with joy. The heroic age of Methodist preachers, in all that appertains to genuine heroism, is not surpassed. The first preachers of the West were brave men—men who were not afraid of toil or hardship, or suffering or death.[38]

The labors of these circuit riders, combined with the fresh fire of the Great Revival, were a potent combination. Before Red River, there were approximately six hundred Methodists in Tennessee; shortly afterward, there were more than ten thousand, easily making them the largest religious group in the state.[39]

The Baptists, too, benefited mightily from the great swells of revival—at least at first. Between 1801 and 1802, the number of Baptist converts exploded. Churches that had reported no converts for years were baptizing twenty or more during some of the protracted meetings. For example, in the Holston Association 27 churches reported 59 additions in 1800; in 1802 36 churches reported 793 baptisms.[40] Though the farmer-preacher leadership of the Baptists was no competition for the Methodist circuit riders, the Baptists nevertheless moved powerfully throughout the state, particularly into West Tennessee when that region opened to settlement in 1818.

But the full impact of the revival was dampened within Baptist communities due to internal divisions and strife. The various factions within the fiercely independent communion initially fought over the question of a statewide organization and how such a body would preserve or threaten their beloved autonomy. More serious was the controversy over missions organizations. Strident opponents of missionary societies saw them as unscrupulous and greedy. They demanded that all missionary organizations disband and refused to fellowship with any churches that supported them. Tennessee became a stronghold of anti-missions sentiment, and hardly a Baptist church in the state was left unscathed by the controversy.

The Baptists also fought over doctrine, particularly the restoration ideas of Alexander Campbell. The fiery Campbell, who arrived in America from Scotland in 1809, called for the dissolving of denominational distinctions and a return to "New Testament Christianity." He insisted that the Bible was the only "sure guide to heaven," that ministers should be treated as equals with those in their congregations, and that all religious institutions should be dissolved "into union with the Body of Christ." Adherents to this school of thought were called "Reformers," and they caused heavy losses among the Baptists, the number of Baptist churches in Middle Tennessee dropping, for example, from forty-nine to eleven.[41] Though the Baptists experienced explosive growth in the wake of revival, these internal feuds distracted them from the tasks of ministry and ultimately cost them very dearly.

The Presbyterians—the real founders of the Christian culture in Tennessee—no doubt wrestled with the implications of the Great Revival more than any other body. Revivalism was emotional; Presbyterianism was not. Revivalism was Arminian, focused on man's free will; Presbyterianism was Calvinistic, focused on God's providence. Revivalism emphasized individualism and personal experience; Presbyterianism emphasized covenantalism and corporate destiny. Revivalism put experience above understanding; Presbyterianism put doctrine above sensation. As a result, the old Reformed community, which had played such a strategic role in the early days of the state, began to distance themselves from the movement. And consequently, they began to distance themselves from the populace at large, who were enthralled and enchanted by the fervor of faith they saw in the revivals.

As if that was not bad enough, declining numbers and a sudden drop-off of enthusiasm for Presbyterian ministry brought about a new difficulty for the Presbyterians: the pressing need for more ministers. Most of the promising young pastoral candidates were attracted by the revivalistic sentiment. In addition, the high educational standards of Presbyterians necessarily kept their leadership circles small. Younger ministers who had been influenced by the revivals began to call for a lowering of these standards—a dangerous proposal on a par with the dogmas of Catholicism to most of the older Presbyterians. But the younger men asserted that the practical crisis simply could not be ignored. In 1802 the Transylvania Presbytery, which included Tennessee's Cumberland region, sought to lower its educational standards and to appoint men without the traditional education as "exhorters." But that was not enough for the more reform-minded. Shortly thereafter, a rogue Cumberland Presbytery was carved out of the Transylvania organization. It readily licensed and then ordained men who lacked the standard theological training. The battle lines were drawn, and they clearly fell largely between revivalistic and anti-revivalistic factions. When a presbytery investigating commission—meeting interestingly enough at the Gasper River Meeting House where the Great Revival took place—ordered the Cumberland Presbytery to dissolve, the Tennesseans first appealed and then, after a period of years, declared themselves independent on February 4, 1810. The new Presbytery, led by Finis Ewing, Samuel McAdow, and Samuel King, became the "first denomination to be organized in Tennessee."[42]

It may be, as one historian has written, that "a bit more light, a bit more of love, a bit more of patience on both sides, would have prevented this rupture."[43] Yet youth and the zeal of the convert often stretch old bodies beyond their limits, denominations being no exception. The Cumberland Presbyterians, once free of restraint, became some of the most intriguing innovators on the frontier. They modified and diluted their Calvinist heritage, embraced revivalism, adopted the Methodist circuit rider system, and used the camp meeting with astounding success. Within three years they had more than sixty congregations.[44]

But the Cumberland Presbyterians were not the only group to break from their Reformed moorings. At the center of yet another rift was Barton Stone. Immensely impacted by the revivals at Red River and Cain Ridge, Stone led five ministers and a number of churches out of the more traditional Kentucky synod and into an independent Springfield Presbytery. A year later, yearning to do away with denominational distinctives altogether, the presbytery dissolved itself and issued the tongue-in-cheek "Last Will and Testament of the Springfield Presbytery." Calling themselves simply the "Christian Church," the group determined to have no creeds whatsoever save the Bible. It was a rather inauspicious start for what would prove to be one of the most powerful and significant movements in the nation.

3.2 *Hellfire and Brimstone*. Frontier revivals were often fearsome events. Not only was the preaching passionate and unrelenting, but the specter of dozens—or perhaps even hundreds—of repentant sinners crying out to God for mercy was more than a little unnerving. Nevertheless, Americans flocked to hear such men as George Whitefield, Samuel Davies, and Jonathan Edwards in droves. Indeed, there was hardly a single person who was unaffected by the Great Awakening.

In 1812 Stone moved to Tennessee and began organizing Christian Churches, starting with one at Mansker Station near present-day Hendersonville. Like many of the young Cumberland Presbyterian leaders, Stone borrowed the methods of the circuit riders and planted numerous churches in Sumner and Wilson counties, encouraging the fledgling movement with his monthly journal, *The Christian Messenger*, which he published until his death in 1826.

Historian Herman Norton has concluded that "the activity of the revival and immediate post-revival period literally gave birth to religion in the state."[45] The transforming power of the revival in the life of the state can indeed hardly be measured. Valiant though the Scots-Irish pioneers of Christianity were in the early history of Tennessee, they were eventually swamped by the waves of settlers who left religion and the civilization it produced on the other side of the mountains. The over-mountain regions became spiritual swampland. It seemed that only something as jarring, as sweeping, and yet as intensely personal as the Great Revival could cleanse the land and its people in the crashing waves of God's glory and holiness. The impact of the revival in Tennessee alone, much less in the rest of the country, was felt for generations.

THE GREAT QUAKE

The first decade of the nineteenth century began with a spiritual earthquake. It ended with an earthquake that was all too physical. Between the sixteenth of December 1811 and the seventh of February 1812, a series of earthquakes struck the entire Central Mississippi region. Together these came to be known as the New Madrid Earthquake, the second most powerful in the history of the world. Its force was astounding. Trees snapped like twigs by the thousands. Whole herds of buffalo were knocked down, rose, fell again, and in panic stampeded the prairie. Over seven hundred miles away President James Madison awoke from a sound sleep and wondered about the rumbling sound that disturbed his rest.[46]

The quake was so disorienting that the Mississippi River flowed backwards for hours, and its course changed permanently.

Directly across the Mississippi from New Madrid and only a few miles away from the river, near the border of Kentucky and Tennessee, a monstrous section of ground sank as if stepped upon and mashed down by some gigantic foot and water from subterranean sources gushed forth in fantastic volume and quickly filled the huge depression.[47]

The result was Reelfoot Lake. In Nashville, the earthquake split the ground and caused springs to flow, forming warm pools that drew the curious and the recuperating for years to come.

That the earthquake occurred on the eve of the War of 1812 and that comets and others signs were evident in the sky at the same time provided too tempting a parallel with certain biblical prophecies for men to remain at peace. Earthquakes, wars, signs in the heavens—it was all too much. The effects on the wayward throughout Tennessee were startling. As one observer wrote, "It was a time of great terror to sinners."[48] People associated the quakes with the judgment of an angry God, and with each new tremor hearts shook free their wickedness. "Preachers were everywhere implored to preach and to pray for the people; there was a great awakening among the inhabitants, while men's hearts failed them, and their knees smote together with fear." The membership of the Western Conference of Methodists jumped from 30,741 to 45,983.[49]

Yet circuit rider Peter Cartwright was unimpressed: "Though many were sincere, and stood firm, yet there were hundreds that no doubt had joined from mere fright."[50] This was very close to the conclusion of Methodist historian James McFerrin:

Such is poor, guilty human nature—the preaching of the gospel, the proclamation of mercy through Christ, the goodness of God, fail to bring men to repentance; and then, when judgments come, they tremble and fear, and, like the wicked in the last day, call for rocks and mountains to hide them from the face of God. How much genuine piety results from this state of things, is not for man to determine; but it is evident that when the alarm is over, and the apparent danger is past, many turn, like the sow that was washed, to wallowing in the mire.[51]

The earthquake was also a signal for Tennessee Indians. Some saw it as confirmation of the spiritual powers of Tecumseh. In his efforts to unify the eastern tribes against the encroachments of the white man, Tecumseh had promised a sign. One month after a sign appeared in the sky, he would stomp his foot and "shake down the houses." And amazingly, in the middle of November a sign did appear, a brilliant greenish trail of fire streaking across the sky from the southwest. Thirty days later, on December sixteenth, Indians throughout the Mississippi region rushed from their violently shaken homes to look at each other in astonishment and shout, "Tecumseh!"[52]

Yet other signs also seemed to confirm a spiritual meaning for the earthquake. For quite some time before the quake, leaders of the Real People of East Tennessee had been receiving dreams and visions calling for a return to their traditional religions. The messages purportedly came from the spirits of the Real People's ancestors, who were apparently disturbed that their descendants had given up so much of their land and their tradition to the ways of the white man. In one vision, ghost riders approached three Cherokee and spoke to them:

> Don't be afraid; we are your brothers and have been sent by the Great Spirit to speak with you. The Great Spirit is dissatisfied that you are receiving the white people in our land without distinction. You yourselves see that your hunting is gone—you are planting the corn of the white people—go and sell that back to them and plant Indian corn and pound it in the manner of your forefathers; do away with mills. The Mother of the Nation—Selu, the Corn Mother—has forsaken you because all her bones are being broken through the grinding.[53]

These visitations made the already daunting task of sending missionaries to the Indians even more difficult. Some Indians accepted the wisdom of the missionaries that said the earthquake was not the end of the world but a sign sent by God to show sinners how horrible judgment could be. Others believed the quake was just what they thought spirits had told them: a sign against the whites, a warning for the Real People to return to their ways before they were lost forever.

No matter how the quakes were interpreted, though, Tennesseans both red and white sensed that this extraordinary phenomenon was a warning. Change was upon them. Life could not go on as it had before. The new century meant new ways, new challenges, and new enemies. There was no returning to the past for white man and red man alike, as the decades just ahead would quickly reveal.

PROFILE 3 *Betwixt and Between*

We are in the world yet not of it. That is, of a certainty, a fact yet to cause no little tensions in our endeavors.

George Whitefield

*E*very revival movement in American history is measured against the rule of the nation's first—and greatest—popular revival. It was a remarkable spiritual awakening that was sparked in large part by the labors of a single man.

He was America's first celebrity. Though just twenty-five years old when he began touring the sparsely settled colonies in 1738, George Whitefield was an immediate sensation, and he remained so for the rest of his life. Over the next thirty years, amidst some seven visits from his native England, he would leave his mark on the lives of virtually every English-speaking soul living on this side of the Atlantic—from the cosmopolitan businessmen of Philadelphia and the seasoned traders of Boston to the yeomen farmers of Virginia and the frontier adventurers of Canada.

He literally took America by storm. Wherever he went, vast crowds gathered to hear him. Commerce would cease. Shops would close. And farmers would leave their plows mid-furrow. One of his sermons in the Boston Common actually drew more listeners than the city's entire population. Another in Philadelphia spilled over onto more than a dozen city blocks. Still another in Savannah recorded the largest single crowd ever to gather anywhere in the colonies—despite the scant local population.[1]

All the greatest men of the day were in unabashed awe of his oratorical prowess. Shakespearean actor David Garrick said, "I would give a hundred guineas if I could say *oh* like Mr. Whitefield." And Benjamin Franklin once quipped, "He can bring men to tears merely by pronouncing the word *Mesopotamia*."[2]

Yet despite his wide acclaim, Whitefield was often persecuted for his faith. Hecklers blew trumpets and shouted obscenities at him as he preached. Enraged mobs often attacked his meetings, robbing, beating, and humiliating his followers. Whitefield himself was subjected to unimaginable brutality—he was clubbed twice, stoned once, whipped at least half a dozen times, and beaten a half a dozen more. And he lived constantly under the pall of death threats. Once he recorded in his journal: "I was honored with having a few stones, dirt, rotten eggs, and pieces of dead cats thrown at me. Nevertheless, the Lord was gracious, and a great number were awakened unto life."[3]

3.3 *George Whitefield.* **Though the actual founder of Methodism, George Whitefield yielded leadership of the movement to John Wesley in order to devote his full attention to evangelism in both England and the Americas. His brilliant oratory and simple gospel theme made him a sensation on both sides of the Atlantic. Without a doubt, he was the primary human agency behind the Great Awakening.**

Amazingly, it was not just the profane who condemned Whitefield's work. He was also opposed by the religious establishment. Accused of being a "fanatic," he was often in "more danger of attack from the clergy than he was from the worldly."[4] As a result, biographer Arnold Dallimore says, "Whitefield's entire evangelistic life was an evidence of his physical courage."[5] Though often stung by the vehemence of the opposition he faced, he refused to take it personally, attributing it rather to the "offense of the Gospel."[6] According to J. I. Packer, most of the English-speaking Christians in Whitefield's day "had taken up with a moralistic, indeed legalistic, recasting of justification by faith." In fact, he says, "Faith had ceased to be self-despairing trust in the person, work, promises, and love of Jesus Christ. It had become a moral life of good works lived in hope of acceptance at the last day." Whitefield believed that this sort of faith was merely "the religion of the natural man masquerading as Christianity."[7] Nevertheless, such a religion was popular and accepted. It always is. Thus, despite the fact that Whitefield obviously struck a sensitive chord among the people when he proclaimed the doctrines of grace, he just as obviously stirred up fierce opposition among both the ungodly and the religious, who always have been and always will be united in their animosity toward the gospel.

Whitefield emphasized that a comprehension of grace would naturally prompt wholehearted righteousness, thus there was actually no contradiction between the requisites of Christian holiness and the prerogatives of Christian liberty. And that was equally an offense to the man who desired no accountability to a moral standard whatsoever and the man who desired to reduce the faith to a series of ethical demands. To both the lawless and the legalist, Whitefield's message of life in Christ was intolerable.

And so it ever has been, and will be. The revivals that swept across Tennessee during the first decade of the nineteenth century were no different. As a result they wrought a double-edged sword. As in Whitefield's day, the leaders of the revival were caught betwixt and between—they saw some reject their message out of hand, others accept the method and all that went with it but fail to comprehend the message. Thankfully, there were still others who grasped the message and were thus forever changed.

4

$\mathscr{P}$aths of $\mathscr{H}$ope,
$\mathscr{T}$rails of $\mathscr{T}$ragedy

*The mystery of history is its integration of the great with the base,
the joyous with the grievous, the magnificent with the banal, the
hopeful with the tragic.*

Timothy Maury

$\mathscr{I}$n His great high priestly prayer, Jesus prayed that his disciples
would "be one" as He and the Father "are one."[1] Alas, the pages of
Church history give little evidence that His disciples have taken
this unity as seriously as Jesus did. Yet, whenever Christians have
actually demonstrated a measure of authentic unity, it has most
often been during times of intense spiritual renewal. In such seasons of grace, peripheral theological distinctions, cultural barriers,
and even racial animosities dissolved in the face of a fresh vision
of the holy. The Church then felt the thrill of drawing near the
grand design, of fulfilling its purpose and destiny on earth.

It is the heightened joy of the renewal itself that often makes
the time afterward so painful. Suddenly, the special season of
grace comes to an end, and leaders find themselves saddled with
shepherding in the calm valleys a people who have known unity
only on the windy and exhilarating mountaintop. Before long,
what began supernaturally seems to demand exhausting human
effort to sustain. The unraveling begins. Grace degenerates into
legalism. Unity shatters into competition. The movement becomes
institutionalized and builds monuments to its own supposed

glory. The final sign of decline is when people speak of what *was* far more than they speak of what *is*, when the second and third generations define themselves in terms of the first generation's blessings. As H. Richard Niebuhr wrote in his groundbreaking *The Social Sources of Denominationalism*:

> Spontaneous movements of the spirit among men face to face with strange and vast new problems become the petrified traditions of ecclesiastical organizations—traditions which have often lost significance in a new and common environment but which have not lost their power to keep apart to the third and fourth generations the children of long-forgotten frontiers.[2]

Unfortunately, what Niebuhr describes is exactly what the churches of Tennessee experienced in the wake of the Great Revival. Fervent revivalism had brought astonishing growth, and the churches scrambled to build new wineskins for their new wine. Denominations broadened their reach and strengthened their administrative machinery. Local churches enlarged their buildings and extended their ministries. And new schools arose to imbed the lessons of the late renewal in the next generation. Yet when men strive to sustain through institutional administration what has happened only by a sovereign work of grace, they inevitably seem to draw dangerously near to entombing the very work of the Spirit they are trying to perpetuate. This was often the case in Tennessee following the age of revivalism, and it may help to explain why the churches lost so much ground in the latter half of the nineteenth century.

It began with what leaders at the time called a "spirit of competition." The churches had enjoyed an exceptional level of cooperation during the renewal, a blessing many hoped would continue until the return of Jesus. It was not to be, for soon an envious animosity arose between the Methodists and the Baptists, the two biggest gainers from the days of revival. Herman Norton wrote: "As they lined up as the chief contenders for converts, the two denominations, eyeing each other suspiciously, developed attitudes of extreme antagonism and tore into each other's ranks with abandon, casting aside all courtesy and ethics."[3]

This was no quiet ecclesiastical conflict, either. It was a full-blown public clash. Crowds of rowdy Methodists chanted: "I'll tell you who the Lord loves best—it's the shouting Methodist!"[4]

Opposing Baptist throngs retorted: "Baptist, Baptist, Baptist. Baptist till I die. I'll go along with the Baptists. And find myself on High."[5]

This rather silly public display of competition purported to be a concern over doctrine differences, though many suspected it was actually more about a "party spirit" and lack of Christian character. Baptists, who baptized only confessing adults and then only by complete immersion, disdained the Methodist practice of sprinkling, particularly the sprinkling of covenant children. The Methodist practice of open communion was also odious to the Baptists, who carefully "guarded the Lord's table" to admit only the faithful.[6]

Alas, the Presbyterians were not immune from these conflicts either. When Methodist circuit rider Peter Cartwright established a church near present-day Hendersonville, he positioned himself directly across the street from the local Presbyterian church. Cartwright regularly—and loudly—thrashed the Presbyterians and their doctrines in his sermons. And apparently he did so with some success—of the twenty-seven members who helped form the new congregation, thirteen were proselytes from that beleaguered Presbyterian congregation. Even as late as 1845, the Presbyterian Synod of Tennessee complained of the "too successful misrepresentation of the doctrines and polity of Presbyterianism made by the Methodists."[7]

Aside from this spirit of competition, the denominations also wrestled with the more internal matter of organization. The Methodists, whom historian Robert Corlew claims "exerted more leadership in Tennessee church affairs during the antebellum period than did any other body," scrambled to accommodate the astounding growth they experienced during the revival.[8] Accustomed to tending circuits spread over vast stretches of land, the Methodists now found themselves organizing new conferences to care for the multiplying districts. Bishops Asbury and McKendree organized the Tennessee Conference in an 1812 meeting near Portland, Tennessee, at a time when membership in the state was around seventeen thousand.[9] Though this conference initially included territory outside of Tennessee, it was later reduced to Tennessee and part of Kentucky and in 1820 again reduced to include only Tennessee. In 1824 the Holston Conference was formed east of the mountains, and the Memphis Conference arose west of the mountains in 1840.

In the three decades leading up to the War between the States, the Methodists threw themselves into a frenzy of activity. Each of the three conferences published journals that merged in 1854 to become the *Nashville Christian Advocate*. Like all the denominations in the state, the Methodists found that these decades were prime for building schools. In 1827 Holston Seminary opened in New Market, ten years later becoming Holston College. Methodists also established East Tennessee Female Institution in Knoxville and in 1857 supported Athens Female College. These were not the only schools built for women, though, for during an astonishing five-year period beginning in 1848, Methodists founded Clarksville Female Academy, Soule Female College at Murfreesboro, Pulaski Female School, and Tennessee Female Institute at Columbia.

The success of the Methodists in these years is a tribute to the spirit of the circuit rider, the spirit of men like Francis Asbury, that lived on in the movement's leaders. Like Asbury, who crossed the mountains sixty-two times and preached more than fifteen thousand sermons,[10] Tennessee Methodists in the first half of the nineteenth century were visionary, hardworking, self-sacrificing, and armed with an Arminian, democratic theology that readily appealed to the hearts of frontier folk. Methodists could boast by this time more than one thousand churches between Memphis and Bristol and at least one church in every county.[11]

The Baptists met with only slightly less growth than the Methodists, but found themselves wrestling far more with matters of church organization. Though their practice of local church autonomy brought many benefits, it also made cooperation among the churches a challenge. By 1812, the eleven thousand Baptists in the state found themselves divided amongst six Associations: the Holston and Tennessee in the east, the Cumberland and Concord in the middle, and the Western and Forked Deer in the west. But, sadly, they were divided by far more than mere regional jurisdictions. "When Robert B. C. Howell came to Nashville from Virginia in 1835 to pastor the First Baptist Church, he found at least ten distinct Baptist sects whose members refused to take communion even with one another."[12] Believers broke fellowship and drew up battle lines along issues like whether historic creeds had any legitimacy whatsoever, whether missions organizations should exist, whether there was a biblical basis for Sunday schools and Bible societies, and even whether unity was actually desirable among the various associations.

Despite much opposition, a "Convention" arose in Nashville, which in 1842 was replaced by the General Association of Tennessee Baptists. Unable to unite the disparate organizations and theologies of such diverse groups as the Missionary Baptists, Gospel Mission Baptists, and Primitive Baptists, the Association nevertheless accomplished much in other arenas in the decades before the War between the States. In 1835 Robert Howell started a journal called *The Baptist* in Nashville that, though plagued by financial problems, remained in circulation for many years. Later it was renamed *Tennessee Baptist*, and under the editorial hand of James R. Graves, it became very influential across all administrative and jurisdictional boundaries. In matters of education, Baptists were initially plagued by debates as to whether higher education should even exist. Only after college-bound youths began attending the schools of other denominations did the church act. The Baptists built Union University, Mossy Creek Baptist Seminary—later Carson-Newman College—and a college for women in Murfreesboro founded in 1848 as Female Institute and later renamed Eaton Female College after its founder. The disadvantages of schism and a slow start in matters of education aside, by 1860 the Baptists had thirty-five thousand members in nearly seven hundred churches and, like the Methodists, could boast of at least one church in every county.[13]

Of all the state's Reformed churches, the Cumberland Presbyterians allowed the winds of revival to carry them the furthest. By 1814, traditional Presbyterians trailed their Cumberland brethren numerically, who ranked third in the state behind the Methodists and Baptists. The path was rocky for the Cumberland movement at first, though. Initially, only three ordained ministers remained of those who left traditional ranks: Finis Ewing, Samuel King, and Samuel McAdow. Unwilling to despise the day of small beginnings, the men pressed on and by 1817 had three presbyteries. After more hard work and prayer, the young denomination reported over 1,100 new members in 1819, over 2,500 in each of the next three years, and by 1825 more than four thousand additions annually. By 1835, the Cumberland Presbyterians had seventeen thousand members in thirty-five presbyteries, and by 1860 their numbers had doubled.[14]

To give their expanding movement focus, the fledgling denomination started a publication in 1832 called *The Revivalist*, which remained in circulation until 1840. They also started schools, though they were less energetic in this than other churches because they had seen what they thought was a detrimental effect of education on traditional Presbyterians. Nevertheless, they established two schools during these decades. Cumberland University was founded in Lebanon in 1842, and in the same year Bethel Seminary was founded at McLemoresville. In 1847 Bethel became a college and by 1858 had 165 students.[15]

The traditional Reformed Presbyterian ranks suffered for the success of their Cumberland brethren and in turn concentrated most of their efforts on their native strengths of education and administration. In 1817 the Synod of Tennessee was formed. It was followed by the Synod of the West in 1826. Each contained four presbyteries, but this multiplication of jurisdictions was not designed to accommodate growth. Instead, the administrative reorganization was prompted by a desire to focus the presbyteries on smaller geographical regions. In fact, the number of the traditional Reformed churches was in sharp decline. No presbytery had more than fifteen congregations and ten ministers, and rarely did new members exceed thirty in any presbytery. By 1834, the Tennessee Synod, located in the east where the Presbyterians were strongest, reported only sixty-four churches and fewer than six

4.1 *David Lipscomb.* One of the early leaders in the Church of Christ that grew out of the great backwoods revivals, David Lipscomb was influential in bringing organization to the reform movement. He founded the Nashville Bible School, which later became David Lipscomb University.

thousand members. By mid-century, Presbyterians numbered only two hundred churches statewide.[16]

Nevertheless, the Presbyterians exceeded all other denominations when it came to educational leadership. In the early years of Tennessee, Presbyterians established schools almost as readily as they did churches. Thomas Craighead started Davidson Academy in Nashville, which eventually became Davidson College, merged with Cumberland College, and took the name University of Nashville. Its first president, Presbyterian minister Philip Lindsley, was one of the most remarkable educational leaders in the state's history. Meanwhile, Hezekiah Balch founded Greeneville College, Samuel Doak founded Tusculum Academy along with his father, John Doak, and Isaac Anderson started what became Maryville College. To support these efforts, the Synod of Tennessee began publishing the *Calvinistic Magazine* at Rogersville in 1826, which was later replaced by *The Christian Observer*, published for Tennessee Presbyterians in Richmond, Virginia.

Though not formally a denomination, the Christian Church evolved into a loose affiliation something akin to that of the Baptists. The followers of Barton Stone and Alexander Campbell united in 1832, and the movement became variously known as the Disciples of Christ, the Churches of Christ, the Christian Churches, and the Restoration Churches. In 1842 a "cooperative" of Nashville churches joined for evangelistic work and soon cooperatives formed at the district level much like the Baptist associations.

When a national movement organized in 1849, the Tennessee churches—which by 1850 had 106 congregations and more than twelve thousand members—were comfortable enough with such structures to join.[17]

This nondenominational structure functioned much like a denomination. In 1842, the movement started publishing *The Bible Advocate* in Paris and later the *Christian Review* in Nashville. When the *Review* ceased circulation in 1853, Tolbert Fanning and David Lipscomb began publishing the influential and long-lived *Gospel Advocate*. Schools also proliferated within the movement. Tolbert Fanning chartered Franklin College in 1844, which was located where the Nashville airport is today. A sister school for women, Minerva College, was also opened to give "suitable facilities to girls for acquiring a classical, mathematical, and scientific, as well

4.2 *Nashville Bible School.* The reform movement that Barton Stone and Alexander Campbell helped ignite came to maturity as their young disciples began to establish educational institutions throughout the West. The Nashville Bible School—founded by one of the most able of those young disciples, David Lipscomb—eventually became the thriving David Lipscomb University.

as an ornamental education."[18] In 1848 Burritt College was chartered and named for a well-known blacksmith whose writings on social and economic subjects were widely read. Located high atop the Cumberland Mountains and purposely secluded from transportation and communication, the school was intended as a place of the most serious study and concentration. Supporters must have been shocked in 1858, then, when an effort to limit student drinking by destroying the stills in the surrounding area resulted in the burning of the president's home. Homeless and despised, the poor man was forced to resign.[19]

*N*EW *M*OVEMENTS

Several new movements joined the five major denominations in the decades before the war. Episcopalians, though initially hindered by lingering attitudes toward the Anglican English following the American Revolution, finally entered Tennessee through the ministry of James Otey. A Virginian who came to lead Franklin's Harpeth Academy in 1821, Otey was profoundly affected when a friend gave him a *Book of Common Prayer*. As a later bishop wrote, "That prayer book in God's providence made Otey a Christian and a churchman."[20] Otey soon met with such fierce prejudice because of his Episcopalian faith that he left the state. He used his time away, though, to prepare for the priesthood and in 1825 returned to Franklin to reopen Harpeth Academy and to begin holding Episcopal services. At first, his congregation met in the Masonic Hall in Franklin, but in 1827 Otey organized St. Paul's Episcopal Church, the first Episcopal church in the state. Later, Otey's exceptional gifts and tireless efforts enabled him to organize St. Peter's Church at Columbia and to begin holding the services in Nashville that led to the formation of Christ Church in 1829.

In that same year, Bishop John Ravenscroft of North Carolina arrived in Nashville to preside over a convention at the Masonic Hall. At this meeting, the Episcopal Diocese of Tennessee was formed. The Episcopal Church in Tennessee grew slowly, though, and largely among the urban upper class. In 1834, when Otey became the bishop of the diocese, there were only eleven churches and nine clergymen. Christ Church of Nashville had thirty-four members and St. Paul's of Franklin had twenty-three. By 1860, the denomination had twenty-six parishes with around 1,500 members.[21]

The Episcopalians had a different approach to education from any other denomination. Rather than focusing on building colleges, Episcopalians devoted themselves to establishing secondary academies. Thus it was not until 1860 that Bishop Leonidas Polk laid the cornerstone for the first Episcopalian school in the state, the University of the South. Situated on a ten-thousand-acre mountaintop campus, the construction progressed well until the outbreak of hostilities in the War between the States. Bishop Polk, who served as a Confederate general, was killed in that tragic conflict. It was not until after the war that Bishop Charles Quintard led the school to completion in 1868.

The Lutherans also joined the growing number of Christian denominations in Tennessee at this time. The first Lutheran congregation was the Shofner Church near Shelbyville in Middle Tennessee. In 1820 the Tennessee Synod was founded, largely through the labors of Paul Henkel, an author and early missionary to the state. Lutheran numbers grew through German immigration more than through conversion, and since available clergymen rarely filled demand, members often changed to other denominations out of pastoral necessity. What leaders the denomination had were insistent upon "the preeminence of the Holy Bible . . . and the Augsburg Confession of Faith as a pure emanation from the Bible." On the eve of the War between the States, the Lutherans had eighteen churches, most of them in the eastern portions of the state.[22]

Catholicism, too, established itself in the state during these years. Catholics had been in Tennessee from the early days of the French traders, among whom Timothy Demonbreun was the best known. After serving under Montcalm at Quebec, Demonbreun moved into Illinois in 1759 and later worked his way up the Cumberland to French Lick, the site of present-day Nashville. He stubbornly retained his Catholic faith despite all efforts by Nashville Protestants to convert him, and he loved to display his prized silver crucifix, a treasure he had brought from France. Though he probably celebrated Mass very few times in his years on the Cumberland, priests did occasionally venture down from Kentucky, and on these occasions Demonbreun presumably found the Eucharist all the more sweet for its infrequency. One of the priests who joined Demonbreun in Nashville for short occasions was Stephen Badin. This Catholic stalwart preached before the state legislature in 1808, and though tempted to plant himself in Nashville, eventually turned toward Knoxville and spent the rest of his life planting churches there.

A second missionary, Robert Abell, officiated at the first public mass in Nashville in 1820. Thereafter, the Catholics shared a meeting house with Protestants and were visited twice a year by a priest. Finally, in 1830, a parish was formed, but it was not until Richard Pius Miles became the bishop of the newly formed Diocese of Nashville that the Catholics received the galvanizing energy they so needed. Bishop Miles was a visionary leader who surprised Catholics and Protestants alike with his fire and industry. He quickly "organized his diocese, launched a seminary and a school for boys, gathered around him a number of capable nuns and priests, established an orphan's home and a hospital and built a Cathedral, later to be called St. Mary's."[23]

The growth of Catholicism received a boost from the dramatic influx of Irish Catholic immigrants in the mid-1800s, who largely settled in Chattanooga, Memphis, and Nashville. Their presence was a force to be reckoned with. In Memphis, for example, more than one-fifth of the eighteen thousand citizens were Irish—and were largely Catholic.[24] Though they unfortunately met with deep-seated hatred, the Catholics of Tennessee remained faithful under the leadership of Bishop Miles. He was, as Herman Norton wrote, "a man of wisdom, patience, and education" who "maintained his dignity in the midst of the intolerant attacks and won the confidence and friendship of many broad-minded Protestants as he continued to extend Catholicism."[25]

Judaism also entered Tennessee during these critical decades. Jews first arrived in the state as early as 1790 and were sprinkled throughout the state by 1840. A census in that year records 160 Jewish families in Davidson County.[26] In 1851 the congregation chartered as *Khal Kodesh Mogen David*, the "Holy Congregation of the Shield of David," began in Nashville, and at about the same time the *B'Nai Israel Synagogue*, "the Children of Israel Congregation," started in Memphis. Tensions developed between strict orthodoxy and more moderate, reformed approaches to the faith, but it was not until 1862 that a Reform congregation began in Nashville. At this same time, during the war years, a small congregation began in Knoxville called *Beth El*, the "House of God." Jews in Tennessee had few rabbis, but fortunately those they did have were men of strength. The founder of *Khal Kodesh Mogen David* in Nashville was the Russian-Pole Alexander Iser, a pioneer who is remembered with affection in the city to this day.

STORMING THE BASTIONS OF FREEMASONRY

In the decades before the War between the States, Americans took a good look at their society and started planning changes. Moved partially by the reforming influence of the revivals and partially by a democratic confidence in man's ability to improve himself, Americans identified their society's ills and took aim. Every problem seemed to have an organization intent on removing it, and every citizen wanted to prove himself a supporter of "the cause," whatever it was. Of particular concern to many Americans were the strength and number of secret societies in the country, and it was this concern that brought the power of the Freemasons to national attention.

It is virtually impossible to overestimate the influence of freemasonry in the early history of Tennessee. The earliest settlers to venture over the mountains brought with them affiliations with the Masonic lodges of Europe, and the eastern colonies and pioneers like Timothy Demonbreun kept Masonic convictions alive even in the remotest parts of the wilderness. In time, the ranks of Tennessee Masons included some of the most prestigious and influential names in the history of the state: Robertson, Donelson, Jackson, Blount, Sevier, Polk, Roane, Grundy, Rhea, Dickson, Houston, and Johnson.

As unusual as it may sound today, freemasonry then was almost inseparably linked with church life. Since the lodges were usually the earliest and grandest buildings in a community, they provided meeting space for congregations without buildings of their own. "The close relationship between the Masonic order and the church in antebellum society is manifested in the number of buildings shared by the two institutions," wrote Mayme Hart Johnson in her *A Treasury of Tennessee Churches*,[27] and the evidence for this pattern abounds. The Methodists of Cornersville met in the Greek Revival Lodge of that city, as the Presbyterians did in Bolivar. Similarly, the Masonic Hall of Franklin was the first home of many of Williamson County's churches from the time of its completion in 1828.

These halls were also the seats of power and officialdom in the young state. They hosted state and county courts, town councils, treaty signings, land deals, and even the occasional visiting dignitary. In 1824 General Lafayette, French hero of the American Revolution, made a return tour of the United States that included a stop in Nashville. There he was hosted by his fellow Masons and had the honor of meeting the oldest Mason of the region, Timothy Demonbreun. In fact, the Masons were so closely linked to the government of Tennessee that for nearly thirty years, from 1824 to 1853, the state legislature met and conducted its business in the Masonic Hall of Nashville.

Yet the Masons offered more than their buildings to the bustling society of early Tennessee. "Freemasonry was in those days not only a fraternal order but a real center of political power in the state, a ready made network of friendships that could offer the young politician quick access to high places." The Masonic leadership were the power brokers in the new state. They defined the elite, guarded the gates to the halls of authority, and set the direction of the state through a network of influential relationships and unofficial understandings. To run afoul of the Masonic leadership was political suicide. Even Congressman Sam Houston, upon finding himself slandered in Masonic circles, labored tirelessly to clear his name in fear that a black mark upon his Masonic record meant political doom.[28]

But beginning in the late 1820s, the Masons came under attack. This assault was powered in part by a group called the Anti-Masons, who united in opposition to all secret orders. Much of their energy was devoted to ending the political career of Andrew Jackson, well-known as a Masonic Grand Master. Another force behind this assault was the story of Captain William Morgan. A former Mason, Morgan was murdered after he published a damaging exposé of Masonic practices and beliefs. When both the tale of his murder and the details of his exposé reached the public, a national outcry arose against the Masons. The most effective force of opposition to freemasonry, though, was revivalistic Christianity. The revivals of the early nineteenth century had revealed the power of religion to transform men's souls. In time, Christians sought to channel this same power toward the transformation of society. The leader of this unique amalgamation of revivalistic fervor and social gospel progressivism was unquestionably Charles Finney.

Finney was converted when he began reading Scripture to better understand the biblical references in American law books. He became a fiery evangelist, widely known for crusades of such emotional power that entire towns were gripped by his message. Finney's ministry led to revivalistic passions among tens of thousands, but his ultimate goal was the conversion of society. Not until believers changed their world was the full work of the gospel done, he believed: "Now the great business of the church is to reform the world," he insisted, "to put away every kind of sin. The

Church of Christ was originally organized to be a body of reformers."[29]

It was as Finney called the faithful to bring all of society into
harmony with Scripture that freemasonry became a target. Finney
had himself been a Mason before his conversion, and he believed
that the organization was completely at odds with biblical
Christianity—its secrecy, its arcane symbolism, its strange rituals,
and its aredemptive worldview all seemed to him to be gross vio-
lations of Christian dogma. In his many revival meetings throughout the country, he insisted that the truly saved must renounce
freemasonry as they would any other sinful practice:

> I wish, if possible, to arouse the young men who are Freemasons
> and Christians, to consider the inevitable consequences of such a
> horrible trifling with the most solemn oaths, as is constantly prac-
> ticed by Freemasons. Such a course must and does, as a matter of
> fact, grieve the Holy Spirit, sear the conscience and harden the
> heart.[30]

Soon, other ministers joined Finney's public stand against
freemasonry. "A leader in the Christian Church questioned
whether a man ever became more spiritually inclined after he
turned 'to the ribbons, the apron, or the mystic symbols of a secret
conclave.'"[31] Even President John Quincy Adams spoke out against
the lodges. The attacks were devastating. Lodges were disbanded,
and thousands fled from the order. By 1838, only two lodges
remained in East Tennessee where dozens had once enjoyed
prominence, and never again did the lodges or the Masonic net-
works enjoy the power they once knew.

*T*HE *T*RAIL *W*HERE *T*HEY *C*RIED

While the churches of Tennessee fought their doctrinal battles, built their organizations, and extricated themselves from

Masonic entanglements, one of the most horrifying events in American history unfolded. The government of the United States forced the Cherokee Nation to abandon its lands, homes, and possessions and move west of the Mississippi River. The depth of the suffering this caused among the Real People can hardly be comprehended. But the dispossession was also tragic because of what it meant for the nation as a whole, because of the cynical lie it made of so much of what Americans believed about their nation. The removal symbolized the victory of greed over destiny, of wickedness over character. It has become a monument to our national loss of innocence and to our departure from the nobility of the original American dream.

When the Pilgrim Fathers composed their Mayflower Compact while drifting off the shore of the New World in 1620, they wrote that they had sailed "for the glory of God and the

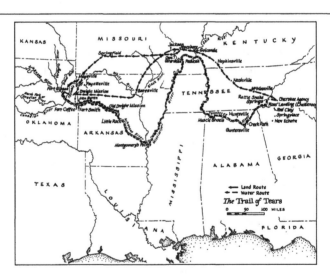

4.3 *The Trail of Tears*. The tragic removal of the Cherokee Nation from its ancestral homeland in 1838 concluded in one of the most shameful episodes in American history—the utter decimation of a peaceful, independent, and Christian civilization by force of law. The long march to the Oklahoma Territory—which was itself to be appropriated from the Native American nations exiled there—was horrific, and the human loss was incalculable.

advancement of the Christian faith." This meant not only the building of a new and biblically based society, but also the evangelization of the natives. As their leader, William Bradford, wrote, "seeing we daily pray for the conversion of the heathens . . . to them we may go . . . that they may be persuaded at length to embrace the Prince of Peace, Christ Jesus, and rest in peace with him forever."[32] But this vision was not new. Even Columbus had written on his first voyage that "it was the beginning and the end of this enterprise that it should be for the increase and the glory of the Christian religion. No one should come to these regions who is not a good Christian."[33] He believed, "Charting the seas is but a necessary requisite for the fulfillment of the Great Commission of our glorious Savior."[34]

Sadly, the purity of this early hope was quickly lost. From the time of the Jamestown colony, where Indian generosity was met with greed and deception, the settlers quickly forgot the purposes of their fathers and rushed to exploit the riches of the New World without much regard for the "savages" who owned them. The hostility that resulted between white man and red—in the bloody King Philip's War of New England, in the horrible French and Indian War, and even in the American Revolution—proved that baser instincts had replaced the nobler purposes of earlier generations.

Nevertheless, by 1794 there was a general peace west of the Appalachians, and this gave George Washington's administration a chance to implement policies designed to "civilize" the Indians in the hope of making them equal citizens in the new nation. The acts of Congress that ensued challenge modern theories about the separation of church and state. In 1787 Congress ordained special lands "for the sole use of Christian Indians" and reserved land for the Moravian Brethren "for civilizing the Indians and promoting Christianity." This was followed by a 1796 law entitled "An Act regulating the grants of land appropriated for Military services and for the Society of the United Brethren, for propagating the Gospel among the Heathen."[35] Thomas Jefferson signed an extension of this law three times during his term in office and even petitioned Congress to ratify a treaty with the Kaskaskia Indians that provided a federal stipend for a Catholic priest and funds to build a church. Dozens of similar acts were passed. Looking back upon these efforts in 1828, John Quincy Adams told Congress that the Indians were "considered as savages, whom it was our policy and our duty to use our influence in converting to Christianity and in bringing within the pale of civilization."[36]

Christian missionaries were on the forefront of this effort, and while their devotion cannot be faulted, many of them found it difficult to distinguish between the work of making Christians and the work of making Americans:

> The missionary's role was to provide the schooling and the moral training to "wean" the Indians from their savage customs so that they, or their children, would blend easily into the cultural institutions of Euro-American society. In short, the melting pot idea of assimilation was to be promoted by mission schools for the Native Americans in the same way that public schools would assimilate incoming aliens from the non-English nations of Europe. To Christianize was to Americanize.[37]

This is not to say, however, that all missionaries were but pawns of federal policy. Yet the fact is that most missionaries unfortunately saw the process of making the Indians Christians and the process of making the Indians Americans as one and the same—and this is the very perspective that doomed so many of their efforts.

Among the Cherokee, this failure was particularly tragic given that the Real People were, as we have seen, so quick to adapt to new ways. The problem was that the missionaries who moved into the Cherokee Nation—Moravians at first, then Presbyterians, and finally Baptists, Congregationalists, and Methodists—found little of redemptive value in Cherokee culture. They saw the Real People as mere savages and immediately concluded that making them Christian meant not transforming their culture but destroying it. Rather than incarnate the gospel into the thought-forms of the Real People, the missionaries treated the Cherokee culture as an enemy and refused to capture its powerful symbolism and lore for their purposes.

The missionaries made their first mistake when they refused to learn the native language. White missionaries found this language difficult and lacking some of the essential terms needed to communicate the gospel. Rather than develop new terms and adapt symbolism as the writers of the New Testament had, most missionaries to the Cherokee insisted upon using English alone in their schools and churches. When one Moravian missionary was asked to translate some paragraphs of Christian doctrine into Cherokee, he reported that "for matters of that nature neither words nor expressions are available in this language." Not finding terms for grace, redemption, sin, hell, repentance, or forgiveness already in the Cherokee language, most missionaries concluded that it was "incapable of conveying any idea beyond the sphere of the senses; there seems to be no other way left by which the spiritual or temporal good of these people can be promoted than by teaching them in our language." As one Moravian wrote, God is surely "graciously pleased with the praise of these little brown ones who indeed at this time understand very little of that which they sing."[38] Unfortunately, the Real People had to learn English to become Christians.

The missionaries also refused to respect the communal life of the Real People. Perhaps they were too shaped by the American values of individualism, private property, and competition, or perhaps they truly did not understand the redemptive strengths of Cherokee tribal life. Whatever the reason, when the missionaries encountered the Real People's communal farms and granaries, for example, they immediately tried to replace them. "Under Christianity the tribal granaries that provided public relief when harvest failed would cease to exist; the hospitality ethic would be abandoned; every family would be on its own to thrive or starve."[39]

The missionaries also disappointed the Real People in the practice of healing. For the Indians, healing was an integral part of religious life. The *Adawehi* conjurers were as much healers as they were priests. The Real People expected that right religion meant health for the individual and the community, that healing demonstrated the power and truth of faith. The missionaries who entered

the Cherokee Nation in the early 1800s were from Christian traditions that separated healing from faith. American Christians had
made healing a secular aspect of their lives, separating it from any
and all of its spiritual components. Their version of Christianity
was essentially dualistic—dividing body and soul, heaven and
earth, sacred and secular. Indian religion, on the other hand, was
"transcendental, mystical, monistic." The Real People could not
understand how the Christian God could be more powerful than
theirs and yet offer no solution for their illnesses. When a missionary pastor told one man that he could not take his son to the
Adawehi for treatment, the man obeyed but returned angrily to the
next church meeting with his son in his arms. "He held out to me
the arm of his little boy," the missionary wrote later. "It was almost
covered with sores." The father angrily shouted, "There, those
may be there till he dies. I shall not doctor them." The church
members saw this and were outraged. Later, the missionary sadly
reported, "The whole church forsook me."[40]

For those missionaries who overcame their cultural preju-
dices and learned to appreciate the subtleties of the Real People's
worldview, the work of evangelism was both fruitful and reward-
ing. Daniel Butrick of the American Board of Commissioners of
Foreign Missions in Boston arrived in the Cherokee Nation in 1818.
Choosing to live with a Cherokee-speaking family in order to learn
their language, Butrick gained insight most settlers never enjoyed.
"In many respects," he said, "their language is far superior to ours;
theological concepts of every kind and degree may be communi-
cated to this people in their own language with as much clearness
and accuracy as in ours." As he grew in understanding of their language, Butrick also grew in compassion. He was distressed to find
that other missionaries were full of "pride and superiority," that
"they will not come down far enough to take hold even of their
blankets" to help. Butrick boldly defended the rights of the
Cherokee to his own government and this, coupled with his
respectful, compassionate evangelistic work, won him not only
souls, but a place of honor among the Real People.[41]

Perhaps the greatest example of an effective missionary to the
Cherokee was Evan Jones. He began serving as a missionary for

the Northern Baptists in 1821 and was initially as "ethnocentric and aggressive as any other missionary." Unlike many of those missionaries, though, he changed. He learned the language so well that he was able to translate the entire Bible into Cherokee when Sequoyah completed his "syllabary" in 1821. This important tool brought literacy to the Real People, and Jones's Bible translation was the first literature many of them read. But Jones went further. He lived in the homes of the Real People, ate their food, understood their problems, and showed himself a faithful friend. Jones quickly realized that the best evangelists to the Cherokee were the Cherokee themselves. He began training converts to preach and start churches, and the greatest testament to his labors were the many Cherokee-speaking, Cherokee-pastored churches that dotted the southeast.[42]

Jones's efforts on behalf of his friends continued until his death in 1872. Even when he was forced out of Georgia for championing the Indians' cause, Jones simply relocated to New Columbus, Tennessee, and continued to preach throughout the Cherokee Nation, accompanied always by the small army of Cherokee ministers he had trained. As Cherokee historian William McLoughlin has written, Jones:

> worked chiefly with the full-bloods, sided with the great majority of the Cherokees against Andrew Jackson, walked with them on the Trail of Tears, served as a chaplain in one of their regiments during the Civil War, and had the unique honor of being officially admitted as a full member of the tribe with a pension from the Cherokee treasury for his long and faithful service to the Cherokee Nation.[43]

Clearly, Evan Jones was an example of what compassion, hard work, and humility could accomplish.

Because of the efforts of men like Jones, and despite the haughty, bumbling efforts of some missionaries, the Real People did begin to turn toward Christianity in considerable numbers. In fact, as Davidson has written, the Real People "had become in large measure a Christian people."[44] Often, this was because the Real People saw the truth in the Christian message despite the questionable example of some of the Christians they knew. When a Cherokee translation of the Scriptures was read to the old Chief Yonagunski, he said, "It seems a good book; it is strange that the white man, who has had it so long, is no better than he is."[45] It may also be, though, that the Real People were simply willing to adapt to American ways as a means of survival. After an 1827 Constitution established an independent Cherokee Nation, Chief John Ross helped secure the passage of "a constitutional provision excluding anyone who disbelieved in the Christian God from holding office or giving testimony in a court of law."[46] Clearly a move to win the favor of the American government, the move also reflected the personal Christianity of many of the Cherokee leaders and the mounting recognition that Christianity offered the best hope for the future. Young Cherokee leaders and intellectuals were eagerly turning to Christianity. One shining example was Elias Boudinot, editor of the *Cherokee Phoenix*, who had even translated the Greek New Testament into the Cherokee language.

Sadly, all these efforts to win the blessing and acceptance of Americans were in vain. Since 1802 an agreement had existed in which Georgia agreed to cede its western lands for a federal promise to extinguish Indian land titles "as early as the same can be peaceably obtained on reasonable terms."[47] In 1828 Georgia used the 1802 agreement as pretext and moved to assume control of all Cherokee land within its borders, thus dissolving the citizenship, the legislature, and the laws of the Cherokee Nation. The real reason for Georgia's actions, though, was that gold had been discovered on Cherokee land. Greed reigned, and white speculators flooded onto the ancient land of the Real People. The problems of the Indians grew worse when Andrew Jackson was elected president in 1829. Jackson, who encouraged mission work among the Indians as a "civilizing force," believed that all Indians should be removed beyond the Mississippi River for their own protection.[48] In 1830 Jackson pushed through a Removal Bill that empowered him to exchange land in the west for Indian land in the East—and with this the legal basis for a gross injustice was complete.

The Removal Bill generated significant opposition. Even fellow Tennessean Davy Crockett opposed Jackson in Congress.

Chief John Ross refused to sign the treaty, and a lawsuit before the Supreme Court upheld his claim. In the majority opinion, Chief Justice John Marshall stated that the "Cherokee Nation is a distinct community occupying its own territory, in which the citizens of Georgia have no right to enter but with the assent of the Cherokee themselves." President Jackson fumed and is supposed to have said, "John Marshall has made his law, now let him enforce it."[49] While the political battles continued, Georgia secretly began distributing the Cherokee lands by lottery. Taking matters into their own hands, a minority faction called the "Treaty Party" signed a removal treaty at New Echota in direct violation of Cherokee law and quite contrary to the wishes of most Cherokee. Among the American officials present was Tennessee Governor William Carroll. Though the majority of the Cherokee Nation claimed no association with the treaty, the United States Senate ratified it, and President Jackson proclaimed that, as of May of 1836, the Cherokee had two years to move across the Mississippi.

The agonies that then descended upon the Real People have few parallels in American history. Their trials often began when invaders stormed their towns, burned their homes, and dug up the

4.4 *John Ross.* The influential chief of the Cherokee Nation at the time of the removal, John Ross was a man of refined culture and high Christian character. His father was a Scots-Irish immigrant who married a beautiful woman of Cherokee ancestry. His love of his heritage—both Celtic and Cherokee—made him a formidable leader of unbending conviction and courage. Though marred by the tragedy of the Trail of Tears, his years of leadership were marked by constancy and commitment.

burial grounds of their ancestors to claim the loot buried with the dead for the journey to the "Nightland." The Real People were then corralled into stockades and embarkation depots built in the belief that they would only be used for a few weeks at a time. Instead, thousands spent blistering summers and icy winters in crowded, filthy camps where cholera claimed hundreds of lives. More than two thousand died in these hellish conditions before the long journey to exile even began.[50]

In its callous ineptitude, the U.S. Army routinely forced the Indians to travel in the worst of seasons and without the merest thought for the physical needs of so many thousands. Yet it was just in this moment of heartless treatment by a supposedly Christian nation that the Christians among the Real People revealed the glory of their faith. Missionaries who traveled with the Indians, Evan Jones among them, reported that they were tending to what amounted to a miniature revival. Jones told of "an almost constant round of religious meetings and scores of baptismal ceremonies." So many were converted that the Baptists counted 175 new members, and Jones baptized as many as fifty-six new believers a day.[51]

> In the midst of much anxiety and urgent haste in the preparation for removal, it is a matter of sincere and humble gratitude that the gospel is making advances altogether unprecedented in the Christian history of the Cherokees. The pressure of their political troubles appears to be overruled to the spiritual advantage of the people. The sentiment of the poet appears to be happily realized in them. Behind a frowning providence, he hides a smiling face. . . . Yesterday . . . I baptized fifty-six hopeful believers in the Lord Jesus Christ in the presence of an immense concourse of serious and attentive spectators.[52]

Witnesses to this amazing spectacle of grace were deeply moved. One who watched the Indians prepare a makeshift chapel commented wryly, "These savages, prisoners of Christians, are now all hands busy, some cutting and carrying posts, and some preparing seats, for a temporary place of preaching tomorrow." Jones noted:

On one Sabbath, by permission of officers in command, they went down to the river and baptized five males and five females. They were guarded to the river and back. Some whites present affirm it to have been the most solemn and impressive religious ceremony they ever witnessed.[53]

Even the guards had opportunity to see genuine Christianity displayed in the midst of misery and suffering. As Jones wrote:

I believe that the Christians, the salt of the earth, are pretty generally distributed among the several detachments of prisoners, and these Christians maintain among themselves the stated worship of God in the sight of their pagan brethren and of the white heathens who guard them.[54]

Yet as wonderful as reports of conversions and worship services on the journey were, they could not mask the agonizing torture of every step. The imagination fails to fully envision what such an experience must have been like: the screaming children, the sickness, filth, blood, vomit, and death. One hardened war veteran later reported, "I fought through the Civil War and have seen men shot to pieces and slaughtered by thousands, but the Cherokee Removal was the cruelest work I ever knew."[55] From May of 1836 to March of 1839, more than seventeen thousand Cherokee were forcibly marched westward. Of these, more than four thousand died.[56] The Cherokee named this horror *nunna-da-ult-sun-yi,* "the trail where they cried."[57] Perhaps in its memory it is not just the Cherokee who ought to weep.

William Wirt, the U.S. Attorney General who represented the Cherokee before the Supreme Court, spoke truly when he said: "We may gather laurels on the field of battle, and trophies upon the ocean, but they will never hide this foul blot upon our escutcheon. 'Remember the Cherokee Nation' will be answer enough to the proudest boasts that we can ever make."[58]

Profile 4   *As a Man Thinketh*

> *The end of learning is to repair the ruins of our first parents by regaining to know God aright, and out of that knowledge to love Him, to imitate Him, to be like Him as we may the nearest by grace.*
> John Milton

The students at Tennessee's earliest schools, academies, and colleges were educated according to the great traditions of the Christian classical heritage. Like their predecessors a generation earlier in the fledgling colonies along the eastern seaboard, they were the beneficiaries of a rich legacy of art, music, and ideas that had not only trained the extraordinary minds of our Founding Fathers but had provoked the remarkable flowering of culture throughout western civilization. It was a pattern of academic discipleship that had hardly changed at all since the dawning days of the Reformation and Renaissance—a pattern, though, that has almost entirely vanished today.

Indeed, those first Tennesseans were educated in a way that we can only dream of today despite all our nifty gadgets, gimmicks, and bright ideas. They were steeped in the ethos of Augustine, Dante, Plutarch, and Vasari. They were conversant in the ideas of Seneca, Ptolemy, Virgil, and Aristophanes. The notions of Athanasius, Chrysostom, Anselm, Bonaventure, Aquinas, Machiavelli, Abelard, and Wyclif informed their thinking and shaped their worldview.

The now carelessly discarded traditional medieval trivium—emphasizing the basic classical scholastic categories of grammar, logic, and rhetoric—equipped them with the tools for a lifetime of learning: a working knowledge of the timetables of history, a background understanding of the great literary classics, a structural competency in Greek- and Latin-based grammars, a familiarity with the sweep of art, music, and ideas, a grasp of research and writing skills, a worldview comprehension for math and science basics, a principle approach to current events, and an emphasis on a Christian life paradigm.

The methodologies of this kind of classical learning adhered to the time-honored principles of creative learning: an emphasis on structural memorization, an exposure to the best of Christendom's cultural ethos, a wide array of focused reading, an opportunity for disciplined presentations, an experience with basic academic skills, and a catechizing for orthopraxy as well as orthodoxy.

The object of this kind of classical education was not merely the accumulation of knowledge. Instead it was to equip a whole new generation of leaders with the necessary tools to exercise discernment, discretion, and discipline in their lives and over their callings. Despite their meager resources, roughhewn facilities, and down-to-earth frontier ethic, they maintained continuity with all that had given birth to the wisdom of the West. It was the modern abandonment of these classical standards a generation later that provoked G. K. Chesterton to remark:

4.5 *Classical Education.* One of the first tasks that Christian missionaries to the Tennessee frontier undertook was the establishment of academies and schools for the education of the young. For the most part, these schools were modeled on the time-tested Classical methodologies that had already served the early American republic— and indeed, much of Western Civilization—so well.

The great intellectual tradition that comes down to us from the past was never interrupted or lost through such trifles as the sack of Rome, the triumph of Attila, or all the barbarian invasions of the Dark Ages. It was lost after . . . the coming of the marvels of technology, the establishment of universal education, and all the enlightenment of the modern world. And thus was lost—or impatiently snapped—the long thin delicate thread that had descended from distant antiquity; the thread of that unusual human hobby: the habit of thinking.[1]

Sadly, it was the church that actually provoked that modern abandonment. Its new emphasis upon personal experience over and against the time-honored traditions of education induced it to emphasize immediate things rather than invest in permanent things. Those early students in Tennessee's rugged frontier schools were among the last generation to receive that kind of comprehensive intellectual and spiritual training. Thus a whole new generation of Tennesseans were left without the requisite tools of leadership, and this at the very time when the pressures of modernity most demanded that a new standard of leadership emerge. Much of the tragedy of the days that followed may well be attributed to the fact that men and women entered onto the battlefield bereft of shield or spear.

5
A War of Brothers

No matter what your country's cause or quarrel, it is enough for the patriot to know she is in a war. It is your duty to espouse her cause— and then to pray for good providence whatever the outcome.

Gideon Pillow

It was August 22, 1831, and life on the plantations of tidewater Virginia was uncommonly still. With the heavy work of harvesting yet a month off, more than one plantation family had decided to attend the camp meetings in South Carolina, leaving what work there was to do in the hands of trusted slaves and overseers. It was this lull in the normally bustling life of Southampton County that gave Nat Turner his opportunity. Long had he dreamed of this moment, his moment of destiny, when a slave rebellion under his leadership would sound the trumpet of deliverance throughout the South. He was the chosen instrument. He was certain of it. Hadn't he fasted and meditated for hours in the woods? Hadn't he seen visions of "white spirits and black spirits engaged in battle . . . and blood flowing in streams?" And when he asked for a sign, hadn't it come; the bluish haze of an August eclipse answering every doubt in his mind? This was truly the moment. He was truly the man.[1]

With seven others Turner quietly padded to the house of his owner, Joseph Travis, and found the master and his family sleeping. White sheets turned wildly red as the intruders skillfully slit the throats of the still-slumbering family. Then, on to the next plantation, and the next. Over the following two days, Turner gathered some seventy-five undisciplined insurgents and made his way toward the county seat, Jerusalem, killing fifty-five whites as he

went. But Turner and his mob never made it to Jerusalem. The
state militia and armed townsmen stopped the raid three miles
from the city, chasing the escaped slaves into the swamps and gun-
ning them down from horseback. Turner eluded capture for two
months, and the nation panicked. The sleepy family farms and the
handful of plantations where whites had lived and worked and
ruled without fear now had the feel of besieged fortresses. But
finally Turner was caught, tried, and hanged. To make sure his
remains weren't used for martyr's relics, the body was given to
doctors who melted it down into grease.[2] The nation breathed a
sigh of relief . . . for the moment.

In New England a similar trumpet call had already sounded.
On January 1, 1831, a journalist by the name of William Lloyd
Garrison issued the first edition of *The Liberator*. With his promise,
"I am in earnest; I will not equivocate; I will not excuse; I will not
retreat a single inch; and I will be heard," Garrison launched his
battle for complete and immediate emancipation of all slaves.[3] The
cry thundered in the ears of Boston society and then throughout
the United States. This was new, radical, unheard of. Slavery had
been considered a national problem for quite some time now. And
gradually the nation had begun to deal with it. It barred the slave
trade at the turn of the century, and slowly one state after another
had abolished the institution altogether. It was generally assumed
that this trend would naturally continue. Slavery was dying out,
most believed.

Such reasoning was lost on the firebrand Garrison, however.
Declaring war on moral moderation, he wrote:

> Tell a man whose house is on fire, to give a moderate alarm; tell him
> to moderately rescue his wife from the hands of the ravisher; tell the
> mother to gradually extricate her babe from the fire into which it
> has fallen; but urge me not to use moderation in a cause like the pre-
> sent . . . The apathy of the people is enough to make every statue
> leap from its pedestal and to hasten the resurrection of the dead.[4]

Two blasts of the trumpet; two very different men. Yet once
their call was heard, American society was never again the same.
As late as 1827, most antislavery societies existed in the South, and

all four of the nation's abolitionist papers were published in slave states. This ended with the work of Turner and Garrison. Fearing more uprisings like Nat Turner's, the southern and border states were thrown into such a reactionary frenzy that slavery became even more entrenched than before. All too often the genteel ways of the "Old South" were lost in the paranoid panic of a culture awaiting assault. In some places it became a crime to teach a slave how to read. In others, the mail could no longer be used to distribute abolitionist literature. And in still others, black ministers were no longer allowed to conduct unsupervised services for slaves. Indeed, chains and whippings appeared where they had never been known before. In Tennessee, the Constitutional Convention of 1834 withdrew the voting rights of freed blacks, rejected proposals for gradual abolition, and made it practically impossible for future legislatures to pass any law allowing "the emancipation of slaves without the consent of their owner or owners."[5]

Abolitionists reacted in turn. The nation became emotionally and practically polarized. The rhetoric on both sides seemed only to exacerbate the conflict. The renowned Presbyterian theologian and historian Robert L. Dabney later wrote:

> Before the Abolitionists began to meddle with our affairs, with which they had no business, I remember that it was a common opinion that domestic slavery was at least injudicious, as far as the happiness of the master was concerned. I do believe that if these mad fanatics had let us alone, in twenty years we should have made Virginia a free State. As it is, their unauthorized attempts to strike off the fetters of our slaves have but riveted them on the faster.[6]

Thus the lines were drawn, and as the nation approached the mid-century mark, attitudes continued to harden on both sides until finally the bloodiest war in American history brought the issue to a bitter end.

Perhaps due to the clamor of controversy, the din of the saber rattling, and the rousing of rhetoric, hardly anyone seemed to notice that there was in fact another way. In England, a Christian member of Parliament named William Wilberforce was at that very moment leading a peaceful movement to outlaw slavery.

5.1 *Leonidas Polk*. The renowned Bishop of Louisiana prior to the outbreak of hostilities between the North and South, Leonidas Polk served as a Major General in the army of the Confederacy. He was a pious man and a visionary leader who sought to preserve not slavery but southern culture and independence. In 1857 he laid the cornerstone of the University of the South atop Monteagle in Tennessee—though the school was unable to open until after the war.

Wilberforce had been the recipient of the last letter John Wesley ever wrote, a letter that encouraged him to fight the evil of slavery. Taking the charge seriously and preaching a bold and disciplined variety of the faith he called "Real Christianity," Wilberforce's efforts led first to the abolition of the British slave trade in 1807 and finally to the abolition of the institution itself in 1833.[7] This latter achievement, the Emancipation Act, went into effect shortly after Wilberforce's death and was his greatest monument. Thus with the stroke of a pen and largely due to the efforts of a single, tireless, Christian politician, slavery was peacefully outlawed in the British Empire. What a lesson this might have been for those who were to suffer so much over the issue in America.

Of course, though, the regional crisis in America that ultimately led to a very uncivil war was not just about slavery. Indeed, many argued that it wasn't about slavery at all. The fact was, the vast majority of Southerners didn't own slaves. Its chief heroes actually abhorred the institution—including such stalwarts as Stonewall Jackson, Robert E. Lee, Alexander Stephens, and Patrick Clebourne. Meanwhile, several slave states remained in the Union and fought with the North, including Delaware, Maryland, Missouri, and the District of Columbia.

Instead, much of the regional conflict centered around such matters as state sovereignty, tariffs and duties, federal taxation, foreign policy, and even maritime law. And it was also about religion. The South was a bastion of theological conservatism. The North, on the other hand, had largely given way to successive tides of theological liberalism, including a wholesale acceptance of Unitarianism and, later, of transcendentalism. Some Northerners thought the South was clinging to outdated theological ideas—not the least of which were the hermaneutical props it had set up to justify slavery—and thus was hindering America in her spiritual evolution as an enlightened society. Such thinking fed abolitionist sentiment and even moved a group of wealthy industrialists, called the Secret Six, to finance a firebrand anarchist named John Brown in hopes of sparking a war to cleanse the nation from the sins of the South.[8]

$\mathscr{T}$HE $\mathscr{D}$EPARTED $\mathscr{G}$LORY

Sadly, the churches merely rode the shifting tides of society in these years, maintaining no prophetic distance from which to speak to a nation in crisis. Garrison and Turner divided the people of God as surely as they divided the rest of society. No one saw this more clearly than American statesman and orator Henry Clay. In an interview with the *Presbyterian Herald* of Louisville, Kentucky, held just weeks before his death in 1852, Clay chastised the churches of America for failing to rise above the partisan fray:

> I tell you this sundering of the religious ties which have hitherto bound our people together, I consider the greatest source of danger to our country. . . . If our religious men cannot live together in peace, what can be expected of us politicians, very few of whom profess to be governed by the subject of slavery? When the people of these states become thoroughly alienated from each other, and get their

passions aroused, they are not apt to stop and consider what is to their interest.[9]

If the preachers would only keep the churches from "running into excesses and fanaticism," Clay thought, the politicians could control the masses. But he admonished the reverend gentlemen that "yours is the harder task; and if you do not perform it, we will not be able to do our part." Then Clay concluded: "That I consider to be the greater source of danger to our country."[10]

It appears that the old statesman was right, for as the story of each denomination reveals, when the churches split over the very issues that were tearing the rest of the nation apart, all hope for a peaceful resolution was dashed.

The Presbyterians were the first to split. Since 1801, the Presbyterians and Congregationalists had worked together under a Plan of Union, but in 1837 the General Assembly of the Presbyterians chose to end the arrangement because they felt the Congregationalists weren't sufficiently Reformed in their theology. Many suspected, though, that the real issue was slavery. The denomination broke up into a "new school," liberals who maintained moderate antislavery sentiments, and an "old school," staunch Calvinists who reluctantly allowed for the legitimacy of slavery. The Synod of Tennessee in the east identified with the "new school," while the Synod of West Tennessee remained with the "old school." Typical of the "new school," the Holston Presbytery in eastern Tennessee adopted a statement that declared:

Slavery is not necessarily sinful or sin *per se*. . . . It is not a permanent or desirable institution, and is to be continued no longer than the good of the master and the slave require it. . . . The Gospel is the remedy for it and Christians should strive for its removal in the spirit of the Gospel. . . . Christians living in the midst of slavery have piety and the intelligence sufficient to qualify them to judge of and to do their duty in the circumstances. Hence the perpetual agitation of this subject is to be avoided, especially as the disastrous result of such agitation have been seen in retarding the day of universal emancipation.[11]

In 1857 yet another a split occurred between the northern and southern branches of the "new school." The Synod of Tennessee affiliated with the southern branch, joining the Synod of the West, which itself had by then divided into the Synod of Memphis and the Synod of Nashville. Confusing enough? Even the protagonists had a difficult time keeping track of who was who and what was what.

The Baptists were equally fractured. In 1835 the editor of the Nashville *Baptist,* irritated by northern abolitionism, wrote, "Southerners . . . will dispose of the matter as they think properly, all the agitations of the Northerners to the contrary notwithstanding." Northern Baptists were equally resolute in their assertion that the perpetuation of slavery was sin. In an 1844 national meeting, suspicious Southerners asked if the foreign missions board would appoint a slaveholder as a missionary. The answer was a firm no. R. B. C. Howell, pastor of First Baptist Church, Nashville, and editor of *The Baptist,* gave voice to the outrage of the South:

> In deciding that a slaveholder is, on that account, not competent to be a missionary, or an agent, they have done violence to the word of God, and to religion. That which disqualifies a man to perform these duties makes him ineligible to the ministry; and if his moral character is such as to forbid his preaching, I see not why it does not forbid his membership in the Church; no slaveholder, then, should dare to connect himself with the Church, or pretend to religion! Thus do they unchristianize us all.[12]

The next year, disaffected Baptists from the South organized the Southern Baptist Convention in Augusta, Georgia. Though the Tennessee Baptists were not involved in the Augusta meeting, the Tennessee General Association approved the new organization in a meeting held in October 1845. Six years later the convention met in Nashville.

The Methodists had been some of the most stalwart opponents of slavery in America; the Tennessee Conference typically declared in 1824 that "slavery is an evil to be deplored and . . . it should be counteracted by every judicious and religious exertion."[13] Nevertheless, the growing regional animosity split them as well. Abolitionism captured the hearts of northern Methodists, and by 1836 the familiar lines were drawn. In 1840 the breakaway Arminian Wesleyan Methodist church was organized, comprised largely of impatient northern abolitionists, but it was the 1844 General Conference that set the stage for a total split. The conference upheld the suspension of a Maryland minister for refusing to free his slaves and ordered a bishop to cease his duties until he freed slaves he had acquired through marriage. It was more than many could tolerate. Bishop William Capers devised a plan for separation, and in 1845 a group of southern Methodists met in Louisville and formed the Methodist Episcopal Church, South. All the conferences in Tennessee joined.

Most of the other denominations in Tennessee managed to ride out the storm of controversy without splitting. The Cumberland Presbyterians took the stand that the perpetuation of slavery was sin but amazingly, though located chiefly in the South, held together. The Christian Church had no formal organization to divide—and besides, they regarded slavery not as a matter of faith but of opinion. Some churches tried to avoid the subject altogether. Though Pope Gregory XVI issued a letter condemning the slave trade in 1839, so "far as can be ascertained, Bishop Miles made no public pronouncement on the subject of slavery. Apparently, he took the peculiar institution of slavery for granted."[14]

𝒯HE 𝒫LIGHT OF THE 𝒮LAVE

While the churches squabbled, equivocated, retreated, or entrenched, the painful, weary lot of the black slave in Tennessee remained much as it had for decades. Ironically, by law slavery should never have entered the state. Originally, the Tennessee territory was governed by the Northwest Ordinance of 1787, which allowed "neither slavery or involuntary servitude in the said territory."[15] Nevertheless, by 1791 there were 35,691 people living there, 3,417 of whom were black slaves. The floodgates had opened. "By 1800, ten thousand new slaves had crossed the mountains from

North Carolina or come down the valleys from Virginia with the white families to whom they belonged." Between 1800 and 1810, while the white population increased by 137 percent, the slave population increased an astounding 238 percent. The opening of the Chickasaw lands in the west in 1818 prepared the way for the vast agricultural endeavors of western Tennessee and a resulting dramatic increase in the slave population. By 1840, there were more than fifty-six thousand slaves in West Tennessee alone, contributing to a 300 percent increase in the state's slave population from 1810 to 1840.[16] By 1860, there was one black man for every three whites in Tennessee.[17]

Behind these numbers, though, is the story of the humiliation of servility, to say nothing of the human suffering. While Christians seriously debated the fate of the peculiar institution—and even in some cases whether black men had souls—families were routinely torn apart, flesh was bought and sold as mere chattel, and untold abuses occurred. While most slave narratives indicate that masters generally treated their charges fairly well—in fact, they were often better fed and sheltered than the average urban laborer—cruelty was not uncommon, and unrestrained brutality was certainly not unheard of.[18] Yet even those slaves who suffered severe trials nevertheless counted themselves fortunate to have been spared the horrors of the voyage from Africa—a trial that many of their great-grandparents or even grandparents had been forced to endure.

Before the slave trade had been outlawed at the turn of the century, a large number of the New England slave ships had been built specially outfitted with decks only eighteen inches apart. The kidnapped Africans were manacled and forced to lie flat the entire length of the voyage. They had, said one sea captain, "not so much room as a man had in his coffin, either in length or breadth." In this condition, men and women were unable to move for the most basic needs, and the stench of over three hundred natives quickly became unbearable. During storms, when the crew battened down the hatches, the temperature soared, and to the already foul air was added the reek of the sick and the decaying dead. Soon, "the sense of misery and suffocation was so terrible in the tweendecks," as one observer reported, "that the slaves not infrequently would go mad before dying or suffocating. In their frenzy some killed others in the hope of procuring more room to breathe. Men strangled those next to them and women drove nails into each other's brains" In time, "the shrieks of the women and the groans of the dying, rendered the whole scene of horror almost inconceivable."[19] Such was the heritage of the slaves of Tennessee. Not surprisingly, even the majority of slaves, who were relatively well treated many years removed from the wretched transport across the sea, despised their servile state and looked upon their cruel legacy with fear and loathing.

Though their masters and captors sometimes claimed sanction for their peculiar institution in the pages of the Bible, the slaves turned to the Jesus of that very Bible in huge numbers. Forsaking their tribal religions, they embraced the same faith their

5.2 *Slave Religion.* Though they had been made servile at the hands of their masters, slaves often accepted the truth of the gospel message—and often they accepted it with extraordinary passion. A great tradition of fiery preaching, soulful music, vivid folk tales, and ecstatic intercession was established for the emerging African-American church.

masters proclaimed, though usually with far greater passion and desperation. Soon slave quarters echoed with songs of praise and shouts of glory. A British traveler happened upon one such meeting near Memphis and wrote:

> I strolled out in the evening to enjoy the cool breeze and moonlight on the verge of the forest. In a lone house, in a lane, I heard the sound of psalm-singing, about eleven o'clock at night, and stopped to listen to a tune which the Covenanters in the days of their adversity had often uplifted on the hill side, when prepared to contend for their religion to the death. The psalm ceased, and a Negro slave delivered a long extempore prayer like those of the Presbyterians, and using excellent language. The prayer was followed by a sermon, in which the fall of our first parents was described, and its consequences to the human race; "born in sin, and conceived in iniquity," but regenerated through the instrumentality of a Redeemer. The audience consisted of a few Negro men and women, sitting on forms in a loft, lighted by a solitary candle. The preacher could neither read nor write; yet he expressed himself clearly, eloquently, and energetically. I went away pleased and astonished at what I had seen and heard; and thought that though it is a penal offense to instruct slaves in these Southern States, yet with all their enactments, the spread of the Gospel could not be controlled, and that the Negro still found means to gain access to the fountain of living waters.[20]

In time, black preachers were permitted an exceptional amount of freedom in the small farming communities and on the plantations of the South. Often the "slave preacher" was expected to be a mouthpiece of the master, warning against rebellion and stealing chickens. But even if the preacher accommodated some white control of his message, he often did the "real preachin'" in secret meetings. Some slave preachers were widely known for their speaking gifts, and it was not uncommon in some places for the families of the masters to join the slaves in their meetings.

Slave quarters were not the only place the Spirit moved in the black community. Freed blacks exerted tremendous influence in matters of religion. Perhaps the most prominent black religious leader in Tennessee before the war was Reverend Nelson Merry of Nashville. Pastor of the black First Baptist Church, Merry was both dearly loved by the black community and deeply respected by whites, who praised his "character, wisdom, and prudence." His success was astounding. Surviving both the War between the States and the later harassments of the Ku Klux Klan, Merry pastored First Baptist from 1840 to 1884 and saw his membership reach as high as 2,800 black men and women.[21]

But it was exactly this deep Christian faith among blacks that made their continued bondage indefensible. Increasingly, believers both white and black came to see slavery as a force intentionally designed to thwart the message of the gospel. As one slave owner wrote of the evils of slavery on the day she freed her slaves, "They cannot be seen by human powers. They form a part of those hidden things of darkness, which are linked by a chain which reaches into the dominion of Satan, not only here on earth, but into his more complete dominion in the realms of deepest hell."[22] Many Christian masters agreed, yet once they decided to free their slaves they often found that their troubles were just beginning. Such was the case of one young pastor named Jeremiah Jeter. Vehemently opposed to slavery, Jeter fell in love and married a woman who inherited slaves from her parents. The two determined to free their slaves but found the matter not so easily solved:

> I could not free them, for the laws of the State forbade it. Yet even if they had not forbidden it, the slaves in my possession were in no condition to support themselves. It was simple cruelty to free a mother with dependent children. Observations, too, had satisfied me that the free Negroes were, in general, in a worse condition than the slaves. The manumission of my slaves to remain in the State was not to be thought of. Should I send them to Liberia? Some of them were in a condition to go, but none of them desired to. If sent, they would be forced to leave wives and children belonging to other masters on nearby plantations, to dwell in a strange land. Besides, to send away the men who could support themselves and aid in the support of others, and retain the women and children to be supported by my own labors, was stretching my humanity quite beyond its power of endurance. They could not go to Africa. The same insuperable difficulties lay in the way of sending them north. Parents and children, husbands and wives would have to be sepa-

rated, and many of them sent forth to certain starvation, unless they should find charitable hands to support them.[23]

After much agonizing prayer and thought, Jeter decided his only recourse was to sell his slaves. The slaves themselves begged him not to:

> It was not only allowable for me, but my solemn obligation. . . . I should have been recreant to my duty and guilty of inhumanity if, under the circumstances, I had not assumed the relation of master and endeavored to meet the responsibilities arising from it.[24]

How would northern abolitionists ever have understood a man opposed to slavery keeping his slaves because it was the most compassionate, the most Christian thing for him to do? Such were the heartbreaking issues that faced Americans before the outbreak of war.

*T*HE *B*LOODY *S*TORM

With the election of the ultranationalist candidate Abraham Lincoln to the presidency in 1860, the country began to unravel. Lincoln had such little support in the South that in Tennessee his name was not even on the ballot. Fearing what the new administration might bring, South Carolina seceded from the union immediately, followed by Alabama, Florida, Georgia, Louisiana, Mississippi, and Texas, all of which formed The Confederate States of America. When hostilities erupted between Union and Confederate forces at Charleston's Fort Sumter on April 12, 1861, the four-year-long fratricide began.

From the beginning, the conflict proved to be among the bloodiest in history. In the decades prior to the hostilities, the technology of war had advanced without corresponding progress in tactics. With the strategies of the American Revolution and the Napoleonic Wars still in vogue, men used rifles, rather than muskets, and cannons with a range and explosive power unknown in previous wars. The new technology opened up the battlefield and spread the killing over a broader arena, well beyond the range the old tactics allowed for. The result was slaughter on an unbelievable scale.

The imbalance between Union and Confederate industrial strength also guaranteed a bloody outcome. The Union was comprised of twenty-three states with a population of more than twenty-two million people, one hundred thousand factories, 1.1 million workers and 96 percent of all railroad equipment in the United States. The South, by contrast, was comprised of only eleven states with a population of nine million people, twenty thousand factories, 101,000 workers, and only nine thousand miles of railroad. None of the South's factories produced munitions.[25]

Finally, the state of medical science was completely unready to accommodate the demands of this kind of war. The standard field doctor's equipment was crude, resembling a modern tool kit, and the surgical techniques were similarly rough. More men died from the medical care they received after being wounded than they did from the wounds themselves.[26] The many photographs of medical stations surrounded by piles of amputated arms and legs attest to the horrors of the war despite the best efforts of the doctors.

Thus, the human costs of the war were staggering. The Union enlisted 2,325,516 soldiers, more than 360,000 of whom were killed. The Confederate army reached about one million in size and lost more than 260,000. Together the Union and Confederate armies lost more men than in all the other wars of America combined. In fact, in the three days of Gettysburg alone, almost as many men died as in the entire Vietnam war, more than the number of people killed on American highways in an average year.[27] Though the last state to join the Confederacy, Tennessee escaped none of the carnage. Because of her central location between North and South, her strategic waterways, and conducive terrain, the state saw more than her share of conflict. Of the some three thousand battles of the war, 775 were fought on Tennessee soil, more than any other state but Virginia. The Volunteer state bid farewell to nearly forty thousand of her loyal sons, fighting on both sides of the terrible conflict, in what some called "the Brother's War."[28]

As costly as the war was for Tennessee, it could have been far worse. Oddly enough, what prevented more destruction were the quick successes of Union troops. Early in 1862, Fort Henry on the Tennessee River and Fort Donelson on the Cumberland fell to the Union invaders. This left Nashville undefended, and on Sunday, February 23, troops under the command of General Don Carlos Buell formally occupied the capital. The city remained under Union control until the war's end, as did virtually all of Middle and West Tennessee, saving the state from the fate of her southern comrades. Of course, the occupation did not seem a blessing to the citizens of Nashville at the time. Gloom hung over the city, and it grew only heavier when Andrew Johnson arrived to assume office as the Military Governor.

> Wholesale arrests and intimidations became the order of the day and all citizens were suspects unless they otherwise proved their virtue. Public officials, newspaper editors, school teachers, and ministers became the special objects of Johnson's vengeance.[29]

While the occupation spared Nashville the physical destruction of bombardment, the city nevertheless witnessed the most severe kind of moral destruction. It seemed Johnson was more concerned about the political allegiance of citizens than he was their ethics or moral behavior. Thus almost immediately after the occupation, every kind of vice crawled to the surface. One newspaper editor complained that the city was "filled with thugs, highwaymen, robbers, and assassins."[30] In July of 1863, prostitution had become such a severe problem that the authorities rounded up 450 women and put them on a steamboat to Louisville. The authorities there refused the unusual shipment, and the boat made its way to Cincinnati where it was again refused. When the Secretary of State ordered the boat back to Nashville, the Provost Marshall decided to require medical exams and licensing for all the prostitutes. The fees from the licensees were used to support hospitals.[31] Drunkenness, too, plagued the city. On a day that "President

Lincoln had set aside for fasting and prayer—sixty persons went before the recorder's court on charges of public drunkenness. More whisky was drunk in Nashville than in Boston, the *Daily Press* editor asserted."[32]

Memphis experienced similar moral decline from the time it was occupied on June 6, 1862, and in both Middle and West Tennessee the churches, having suffered a near-total shutdown, were unable to rise to the challenge. Denominational activities had ceased almost entirely. Church buildings were either leveled for military purposes, converted to hospitals or barracks, or occupied by the "missionaries" of northern denominations. Ministers of southern denominations were hunted, imprisoned, and even killed by Union authorities, and the loss of leadership was nearly fatal for many churches. Congregations often closed during these years, never to reopen, and those that remained open were usually populated by women and children alone. The Methodists and Baptists lost over one third of their memberships during the war.[33]

*T*HE *G*LORY OF THE *C*AMP

Yet, what the armies of faith lost on the home front they regained in revivals on the battlefield. As unlikely as it would seem in time of war, some of the most powerful revivals of religion yet seen in Tennessee occurred on the campgrounds of armies in the very thick of the war. By 1862, revivals had broken out in the Army of Tennessee, but decline had quickly set in with "soldiers playing cards, swearing, and drinking within a few feet of religious services." By the winter of 1862-63, chaplains in General Braxton Bragg's command were so discouraged that they considered resigning en masse. But at a meeting to discuss the proposal, a Baptist minister, Reverend L. H. Millikan, offered three resolutions:

1. That the souls of the vast multitudes are too precious to be abandoned to perdition.

2. That God is able to give His own called ministers the victory even among soldiers.

3. That the chaplains should enter into a covenant to pray for each other, and that all should at once begin protracted meetings in their several regiments claiming this whole army for the King of Kings.[34]

Agreeing, the ministers gave themselves immediately to prayer and meetings. Within weeks each chaplain reported revivals in his regiment. As one minister wrote in the *Southern Presbyterian* of April 1863, "I have attended many revivals—have had several at my own church—but I have never seen one of such interest as this."[35]

Indeed, before long the biggest problem the ministers had was a lack of help. Crying out for more chaplains and missionaries, one minister wrote that with more preachers, "I think we would have a great revival. I never saw men so anxious to hear preaching. They crowd around the preaching place two or three hours before the preacher gets there." When the Army of Tennessee moved to Chattanooga, Reverend W. H. Browning reported that "there is now a general spirit of revival manifest in every part of the army." The Army seemed transformed: "Instead of oaths, jests, the blackguard songs, one heard the songs of Zion, prayer, and praises of God." Instead of a "school of vice" the Army became "the place where God is adored, and where many learn to revere the name of Jesus."[36]

When Chaplains T. H. Davenport and John B. Chapman of the Twenty-Sixth and Thirty-Second Tennessee Regiments began a series of meetings, the results surprised even them. Their twenty-five-square-foot meeting house had to be expanded to seventy-five by sixty feet to accommodate more than a thousand soldiers at a time. Soldiers assembled morning and night for three months. Davenport described the crowd he had the privilege of addressing:

Every eye is on the speaker; not a head, hand or foot is seen moving, the big tears are stealing down their sunburnt cheeks. Mourners are called, and the large altar is crowded with weeping penitents. Those lion-hearted men who had so often faced dangers, and who would scorn to beg mercy of the foe, are at the feet of Jesus, humbly, earnestly begging pardon and mercy. . . . Nothing was done for vain glory; all were in earnest.[37]

Of another meeting one minister wrote, "Men who never shrank in battle from any responsibility came forward weeping. Such is the power of the Gospel of Christ when preached in its purity." Dozens of similar meetings were held with thousands of lives changed. Some even felt the call to the ministry themselves, for as one chaplain wrote:

> Strange as it may seem to many . . . the call to preach the gospel of Christ came to the hearts of the men of war on the tented field; and no sooner were their carnal weapons laid aside than they buckled on the Divine armor, and, seizing the sword of the Spirit, entered the battle against the power of darkness.[38]

As the war neared an end, the revivals became symbols of what might happen in a better postwar America. The Presbyterians who gathered in Georgia in December of 1865 held tightly to just such a hope:

> That our camps should have been made nurseries of piety, is something not only new and unprecedented in warfare, but may be regarded as an encouraging token of God's purpose to favor and bless our future Zion. If these rich and spiritual gifts are carefully gathered and husbanded for the Master's use, we may soon have occasion to forget our temporal sorrows in the abundance of our spiritual joys.[39]

The longevity and depth of the revivals were largely due to the near-superhuman efforts of the military chaplains. Living in the same conditions as their men and risking their lives daily for the cause of their Christ, these ministers comforted the fearful, held the dying, called the lost to salvation, strengthened the converted, and even advised commanders. Lacking the tools of more traditional pastorates, they used prayer covenants, tracts, Bible distribution, and every variety and size of meetings to proclaim their gospel. The diary of one such servant indicates how much these men lived "on the stretch for God."

> May 17, 1863, 10 A.M., I preached in the Presbyterian Church; house crowded with officers and soldiers; serious attention. At three o'clock, I preached in Bates brigade; a very good time: revival in the brigade. May 19th, I preached in Johnson's brigade; thirty to forty mourners; glorious work in this command. May 20th, I preached in General Polk's brigade; many mourners; several conversions. May 21st, I preached in General Wood's brigade; forty to fifty mourners; fifteen or twenty conversions. May 22nd, I spoke in General Riddle's brigade; a great work here; already more than one hundred conversions in this command.[40]

One of the most remarkable men among these chaplains was E. M. Bounds, known today largely for his powerful writings on prayer. A pastor from Missouri before the war, Bounds was arrested by Union troops for opposing the confiscation of church buildings. His ministry in prison was so effective that following a prisoner exchange he was immediately sworn in as a chaplain and soon found himself in John Bell Hood's Army of the Tennessee. A more war-weary band of soldiers has rarely existed. These veterans had seen many a preacher appeal for converts in the quiet of the camp only to flee to the comforts of home when the firing began. Chaplain Bounds was a refreshing change. The soldiers learned that when the fighting broke out, they could find Bounds on the front lines, exposing himself to danger and drawing fire as he shouted encouragement to "his flock." The men loved him. He was barely over five feet tall and as thin as a rail, and when he made his rounds carrying a full backpack, the men laughingly called him "the walking bundle," for the man could scarcely be seen under the huge load. Bounds always smiled, waved, and turned to the next soul that required mending.[41]

Then came the Battle of Franklin. On November 30, 1864, General Hood launched a frontal assault against the entrenched forces of Union General Schofield near Franklin. It was a hasty, rash move, and in a charge as dramatic as anything seen at Gettysburg, eighteen thousand Confederate soldiers hurled against entrenched Union lines. It was a bloodbath, and Hood lost 6,252 men that day, including thirteen general officers. Many prisoners were taken, among them Chaplain Edward Bounds. For days afterwards, Bounds's heart-wrenching task was to dig mass graves for the very men whose souls he had tended. All the while, though, he sang hymns, quoted Scripture aloud, and offered encouragement to his fellow captives. Finally, after more than two weeks of this horror, most of the prisoners were released on condition that they not take up arms again. Bounds agreed and left for his home in Missouri.[42] His business in Franklin, however, was unfinished.

Early in 1865, he returned to Franklin. With all his heart he had loved the men in those horrible mass graves—he knew their hurts, the names of their wives and children, the shape of their fears—and he simply couldn't leave them there. He conceived a project to properly bury the dead and commemorate their lives. His vision moved a local farmer to donate some land, and during the hot summer of 1865, some 1,496 Confederate soldiers were exhumed and buried in the new cemetery on the hills of the Carnton Farm. He even raised seven hundred dollars to pay local men to tend the graves. But it was not enough. He made a list of

5.3 *Revivals in the Camp.* During the bitter years of struggle—but especially throughout 1862 and 1863—spiritual renewal swept through the camps of the Southern armies. Led by such outstanding Christian Generals as Robert E. Lee and Stonewall Jackson, the Confederate troops often held prayer meetings and gospel services before, during, and after their military engagements.

all the men from Missouri he buried at Franklin and published it in the Missouri newspapers to inform the families and generate even more support. He tenderly kept the list in his own wallet until the day of his death forty-eight years later. Throughout his life, Bounds visited the families of his men, wrote them letters, and even secured scholarships for the children of the men he had prayed with in those smoky Confederate camps. Following the War, Bounds became the pastor of Franklin's Methodist Episcopal Church, led a major revival in that city, and then continued his dynamic writing and preaching ministry in Georgia and Alabama.[43]

LINCOLN AND THE MEANING OF THE WAR

As the war drew to an end, Americans grappled with what had happened and with how Christians should interpret such a cataclysm. Though most of his severest critics are loathe to admit it, the man who perhaps best captured the meaning of the war was Abraham Lincoln. This is surprising for those who know of Lincoln's early attitudes. It is true that he was far more interested in the preservation of the nationalistic Union than he was in any of the particular issues that had divided it—including the issue of slavery. It is true that he expressed grave doubts about the ability of the black man to function in a free society. It is true that he was willing to permit the continuation of slavery for the sake of the preservation of the Union—if that were possible. It is even true that his landmark Emancipation Proclamation failed to free any of the slaves under his jurisdiction and was powerless outside it. And it is true that he was a confirmed skeptic and secularist throughout most of his life and career. Nevertheless, it is obvious that Lincoln underwent a gradual transformation during his final lonely years in office. The death of his son had sent him searching for answers he did not have, and the ministry of a local Presbyterian pastor offered him hope he had never known. Apparently, he was actually converted sometime after the traumatic events on the field of Gettysburg—events that he would later immortalize.[44]

The spiritual transformation he had undergone makes Lincoln's assassination all the more tragic, for he was to have been baptized the morning after John Wilkes Booth fired a pistol shot into his head. In fact, even as Booth opened fire, Lincoln was telling his wife how after the war he wanted to go to Palestine and walk in his Master's steps. They were the last words he ever spoke.[45]

So it is possible that this later, more mature, more sober Lincoln may well have glimpsed the meaning of the war at a depth so many others on both sides missed. In his second inaugural address, he acknowledged that both sides in the war "read the same Bible and pray to the same God, and each invokes His aid against the other." While it might seem strange to some that "men should dare to ask a just God's assistance in wringing their bread from the sweat of other men's faces, let us judge not, that we be not judged." Nevertheless, "The Almighty has His own purposes."

> Woe unto the world because of offenses; for it must needs be that offenses come, but woe to that man by whom the offense cometh." If we shall suppose that American slavery is one of those offenses which, in the providence of God, must needs come, but which, having continued through His appointed time, He now wills to remove, and that He gives to both North and South this terrible war as the woe due to those by whom the offense came, shall we discern therein any departure from those divine attributes which the believers in a living God always ascribe to Him? Fondly do we hope, fervently do we pray, that this mighty scourge of war may speedily pass away. Yet, if God wills that it continue until all the wealth piled by the bondsman's two hundred and fifty years of unrequited toil shall be sunk, and until every drop of blood drawn with the lash shall be paid by another drawn with the sword, as was said three thousand years ago, so still it must be said, "The judgments of the Lord are true and righteous altogether."[46]

On April 9, 1865, five weeks after Lincoln's address, the fighting ended—though the judgment upon both North and South had yet to be fully exacted.

PROFILE 5   *The Novelty
of Nationalism*

*Nationalism and patriotism are the fruit of two entirely divergent
movements; the latter admirable, the former questionable.*

Charles Hodge

*B*y any modern measure, the obstinate resolve of the antebellum South to maintain the principles of regionalism, localism,
agrarianism, and state sovereignty was impossibly exotic and pro-
saic. It appears to us to have defied every common cultural convention and crossed every presumed political boundary. Our
perspective of the world, shaped as it is by the leviathan ideological cudgels of state sectarianism and gargantuanism, simply cannot conceive of such old world idealism. We think in terms of the
neat national categories of union, federalism, centralization, and
corporatization.

In fact, though, it was those categories that were startlingly
novel to the men and women living in the first half of the nineteenth century—even as they had been throughout the entire history of Christendom.

The fact is, the whole idea of nationality—and even the mood
of nationalistic sentiment that gave rise to that idea—is a modern
innovation in the affairs of men. It is an idea that until just a short
time ago was utterly remote from the experience of Western civilization. Even the vocabulary of nationalism is of a very recent vin-
tage; it was not until well into the nineteenth century that the
institutional phrases we take so for granted today, such as "state,"
"polity," "federal," "government," or even "nation," came into
common usage. As short a time ago as the founding of the
American republic, political discourse preferred to speak of "the
commonwealth," "the people," "the confederation," "the common
land," "the public," "the community," or "the cooperative welfare"

in order to avoid the centralizing and unitary implications of "nationhood." The New English Dictionary underscored that distinction as late as 1908 when it stated that the old meaning of "nationality" envisaged "little more than an ethnic unit" but that a wholly new meaning had begun to emerge that stressed the notion of "political unity and independence."

At virtually no time in the past—especially at no time during the age of Christendom—did men identify themselves in terms of a particular nation-state. Instead, they saw themselves as members of a family or a community, or, even more likely, of a faith. Jurisdictions and boundaries were set according to these relational and covenantal loyalties rather than by governmental edicts. Thus patriotism was interpersonal rather than institutional.

Most Americans, whether from the North or the South, generally did not see themselves as citizens of the United States. Their identity was not defined by a temporal state but an eternal estate. Their sense of purpose was rooted in who they were rather than where they were from or what they did. As difficult as it may be for us to comprehend, this is the most significant clue to understanding their motivations, their ideals, their aspirations, and ultimately, their actions. They saw themselves first and foremost as coheirs of a united vision of liberty rather than subjects of a particular magistratical jurisdiction.

Though the systemic and ideological notions of Enlightenment nationalism had gained more and more favor with the western world's political elites since the time of the French Revolution, it was still remote enough from the day-to-day existence of Americans to be practically unnoticed.

That is why any map of the world from those days is so mind-bogglingly indecipherable to us: it portrays a forgotten philosophy as well as a forgotten geography. There did not yet exist such nation-states as Germany, Italy, or Belgium. And the United States were plural sovereignties confederated together, not a singular federal union. The wrenching War between the States was thus at root a struggle between the old world order and the new world order. Slavery became the polarizing pretext for the imposition of a novel nationalism upon the American vision. And thus was the gravest moral issue of the age trivialized by political ideologues. Alas, the more things change, the more they stay the same.

5.4 *The Novelty of Nations.* Prior to the advent of ideological nationalism, the map of Europe was a nearly indecipherable tangle of ancient feudal lands and ethnic territories. This map, representing the boundaries existing just prior to 1745, demonstrates only too clearly the dramatic difference that modern political affairs have had to the historic communities of Western Civilization.

6
A Sunday Between Wars

Freedom is simultaneously a glorious and a dangerous thing. There is no better illustration of that paradox than the history of America—or the history of the church.

Thomas A. Wilson

Free at last! Free at last! Thank God Almighty, We're free at last!" This was the song of the freed slave. "Everyone was a-singing," one ex-slave remembered. "We was all walking on golden clouds." "Yes, child," said another, "the Negroes are free, and when they knew that they were free they, oh! baby! They began to sing. . . . Such rejoicing and shouting you never heard in your life."[1]

They were free. And the song of freedom echoed from every gathering of black men and women in America. It rang out from the "contraband camps" the Union troops set up to care for freed slaves. Despite crowded and diseased conditions, blacks who had never known freedom often got their first taste in these camps and with the help of white missionaries and soldiers learned to read, married "proper," and discovered what it was to be paid for their labors. Evolving eventually into neighborhoods like "South Memphis" and Nashville's "Edgefield," the contraband camps were where many a former slave first heard the news that freedom had indeed been declared throughout the nation.

The song of freedom also rang out from thousands of black veterans of the war. More than twenty thousand free blacks from Tennessee served in the Union Army, fully 40 percent of all Tennessee Union recruits. And some ten thousand free blacks fought for the Confederacy—often side by side with their former

133

masters. In all, blacks participated in at least 410 military engagements, won sixteen Congressional Medals of Honor, and died at a disproportionately high rate. For the black soldier, the song of liberty was a song of gratitude for life itself.[2]

The song of freedom sounded, too, from the ships where black sailors served, from the farms and plantations where ex-slaves chose to remain faithful to their former owners, and from campfires in remote woods where freed slaves vowed never to near white society again. It was heard from the black churches that survived the war and drew freed blacks like familiar beacons in the otherwise foreign wilderness of the white world. And it was heard from the heart of every mother reunited with her children, from every slave who believed he would never be whipped again, and from every man, woman, and child who ever stood up on that long-envisioned day and simply walked away from their field of bondage. *"Free at last, Free at last."*

And what did freedom mean to the generation of slaves who simply walked away from the ordeal of servility? The answer is that it had as many meanings as there were slaves:

> Freedom to some was getting married before a preacher and signing papers and knowing it was for always and not until the next cotton crop. Freedom to others was the right to pick up and go. . . . Freedom was Bibles, freedom was churches, and freedom was gin. Freedom was two names. . . . It was getting up when you wanted to and lying down when the spirit hit you. It was doing nothing, too. How was a person to know he was free if he couldn't sit still and watch the sun and pull on his pipe when he didn't want to do anything else? Over and above this, deeper than this, freedom was land and letters: an opportunity to learn and the right—the means—to earn one's own bread.[3]

Freedom meant, too, that blacks who had worshiped Jesus in the slave quarters and the hidden brush arbors of the plantation, who had felt the Spirit move in the makeshift chapel of an army camp, or who had learned of God's love in the pages of a Bible the contraband camp missionary taught them to read could now meet for church as openly as they pleased and sing and shout as loudly as their gratitude demanded. The day of the black church in Tennessee—and indeed, in all America—had arrived.

THE RISE OF THE BLACK CHURCH

Black churches sprang up in huge numbers after the war and quickly joined black denominations that had existed since the time of the American Revolution. Many of these denominations began for the same reasons as the African Methodist Episcopal Church, for as their *Book of Discipline* states:

> In 1787, the colored people belonging to the Methodist Society of Philadelphia convened together to take into consideration the evils under which they labored, arising from the unkind treatment of their white brethren who considered them a nuisance in the house of worship, and even pulled them off their knees while in the act of prayer and ordered them to back seats. For these and various other acts of unchristian conduct, they considered it their duty to devise a plan in order to build a house of their own.[4]

From this hope for "a house of their own" came not only the African Methodist Episcopal Church in 1816, but also the African Baptist Church in 1809 and the African Methodist Episcopal Church, Zion, in 1820. Following the war, when the new black churches in the South joined these older northern denominations, it was the Methodists who enjoyed the greatest success. This was largely because white Methodist preachers in the South encouraged their black members to establish African churches in their indigenous communities and neighborhoods. These churches multiplied so rapidly that though there were fewer than ten black churches of any denomination in Tennessee before the war, there were enough African Methodist churches by the end of the war to organize a Tennessee conference.

Before long other denominations, sensing the shape of the future, encouraged the establishment of independent black congregations. In 1869 the Cumberland Presbyterians, ever willing to adapt the wineskin for the demands of new wine, organized the Colored Cumberland Presbyterian Church. At the same time, the Christian Church planted dozens of black congregations. The Baptists also drew large numbers of blacks—the historic Baptist emphasis on religious freedom struck a responsive chord in the hearts of the newly liberated. Southern Baptists encouraged the formation of separate black congregations and made them adjuncts of the existing associations and state conventions. Of all the denominations in Tennessee, though, only the Methodist Episcopal Church tried to build congregations where whites and blacks worshiped together. It was, indeed, a noble effort, but tensions quickly arose, and in the end only 10 percent of the denomination's membership in Tennessee was black.[5]

6.1 *Fisk University.* One of the very first universities established for the benefit of former slaves, Fisk University was founded in 1866 by the American Missionary Association and the Western Freedman's Association. Though often harassed by members of the Ku Klux Klan, the school gained worldwide renown and popular support thanks, in large part, to the extraordinary talents of the Fisk Jubilee Singers.

The black man needed not only churches but schools, and the denominations threw themselves into a flurry of school-building to meet the challenge. In 1866 the American Missionary Society opened Fisk School in Nashville and four years later started Lemoyne Normal and Commercial School in Memphis. In the same year that Fisk began, the Methodist Episcopal church founded Central Tennessee College, which opened a medical department in 1874 named for the Meharry family. Northern Baptists founded the Normal and Theological Institute at Nashville in 1867. Seven years later, the school relocated to the present site of Peabody College and in 1883 became Roger Williams University. After moving again, the school ultimately located in Memphis and merged with Howe Junior College. The Presbyterian Church, USA, founded Knoxville College for Blacks in 1872, which became a part of the University of Tennessee system in 1990. The only school founded by a black denomination in the state was Lane College, begun in 1879 by the Colored Methodist Episcopal Church.

Of all these schools, the story of Fisk University's growth is the most remarkable. This was largely due to the popularity of the Fisk Jubilee Singers, founded by George L. White. In 1871, when the school was desperately short of funds, the Jubilee Singers ventured north to raise support. The response was disappointing at first, but when the troupe began singing "Negro Spirituals," their popularity soared. The Singers won wide acclaim in New England, sang for President Grant in the White House, and earned over twenty thousand dollars for Fisk. Buoyed by this success, the group made a European tour in 1873, earning nearly fifty thousand dollars and having their picture painted by Queen Victoria's court painter. In all, the Jubilee Singers earned the school more than $150,000, which by 1900 meant a campus worth $350,000 and 433 graduates.[6] Aside from the benefit to their school, though, the Fisk Jubilee Singers also performed a service for the whole nation by taking the oral tradition of the Negro spiritual and preserving it as an important aspect of black heritage.

*T*HE *R*ISE OF THE *K*LAN

The victories of black churches and schools after the war were all the more astonishing given the fierce opposition arrayed against them. On one March day in 1868, Fisk College students looked up to see the Ku Klux Klan riding in hooded mass along Nashville's Church Street in a blatant attempt to intimidate the students and close the school. Fortunately, the school's leaders and students were courageous enough to see their vision through, but the presence of the Ku Klux Klan and its many allies continued to assure steely opposition to black advancement throughout the South.

Founded in Pulaski, Tennessee, the Klan was supposedly an association for the defense of war widows and orphans against the greedy exploitation of the infamous carpetbaggers and scalawags during the early bitter years of Reconstruction. But the original, seemingly noble, intention of the organization was quickly submerged in a sea of prejudice, malice, and vengeance. The movement was taken over by a rowdy gang of young Confederate veterans who were "hungering and thirsting" for amusement. They drew their name from the Greek word for "circle" or "band," *kuyklos*—a word familiar throughout the South because of the popular Kuklos Adelphon social fraternity founded at the University of South Carolina in 1812—and they used dramatic-sounding titles like Grand Cyclops, Grand Turk, and Grand Magi. For a time their activities were meant "for sheer pleasure of mystery and joke," but when the federally appointed governor, William Brownlow, initiated a host of oppressive antiveteran policies, a storm of bitterness blew throughout the state. The Klan then turned political—and vicious. Intimidating blacks, and particularly frightening them from the franchise polls, became its primary goal.[7]

The Klan's rapid growth, fanned by the harsh winds of southern fear and bitterness, led to its first national meeting in April 1867 at Nashville's Maxwell House Hotel. The organization emerged from the meeting with a bold new strategy:

6.2 *The Ku Klux Klan.* Though originally established for much more benign purposes, the Ku Klux Klan quickly became a weapon of racist terror against African-American families, institutions, and communities. Parading through the streets robed in their trademark white robes, Klansmen became a poignant reminder of on-going racial injustice in both the North and the South.

Reduce blacks to political impotence. How? . . . By stealth and murder, by economic intimidation and political assassinations, by the political use of terror, by the braining of the baby in its mother's arms, the slaying of the husband at his wife's feet, the raping of the wife before her husband's eyes. By fear.[8]

With the Klan's encouragement, the South was soon "honeycombed with secret organizations: the Knights of the White Camelia, the Red Shirts, the White League, Mother's Little Helpers and the Baseball Club of the First Baptist Church."[9]

The organization was styled as an "Invisible Empire" led by a "Grand Wizard." The states became "Realms" headed by "Grand Dragons," and each congressional district became a "Dominion" comprised of "Dens." Though the Klan continued to claim that its sole purpose was protection of "the weak, the innocent and the defenseless, from the indignities, wrongs, and outrages of the lawless, the violent, and the brutal," it had by that time drifted far afield of its founders' original benign intents. The truth was that murders, rapes, and whippings followed the movement wherever it went. Alarmed, the state legislature formed a committee to study the Klan. Concluding that "a perfect reign of terror" existed in many Tennessee counties, the committee reported:

> Klansmen were going abroad . . . robbing poor Negroes, taking them out of their houses at night, hanging, shooting and whipping them in a most cruel manner, and driving them from their houses . . . . Women and children . . . were subjected to the torture of the lash, and brutal assaults . . . committed upon them by these night prowlers . . . In many instances the persons of females . . . were violated, and when the husband or father complained, he had been obliged to flee to save his own life.[10]

The Ku Klux Klan Act, designed to restrict the Klan's activities, brought no convictions, though, and when a man from the governor's office tried to spy on the Nashville Klansmen, he was later found in the Duck River with a bullet in his skull and a rope around his neck. Finally, on February 25, 1869, Governor Brownlow resigned to assume a seat in the U.S. Senate, and the Klan relaxed—at least for a time.

The tragedy of the Klan for the legacy of faith in Tennessee is the sanction it received from many Christian churches. The average Klansman considered himself a Christian, attended a church, and defended his Klan involvement with Scripture. He shared the pews with other men he knew to be Klan brothers and often listened to sermons preached by pastors who were secret Klansmen themselves. In fact, it was through the ready-made networking of churches and Masonic Lodges that the Klan grew so rapidly. The tragedy, though, is not only that the black man came to fear the white man's version of Christianity—excluding as it did most anyone but the white man himself—but that the white churches were often transformed into monuments to the prevailing culture, symbols of a uniquely American form of ideological and nationalistic cultural arrogance. The result was a climate of hatred and suspicion that bound both white and black with chains unbroken for generations.

REBUILDING THE WALLS

Compromised not only by racial hatred and division, the white churches in Tennessee suffered as well from serious internal challenges. In fact, so handicapped were they by the ravages of war and their own feuds that in the four decades following the Civil War "only one state registered less increase in church membership than did Tennessee."[11]

To begin with, the churches were beset with what historian Herman Norton called "a sectarian spirit."[12] The cooperation of the war years disintegrated into a cynical competition for membership that discredited the very message of the church. Additionally, the churches battled, in society as well as the pews, a flood of socially acceptable occultism in the form of séances, Ouija boards, tarot cards, and magic. This trend began as families of the thousands of war dead tried to communicate with their deceased relatives, often stepping inadvertently into the swift waters of necromancy and spiritism.

Yet another hindrance to the churches in these years was their own degenerative doctrinal drift. Not only did theological liberalism, rooted as it was in evolutionary theory and German higher criticism of Scripture, take a tremendous toll on the churches of postwar America, but a preoccupation with the second coming of Christ turned the gaze of many churches idly heavenward and away from the desperate need for evangelism and social action. Living under the promise of the second coming caused many Christians to question why the Church should work to transform a society that God was soon to destroy and from which the Church was soon to be rescued. Not every church responded to the idea of a "rapture" with idleness, though, for many believers heard the message of Jesus' rapid return as a call to gather as many souls as possible before the hour grew too late. Still, the resulting retreat from responsibility on the part of many churches left large segments of society without the leavening influence of the Christian faith they so desperately needed.

6.3 *The Monteagle Sunday School Assembly.* Established in 1882 as a summer retreat center, the Monteagle Sunday School Assembly has served as the locus for teacher training, gospel preaching, and community development ever since. Its 96 acres are divided between cottage residences, recreational facilities, and public forums designed to create a kind of refuge from the hustle and bustle of the world at large so Christian workers and their families can refresh their spiritual sensibilities and hone their ministry skills. Though its exclusively spiritual emphasis has been diluted over the years, it continues to attract some of the best Bible teaching and community fellowship in Tennessee.

Another challenge for the churches was the use of revivals as a technique of church growth. Genuine revivals had continued from the time of the great Red River and Cain Ridge "outpourings" at the beginning of the century. When they were, as some styled them, a "sovereign work," they normally bore a harvest of good fruit. When an "outbreak" occurred unexpectedly, it seemed to have the power to convert the vilest sinner, transform the most wicked community, and leave in its wake strong churches and ministries. Yet, when men planned what looked like revivals in the hope of drawing large numbers, the result was *revivalism*, or revival as a humanly devised method rather than a divinely inspired renewal. In England, Charles Spurgeon encountered this same counterfeit and held forth loudly against it:

> If you want to get up a revival, you can do it, just as you can grow tasteless strawberries in winter, by artificial heat. There are ways and means of doing that kind of thing, but the genuine work of God needs no such planning and scheming.[13]

Many in America shared Spurgeon's thoughts and suspected that the weakness of the Church was due in part to pew-sitters drawn by the "show" of revivalism but who had not confronted the costly claims of discipleship.

What external challenges the churches faced in these years stemmed largely from the impact of the war itself. War usually produces domestic revolution, breaking up the age-old foundations and loosening the grip of the values, traditions, and customs that hold society together. This means change, often rapid, and usually of the kind that makes a society unstable. Survivors, then, find themselves in a shaky, unfamiliar world and often try to salve their lonely disorientation with a headlong rush into materialism designed to compensate for the years of hunger and lack. This was the world the church had to reach in the years following the war, and, as had happened after the American Revolution, they found it hard to regain their prewar strength.

Nevertheless, despite all these difficulties, the churches made valiant efforts to restore their lost glory and shape the postwar world for the better. Their first challenge was to dislodge northern denominations from their buildings. During the years of bloodshed, Secretary of War Edwin Stanton issued an order placing "all houses of worship belonging to the Methodist Episcopal Church, South, in which a loyal preacher appointed by a loyal bishop does not now officiate" under the control of the northern branch of Methodism.[14] Later Stanton issued a similar order pertaining to Baptist churches. In response, northern missionaries flooded into the South to occupy the churches in Union-controlled territory. The impact of these missionaries was dubious at best, for as Herman Norton has written, "The zeal that was manifested by the northern

denominations in forcing themselves into the state was ill calcu-
lated to further either the cause of the Union or religion."[15] These
orders by Stanton were contrary to the spirit of Lincoln's instruc-
tions of 1864 that the "United States Government must not under-
take to run the church" and that only a "military need" should
occasion the northern occupation of a church.[16] Following the war,
many southern churches found it difficult to remove these northern "squatters," particularly since Governor Brownlow encouraged the Union usurpers to remain. Finally, after cooler heads
prevailed, many of the churches were returned to their prewar
owners, and some were even rebuilt with federal funds.

Having reoccupied their church buildings, ministers labored
feverishly to rebuild church life. Denominations resumed their
deliberations, local congregations reignited their ministries, and
church schools, all of which closed during the war, reopened.
Though some schools found it impossible to remain open in the
difficult conditions of the time, a few new schools grew rapidly.
The Baptist State Convention, formed in 1874, established
Southwestern Baptist University at Jackson. Under the wise leadership of Bishop Holland McTyeire, the Southern Methodists fulfilled the dream of a university of their own by opening a school in
Nashville. Taking its name from Commodore Cornelius
Vanderbilt, the school's million-dollar donor, Vanderbilt
University became a major intellectual and spiritual force in the
state. And the Presbyterians, forever in the vanguard of Christian
education, started King College at Bristol in 1868 and
Southwestern Presbyterian University at Clarksville in 1873.

Methodist churches grew rapidly during these years, their
flexibility in doctrine and government serving them well in the
west. Baptist churches multiplied quickly as well, raising not only
the number of disciples in the state but also the number of associations and denominations. Within their fold were the Primitive
Baptists, the Regular Baptists, the General Baptists, the Free Will
Baptists, the Northern Baptist Convention, the Duck River and
Kindred Association of Baptists or Baptist Church of Christ, and
the Two-Seed-in-the-Spirit Baptists. Of the Presbyterians in the
state, the Cumberland Presbyterians were not only the largest

group but also the most innovative. Comprising more than half of all Presbyterians, the Tennessee denomination was but part of a growing network of churches that spanned from Pennsylvania to California. Their fivefold growth in the three decades before the war and their ability to avoid a split over slavery left them well positioned by war's end to effectively meet the desperate needs of the postwar era.

But of all Tennessee denominations, the Churches of Christ experienced the most rapid growth. Before the war, the Disciples of Christ had broken into several factions, with Nashville becoming home to the conservative Church of Christ wing. This was largely due to the influence of Tolbert Fanning. Born in 1810 and converted at the age of seventeen, Fanning was a powerful man in both speech and stature. At six feet, six inches and 240 pounds, he commanded respect for his ability to work his farm as energetically as any other man and yet fulfill the responsibilities of his ministry with equal skill. In 1844 Fanning founded Franklin College in Nashville, and in 1855 he started the *Gospel Advocate,* hoping to encourage unity on the question of missionary societies. Fanning was completely opposed to such societies, as were many other prominent church leaders in his day, believing that only institutions mentioned in Scripture should be used to accomplish the preaching of the gospel. As one acquaintance wrote of Fanning, "He never had much confidence in human plans and human schemes in religion by which to do the work of the church, and, as he advanced in life, and studied the Scriptures more, he had less and less."[17] Both Franklin School and the *Gospel Advocate* closed during the war years, but in the nine years that Fanning lived after the war his ministry was extended more than ever by the support of one of his students, the gifted and passionate David Lipscomb.

Lipscomb was born in Tennessee and received his education under Fanning at Franklin College in Nashville. Though initially he made his living by farming, he began preaching in the 1850s and after the war became the driving force behind the resurrection of the *Gospel Advocate.* The paper appeared in its new form in January 1866, stridently southern in sympathy and completely uncompromising in matters of doctrine. Believing that Scripture reveals not only truth but an authoritative "ancient order," Lipscomb struck out against perceived evils such as instrumental music and "organizations" or "societies." He argued that since instrumental music is not mentioned in the New Testament, it should be forbidden out of hand. Indeed, he believed that the organ was nothing less than an "instrument of Satan." Sunday schools, denominational structures, and missionary societies were also "unbiblical" in his view. "Decrees of Associations, Conferences, Synods, . . . and Romish Councils" were also declared to be "unbiblical," and therefore any "meeting" that gave direction to the local church other than local eldership represented "an improper assumption of power and authority" for which Lipscomb found "no authority in the Bible."[18] To train ministers to adhere to such strictures, Lipscomb founded Nashville Bible School in 1891, which continued the work of Fanning's Franklin College, and which ultimately became David Lipscomb University after its founder's death. The Church of Christ movement took Lipscomb's teaching as its guide and his spirit as the measure of its righteous zeal. By the end of the century, there were more members of the Church of Christ in Tennessee than in all the eight adjacent states combined.

Like the churches, the synagogues of Tennessee added believers and congregations in the turbulent postwar years. New congregations, like the *Mitzpah Congregation* of Chattanooga and the *Beth-El-Emeth* synagogue in Memphis, grew out of Hebrew Benevolent associations designed to tend the Jewish war dead and support local Jewish communities. In Nashville, the venerable *Mogen David* congregation merged with the smaller *Ohava Emes Congregation*, "Lovers of Truth," to form the new *Ohavai Shalom Congregation*, "Lovers of Peace," chartered in 1868. A third congregation in Nashville signaled major changes for the Jewish community. Named *B'nai Yeshurun*, this congregation was far less traditional and more assimilated into the American religious culture than the more orthodox congregations. This meant that men and women could sit together, that organ music had a place in the service, and that most of the service would be in English. To counter this modernist trend, a congregation called *Shaharis* purchased cemetery land next to *Ohabai Shalom*, and this gradually gave way to the *Congregation Sheerit Israel*, Nashville's Orthodox Jewish congregation.

Such visible expansion of Jews in Tennessee did not go unnoticed by the state's anti-Semitic groups, most notably the Ku Klux Klan. A number of secular Jewish organizations arose to stand against the Klan and its ilk, and these grew so rapidly that by 1878 there were six active chapters of the *B'Nai Brith* in Tennessee, as well as organizations like the Independent Order of Abraham and the Free Sons of Israel.

*F*AITH AND *R*EFORM

Like Nehemiah of old, with the sword in one hand and the trowel in the other, the churches of Tennessee not only rebuilt in the years after the war but also moved to counter a disastrous moral decline. They saw many signposts on this road to moral decay, and Sabbath-breaking was considered among the most serious. From the time of the Pilgrims and the Puritans, Sabbath-keeping was a mainstay of both church life and civil government. The War between the States knew no Sundays, though, and in the decades that followed the trend continued. The churches found their assemblies, Sunday schools, and socials in competition with every kind of amusement, and in 1897 even the Tennessee Centennial. Dancing, novel-reading, theater-going, and card-playing also loomed as portents of evil to come, but nothing concerned the churches like the rampant abuse of alcohol.

Though fermented drink consumed in moderation was commonplace in colonial America, attitudes changed in the early nineteenth century. As the population moved west and grain production increased, so did alcoholic consumption. Grain was more easily marketed as liquor, and barrels of whiskey became a convenient medium of exchange. The temptation was too great, and with the weakened Christian culture of the west providing little resistance, drunkenness increased dramatically. In his *Six Sermons on Intemperance,* Lyman Beecher sounded a national alarm:

> Intemperance is the sin of our land, and if anything shall defeat the hopes of the world, which hang upon our experiment in civil liberty, it is that river of fire . . . rolling through the land and extending around an atmosphere of death.[19]

Moved by warnings such as this, the American Temperance Society, founded in Boston in 1826, began promoting voluntary total abstinence. Churches and ministers were the driving force behind this movement, which led to prohibition in at least nine states and by 1850 had a membership of over 238,000.[20]

After the War between the States, the battle against alcohol was carried on by a Prohibition Party begun in 1869 by Frances Willard's Women's Christian Temperance Union and the Anti-Saloon League, which, led by Methodist minister Alpha Kynett, styled itself the "Church in Action against the Saloon." What each of these organizations wanted to prevent were the conditions represented by Nashville's "Black Bottom," a "region of immorality" that was particularly symbolic because it stood within sight of the capitol. One observer described it as:

> A conglomeration of dives, brothels, pawnshops, second-hand clothing stores, filthy habitations . . . accompanied by the daily display of lewdness and drunkenness on the sidewalks and redolent with the stench of every vile odor. . . . no city in America or Europe can present a more disgraceful or sickening aspect of modern civilization.[21]

Increasingly aware of the problem, the churches launched into action with the Methodists characteristically in the lead. Conferences debated, ministers preached, and congregation members flooded into organizations like the Sons of Temperance, the Friends of Temperance, the Order of Good Templars, and St. Mary's Catholic Total Abstinence Society. A great day of victory for antialcohol forces arrived in 1877 when the state legislature passed the "Four Mile Law." The law "forbade retail liquor sales within four miles of any chartered school outside an incorporated town." The scope of the law was fairly limited until community leaders began surrendering their municipal status, seeking chartered schools. Then, beginning in 1877, the legislature added amendments that applied the law to all schools, and this became the legal basis for "drying up the entire state."[22]

The Four Mile Law signaled a major shift for the churches. As Herman Norton wrote, "With its passage, the temperance forces, led by the churches, gradually ceased to rely primarily on sermons, prayers, and moral persuasion and sought to achieve their objectives chiefly through legislation." Even churches known for their staunch defense of the separation of church and state plunged into what critics called "ministry by legislation."[23] The Methodists, Baptists, Cumberland Presbyterians, and the Presbyterian Church, USA, all called for legal action against alcohol. The Roman Catholics, Episcopalians, and Presbyterian Church, US, stayed out of the fray, not being teetotalers. And the Churches of Christ were split, with many following the view of David Lipscomb that God would destroy the evils of whiskey without the power of legislation or the interference of politics.

For many, the battle against alcohol was a holy crusade, a battle to recover "the lost soul of America." Churches debated and even fought over whether wine ought to be served in communion. Others felt that the whole prohibition effort was misguided, wrongly treating alcohol as the sin when the real evil was in the human heart. The issue of alcohol divided churches like nothing had since slavery. In 1883 David Kelley decided to run for governor as the Prohibition Party candidate. A Methodist minister from Gallatin, Kelley expected an endorsement from his own denomination. Instead, he was suspended from the ministry for six months. A firestorm of protest arose, and when it reached the General Conference, the decision was reversed. Nevertheless, bitterness lingered on both sides. Even with the passage of a statewide Prohibition law in 1909—a full decade before the Eighteenth Amendment established nationwide Prohibition—ill feeling over the issue continued to cause tremors in the churches.

THE HOLINESS MOVEMENT

While most Christians saw in prohibition a victory for righteousness, others thought such political influence was evidence of apostasy. The denominations had left the true ministry of the Word of God, they believed, and merged with the state to form an anti-Christian system as wicked as any in the days of the Roman Empire. What men needed was holiness, separation from the world, and a thorough sanctification that only the Holy Spirit could accomplish. On the wings of such hopes arose the Holiness Movement, a rushing river that not only washed through much of American Christianity in the late nineteenth century but also flowed into the unprecedented worldwide revivals of the twentieth century.

The Holiness Movement grew out of the theology of John Wesley and the various streams of the revival that surfaced during the War between the States. Wesley taught a doctrine of Christian perfection known as "entire sanctification," the belief that following salvation there is a separate and instantaneous experience that frees a believer from sin and attunes him to the "higher life." After the war, both Methodists and non-Methodists embraced the doctrine in increasing numbers, and this, combined with an interdenominational concern for the "worldliness" of the church, gave impetus to an entirely new movement. In July 1867 the Methodists sponsored a camp meeting for the promotion of holiness in Vineland, New Jersey, out of which sprang the National Campmeeting Association for the Promotion of Holiness. From this inception until 1883, more than fifty-two "national camps" were held, with the experience of most of them similar to that of the one at Manheim, Pennsylvania, in 1868:

> All at once, as sudden as if a flash of lightning from the heavens had fallen upon the people, one simultaneous burst of agony and then of glory was heard in all parts of the congregation; and for nearly an hour the scene beggared description. . . . Those seated far back in the audience declared that the sensation was as if a strong wind had moved from the stand over the congregation. Several intelligent

people, in different parts of the congregation, spoke of the same phenomenon. . . . Sinners stood awestricken, and others fled affrighted from the congregation.[24]

In many of the meetings, healings were reported, and before long thousands were flocking to hear speakers like Phoebe Palmer, Hannah Whitehall Smith, Charles Cullis, John Inskip, and A. B. Simpson, who wrote the beloved hymn, "Standing on the Promises."

The Holiness Movement generated tremendous interest in Tennessee. As early as 1878, the Nashville *Christian Advocate* reported that "Venerable men are calling attention to it. Multitudes of awakened believers are seeking it. . . . The movement is the natural recoil of the religious mind from the rampant worldliness of the time."[25] As the movement washed through the churches in Tennessee and elsewhere, new denominations formed, as many as twenty-three between 1893 and 1900 alone. Two of these took deep root in Tennessee. In 1895 a union of Holiness churches in Los Angeles, encouraged by former Methodist Phineas F. Bresee, led to the formation of the Church of the Nazarene. More than three thousand Tennessee Methodists joined the new denomination, which in time become the nation's largest Holiness church.[26]

Another Holiness denomination arose in 1886 when eight Tennesseans formed a "Christian Union" to restore "primitive Christianity." The Union chose Richard Spurling as its pastor and later teamed with another gathering in North Carolina in 1896. That same year, during their camp meeting at Shearer Schoolhouse in Cherokee, North Carolina, more than one hundred people "spoke in tongues," a claim becoming common in Holiness meetings by that time. Persecutions broke out against the little group. Houses were burned, chapels were blown up, and the Ku Klux Klan even paid the "tongue-talkers" a visit. When the authorities of Cherokee County arrested some of the persecutors, their victims begged the officials for mercy, and the congregation's enemies were freed. Some of the attenders of the camp meeting later called themselves the Holiness Church at Camp Creek, North Carolina, but eventually they settled on the name "Church of God" in 1906.[27]

The Holiness Movement not only brought new denominations to Tennessee, but also led to one of the most important revivals the state ever witnessed. Toward the end of the nineteenth century, reports of revivals around the country made the many citizens of Nashville hungry for an "outpouring" in their city. Influenced by the Holiness passion for prayer and revival, the Methodists in the city had been praying for two years that God would "send a revival." Bishop George Pierce, bemoaning the sense of "spiritual deadness," declared that the city needed "a revival of religion; a sin-killing, sin-hating, sin-forsaking, debt-paying, God-serving, man-loving religion." Many agreed and blamed everything from "demonic interference" to the neglect of the Negro for the delay.[28] The waiting came to an end, though, when the city's clergymen invited Sam Jones to preach.

Jones was one of the most important revivalists of his day. Just the year before he had created a huge stir in Memphis with his preaching; after a decade of ministry his attributed conversions numbered in the thousands. Born in Alabama to a family of Methodist preachers, Jones began drinking at an early age to ease the pain of ulcers, though his drunkenness ultimately cost him his law practice and his marriage. When his dying father asked him to meet him in heaven, Jones was converted and immediately felt a call to ministry. He was admitted to the North Carolina Methodist Conference as an itinerant preacher on one of its poorest circuits in March 1872. In three years, church membership increased at a rate of two hundred a year, and giving increased 1,200 percent. More than two thousand members were added over the next five years, and in 1884 Jones began to hold large meetings in big cities throughout the South.[29]

In 1885 the Protestant Minister's Association of Nashville was shocked when Jones informed them that no church in the city was large enough for the crowds he would draw and that they would need to build a three-thousand-dollar tent. The incredulous ministers dared the brash upstart to prove himself. Jones preached in Nashville's three largest churches, denouncing the "whisky sellers, drunkards, gamblers, and theatre-goers" who filled the pews of the city. Jones offended J. D. Barbee, pastor of McKendree

Methodist Church, by claiming that if Barbee drew the line where God drew the line, the church would have one hundred members instead of one thousand. The evangelist preached in similar tones at the Tulip Street Methodist Church over the next three days, kicking off a revival that led to 150 conversions and 111 additions to the church.[30]

When the work at Tulip Street Methodist ended, Jones left Nashville insisting that he would return when the ministers granted his request for a tent. Not everyone was eager to comply. During his preaching tour Jones had stated that most of the saloons in the city were owned by Christians. The proud citizens of Nashville were shocked at such a claim, but when the *Daily American* investigated, it discovered that sixty-eight of the eighty-one liquor dealers were indeed church members. This confirmation of Jones's charge only intensified the hunger for revival in the city, and fires began to spark in a number of churches. Dr. O. P. Fitzgerald of the *Christian Advocate* wrote, "The need is felt, the desire is expressed, the pastors are moving and praying men and women are calling upon God for power on high."[31]

6.4 *Samuel P. Jones.* One of the leading evangelists of his day, Sam Jones first came to Nashville in 1885 for a series of revival meetings that stirred the city to its core. He unhesitatingly attacked the corruption and perversion that abounded in the city at the time, and thus won not only a goodly number of converts but a healthy supply of enemies as well. The conversion of one of those enemies—the notorious steamboat tycoon, Captain Thomas Green Ryman—would ultimately leave an indelible mark on the city.

When Jones returned six weeks later to preach in his much-debated tent, the city was at fever pitch for revival. The evangelist startled his crowd at the end of the first night's meeting when he announced a 6 A.M. prayer meeting every morning at McKendree Methodist. Suspecting that "there's many a good Methodist, Baptist and Presbyterian in the city who wouldn't turn over in his bed to save Nashville from Hell," Jones commanded all of his audience to be there, "Dr. Barbee thrown in." More than one thousand people turned out for the morning prayer service, and half of them were men at a time when the pews of Nashville's churches were filled largely with women and children. The news swept the city and increased the numbers attending the afternoon and evening meetings. Jones didn't hold back, but preached against hypocrisy, worldly entertainments, weak ministers, and his favorite target, alcohol. In one meeting, Jones ended his diatribe against alcohol and drunkenness with an appeal to motherhood:

> Never let it be said you added a pang to a mother's heart. There are burdens here on a mother's heart, she can't carry much longer. I tell you, human hearts will carry just so much and then they'll break. There are mothers in this town who, if God don't take 'em to Heaven, will be raving maniacs in twelve months. My mother! My mother![32]

At the end of the meeting, a large man, well known to the audience, strode to the front when the invitation was given. It was Tom Ryman, "a figure of mythic proportions in Nashville," who owned thirty-five steamboats, some of which were "floating dens of iniquity." Ryman and "his boys" had intended to disrupt the meeting and drive the preacher off, but something in Jones's ninety-minute sermon reached the hard-bitten river man, and as he clasped the preacher's hand he proclaimed, "I came here for the purpose stated by Mr. Jones and he has whipped me with the Gospel of Christ."[33]

The city was electric with the news of Ryman's conversion. There was no doubting the depth of the change. Ryman hauled his river friends to the altar, mounted "Scripture boards" on street corners, and sent "gospel wagons," filled with food, medicine, and clothing for the poor, throughout the city. One wagon was even outfitted with its own choir, organ, and pulpit and seemed to always make its way to the city's business district on Sundays to touch the troubled consciences of Sabbath-breakers. He renamed one of his steamboats the "Sam Jones" and converted his riverside saloon into "Sam Jones Hall." "He then had Scripture passages painted over the doorways on his steamers lest passengers ever forgot that they rode on a vessel devoted to God's glory." Ryman's greatest achievement for the faith, though, was one he discussed with Jones the night of his salvation: a huge "Tabernacle" to perpetuate the revival and to serve as a Nashville home for Sam Jones. Between 1889 and 1892, the Union Gospel Tabernacle was indeed built, and Ryman's dream was fulfilled. Not only did the building house some of the most powerful revivals of Sam Jones's ministry, but also stirring revivalists like Dwight Moody, Billy Sunday, and Aimee Semple McPherson. Though still a Nashville landmark, in time the Tabernacle lost its uniquely religious purpose. It was renamed the Ryman Auditorium and ultimately became the "mother church" of country music—home to the "Grand Ole Opry."[34]

Sam Jones continued his ministry until his death in 1906. "He is reputed to have had five hundred thousand converts out of a total of 25 million people in his meetings, most of which were in Nashville."[35] Yet he was the very opposite of the modern image of the evangelist. A reporter of his day wrote:

> Sam Jones is a very insignificant looking person. He is a small, thin wiry-looking man with a firm jaw, pinched face, sallow complexion, a small black mustache, coal-black hair brushed high off a rather narrow forehead, finely lined eyebrows, and hands as small and delicate as a woman's. He is the last person in the world one would expect to be a religious exhorter.[36]

Jones was, the reporter said, much more likely to be "an accomplished second in a duet" or a confidence man "at a county fair." Typically, the little man made no apology, "I weigh 135 pounds, but 132 $\frac{1}{2}$ of that are solid backbone."[37]

6.5 *The Ryman Auditorium.* The original home of the Grand Ole Opry and the "Mother Church of Country Music," the Ryman auditorium was actually built as a gospel tabernacle by Captain Tom Ryman for the evangelist Sam Jones. The Union Gospel Tabernacle, as it was then called, served the city as a beacon light of the muscular "git up and git" faith that Jones preached.

The perceptive in Jones's audience sensed that such bravado was more than empty bluster; it was the studied method of a man desperate to arouse a sleeping church. Jones understood that the church was the key to the nation's destiny. He knew also that in the decades following the War between the States the church in America was in trouble. He was the dynamite to blow it out of its lethargy. He confronted the self-important with the base and the common, dislodged the complacent with the power of discomfiting truth, and exposed the idolatries of the self-deceived. In an age when table legs were covered lest they offend delicate sensibilities, Jones crudely slammed into the facade of a society that had disconnected from the vital Christianity of its founding. He was the perfect tool to crack open the hardened hearts of such a society, and his legacy is perhaps best found in the revivals that crackled through the nation a generation later.

PROFILE 6   *City Upon a Hill*

---

*Posterity: you will never know how much it has cost my generation
to preserve your freedom. I hope you will make good use of it.*
                                                John Quincy Adams

*B*y the end of the nineteenth century most Americans, including most Tennesseans, looked forward to the future with the proud
and certain belief that the next hundred years would be the greatest, the most glorious, and the most glamorous in human history.
They were infected with a sanguine spirit. Optimism was rampant.
A brazen confidence colored their every activity. Hope was the
atmosphere in which they lived and breathed and had their being.

Certainly there was nothing in their experience to make them
think otherwise. Never had a century changed the lives of men
and women more dramatically than the one just past. The twentieth century has moved fast and furiously, so that those of us who
have lived in it feel sometimes giddy watching it spin; but the
nineteenth century moved faster and more furiously still.
Railroads, telephones, the telegraph, electricity, mass production,
forged steel, automobiles, and countless other modern discoveries
had all come upon them at a dizzying pace, expanding their
visions and expectations far beyond their grandfathers' wildest
dreams.

The wrenching disruption of the War between the States was
now past. The moral blight of slavery had been wiped out of existence. Prosperity had returned. Brash vitality and assurance were
now the common currencies of the day. Things couldn't have been
better—or at least so it seemed.

It was more than unfounded imagination, then, that lay
behind the *New York World's* prediction that the twentieth century
would "meet and overcome all perils and prove to be the best that
this steadily improving planet has ever seen."[1]

Most Americans were cheerfully assured that control of man and nature would soon lie entirely within their grasp and would bestow upon them the unfathomable power to alter the destinies of societies, nations, and epochs. They were a people of manifold purpose. They were a people of manifest destiny.

What they did not know was that dark and malignant seeds were already germinating just beneath the surface of the new century's soil. Even as the new epoch dawned, ideological revolutions, nationalistic passions, and unbridled new technological powers drew the entire world toward a century of the unimagined and unimaginable horrors of war, despotism, injustice, prejudice, discrimination, and totalitarianism.

Who could have guessed during those ebulliently auspicious days of anticipation and celebration that a mere handful of ideologues would, over the span of the next century, spill more innocent blood than all the murderers, warlords, and tyrants of past

6.6 *City Upon a Hill.* America was an optimistic and enthusiastic land as it entered the modern era. And Tennessee shared in that optimism and enthusiasm. It seemed that there was nothing—no problem, no dilemma, no obstacle— that the progress of the nation could not overcome.

history combined? Who could have guessed that they would together ensure that the hopes and dreams and aspirations of the twentieth century would be smothered under the weight of holocaust, genocide, and triage?

While the church had been forced to face grave and difficult challenges in the past, its challenges in this new century would be unprecedented. From both within and without the community of faith would be buffeted by forces of fierce virulence. And its response would ultimately determine the destiny of both men and nations.

The founders of the great American experiment in liberty— from the Pilgrim and Puritan pioneers to the Constitutional framers—imagined that this land might be a "city on a hill," a "light to the nations," a "great and final hope for mankind." The difficult days of the twentieth century would test that proposition as it had never before been tested. And, as always, judgment would begin at the house of God.

7

$\mathscr{R}$ivers of $\mathscr{F}$ire, $\mathscr{C}$urrents of $\mathscr{C}$hange

Modernity has made us all mere pilgrims wandering through the wilderness of this world.

John Crowe Ransom

$\mathscr{I}$t was December 31, 1900, and the students of Bethel Bible College in Topeka, Kansas, were filled with anticipation. It was the time of the Watch-Night Service, a New Year's Eve vigil that began with the early Methodists and revived in the late nineteenth century with the Holiness Movement. But the forty students who gathered that night at Stone's Folly, the mansion where the school met, sensed that this particular Watch-Night was going to be different. Their teacher's special assignment had filled them each with a hunger for a fresh encounter with the Holy Spirit. Yes, this Watch-Night was going to be different, but none of the students could have known that what they were about to experience was going to spark one of the largest movements in the history of the American church.

Their teacher's name was Charles Parham. Born in Muscatine, Iowa, on June 4, 1873, Parham began preaching in the Congregational Church when he was fifteen. He later joined the Methodists and through them became involved in the rapidly growing Holiness Movement. He was changed by the message and experience of "entire sanctification," but he believed "that while many had obtained real experiences, in sanctification . . .

there still remained a great outpouring of power for Christians." He also believed that the "gift of tongues" described in the book of Acts should be experienced by modern believers. In October 1900 he opened the College. A short time later, he made the decisive classroom assignment: "According to Scripture, is there some sort of special witness to the fact that a person has been baptized with the Holy Spirit?" After a short season of study, the students determined that the primary biblical sign of Holy Spirit baptism is indeed a supernatural manifestation of unknown languages—the "gift of tongues." And they wanted it.[1]

During the prayer and spiritual searching of the New Year's Eve vigil, a thirty-year-old student named Agnes Ozman remembered that in the Bible the gift of the Holy Spirit with "tongues" was given at the "laying on of hands." She asked Parham and the others to lay hands on her. Parham later wrote of this moment:

> I had scarcely repeated three dozen sentences when a glory fell upon her, a halo seemed to surround her head and face, and she began speaking in the Chinese language, and was unable to speak English for three days. Seeing this marvelous manifestation of the restoration of Pentecostal power . . . we decided as a school to wait upon God. We felt that God was no respecter of persons and what He had so graciously poured out upon one, He would upon all.[2]

Soon most of the students, and even Parham himself, experienced "Spirit baptism" and spoke in "tongues." Endued with this powerful new experience, they were eager to share their testimony with the world.

But the world did not want to hear. For two years Parham and his followers tried to hold meetings to bring others into "Pentecost" but met with nothing but persecution and frustration. The press ridiculed, the churches rebuffed, and the unchurched scorned. Attempted revivals in Kansas City and Lawrence were failures, and it became clear that Parham "was to find no wide acceptance of his new experience for several years." Eventually, persecution even forced the closing of the College:

Both the pulpit and the press sought to utterly destroy our place and prestige, until my wife, her sister and myself stood alone. Hated, despised, counted as naught, for weeks never knowing where our next meal would come from, yet feeling that we must maintain the faith once for all delivered to the saints. When we had car fare we rode, when we didn't we walked. When buildings were closed to us we preached on the street.[3]

This situation changed dramatically, though, when Mary Arthur of Galena, Kansas, reported being healed of a series of chronic ailments under Parham's ministry. News of the healing spread, and meetings that began with a small group in the Arthur home became a three-month series of revival meetings held under a large tent and then eventually in a building on Main Street. The Cincinnati *Inquirer* picked up the story in its January 27, 1904, edition, and soon Parham was holding "Full Gospel" meetings in towns throughout Kansas, Missouri, and Texas. The Texas meetings were astoundingly successful. "It is estimated that by winter of 1905, Texas alone had 25,000 Pentecostal believers and about 60 preachers—all the direct result of Parham's consecrated efforts."[4] To train champions from the Houston revival, Parham opened a Bible school similar to the one in Topeka.

One of the students who enrolled in the school was a black preacher by the name of William Seymour. The son of former slaves, Seymour believed Parham's message of "tongues" as a sign of "Spirit baptism" but had not experienced it for himself. Though the laws of the State of Texas prohibited a black man from studying in a white institution, Parham sensed Seymour's hunger and allowed him to attend classes. He remained at the school until 1906, when he received an invitation to pastor a Nazarene mission in Los Angeles. He accepted the call, but when he arrived and preached his first sermon one morning on the Pentecostal experience from Acts 2:4, he found himself locked out of the church for the afternoon service. Seymour was determined to continue, though, and began holding meetings at the nearby home of Richard and Ruth Asberry. There, on April 9, 1906, seven people, including Seymour himself, received the experience of "Holy

Spirit baptism" and began speaking in "tongues." One participant later reported:

> They shouted three days and three nights. It was the Easter season. The people came from everywhere. By the next morning there was no way of getting near the house. As the people came in they would fall under God's Power; and the whole city was stirred. They shouted there until the foundation of the house gave way, but no one was hurt. During these three days, there were many people who received their baptism who had just come to see what it was. The sick were healed and sinners were saved just as they came in.[5]

Seymour soon purchased an abandoned building a few blocks away on Azusa Street to house the growing crowds, and before long the word "Azusa" was synonymous with both the revival and the Pentecostal experience.

Seymour held meetings three times a day. The crowds that gathered were from every race and nationality, scandalous in those days. Unlike most churches services, the meetings were unorchestrated and spontaneous, filled with prayer, worship, and testimony "as the Spirit led." Few who attended were ever the same again. Arthur Osterberg, the twenty-one-year-old pastor of a nearby church in Los Angeles, reluctantly consented to take his mother to the meetings. His account is typical of the experience of thousands who attended the Azusa meetings:

> I was not entirely in favor of the idea, but I saw as soon as I entered Azusa Street that something unusual was going on. . . . I was critical, but I went in and sat down on the rough boards they used for makeshift pews. A club-footed man of Mexican ancestry and his wife sat down next to me. The service began. There was a long prayer. During it I heard someone behind me sobbing. Then there were others. The sound of their wailing rose like the moan of the wind in the place. This club-footed man beside me became restless and at length made his way to the aisle. He limped up and down. I guess I was the only one watching him. Gradually he ceased to limp. Before my eyes he was cured. He was miraculously healed without anyone praying for him and with no formal "conversion," as we call it, at all. That convinced me there was something different in this meeting from any other that I had ever attended.

Somehow those people had gotten back to primitive Christianity when those things were possible. I closed up my own church and joined the movement.[6]

The huge crowds and dramatic tales of the revival drew the press to the scene. In an April 18 front-page article entitled "Weird Babel of Tongues," the *Los Angeles Times* gave its account of the meetings:

Breathing strange utterances and mouthing a creed which it would seem no sane mortal could understand, the newest religious sect has started in Los Angeles. Meetings are held in a tumble-down shack on Azusa Street, near San Pedro Street, and the devotees of the weird doctrine practice the most fanatical rites, preach the wildest theories and work themselves into a state of mad excitement in their peculiar zeal. Colored people and a sprinkling of whites compose the congregation, and night is made hideous in the neighborhood by the howlings of the worshipers, who spend hours swaying forth and back in a nerve-racking attitude of prayer and supplication. They claim to have "the gift of tongues," and to be able to comprehend the babel. Such startling claim has never yet been made by any company of fanatics, even in Los Angeles, the home of almost numberless creeds.[7]

Pentecostal historians later complained that the reporters "had little interest in the times of tremendous heart-searching and emptying of self that were going on,"[8] but what happened next made complaints about the reports unnecessary. The same day readers chuckled at the accounts in the Los Angeles papers, the city of San Francisco experienced one of the worst earthquakes in history. Fires from the quake lasted for three days, and four square miles of the city were reduced to ruins. The degree of human suffering was staggering. More than five hundred people were killed, five hundred thousand more were left homeless, and the total damage was estimated at $375 million.[9] Leaders at Azusa Street felt that "the Lord was answering our payers for a revival in His own way," for the crowds dramatically increased after the quake and the "manifestations of the Spirit" seemed to intensify.[10]

The "outpouring" in Los Angeles lasted for three years. As news spread of the astonishing signs and wonders, people literally traveled from around the world to drink from the stream then flowing so powerfully through the decrepit building on Azusa Street. Many of these pilgrims returned to their homelands and pioneered Pentecostal missions and churches of their own. In lands as far away as Russia, Pentecostalism spread rapidly. Braving cruel persecution from the Orthodox Church and the Czarist regime, Russian Pentecostals spread their message so effectively that the movement survived the atheistic Communist regime that came to power in 1917 and was still flourishing underground when that regime ended seventy years later. In Europe, the movement touched the lives of thousands and did so just before the meat-grinders of World War I destroyed a generation of young men, many of whom gave witness to their Pentecostal faith in the terror-filled trenches of places like Verdun and the Somme. In Brazil, in South Africa, and in the Orient, Pentecostal missionaries carried the message and fire of Azusa Street with great effect. In time, the Pentecostal movement evolved into the Latter Rain movement, led by men like Oral Roberts, Gordon Lindsay, and William Branham, and still later into the Charismatic movement, becoming one of the largest popular movements in the history of the church.

*P*ENTECOST IN *T*ENNESSEE

The Pentecostal movement spread into Tennessee like wildfire through dry brush. Traveling ministers who had been to Azusa Street carried its message and experiences eastward and left "sanctified, Spirit baptized, tongues-talking" believers in their wake. Sleepy country churches in rural Tennessee caught the Azusa fire from these messengers and began nightly meetings that often met regularly for months. In urban areas, Holiness churches were usually the first to experience Pentecost, and their ecstatic meetings drew the curious and the hungry by the hundreds. It was not uncommon, too, for a member of a more traditional denomination to be "arrested by the Spirit" only to find himself no longer welcomed by his church family. Pentecostal fire moved into the mountain regions of Tennessee as well. Appalachian Pentecostals often added doctrines and experiences of their own to those of Azusa Street, with some groups even believing that their "Spirit-empowered faith" enabled them to handle rattlesnakes and drink poison to the glory of God. And, as in Los Angeles, revival meetings drew white and black seekers together under the same roof. Some scholars have seen in this an important early step toward racial harmony in Tennessee that in some cases paved the way for the Civil Rights movement.

One of the first men to bring the message of Azusa Street to Tennessee was G. B. Cashwell, a man whose meetings helped launch some of the state's largest and most influential denominations. Cashwell was a 250-pound Methodist preacher who joined the Holiness Movement in 1903. When he read a magazine report of the Azusa revival, he immediately wrote to the annual conference of his church, "I am unable to be with you this time, for I am now leaving for Los Angeles, California, where I shall seek for the Baptism of the Holy Ghost." Cashwell fasted and prayed during the entire six-day rail journey to Los Angeles. Upon reaching his destination he went directly to the mission and asked Seymour and several others to lay hands on him. Cashwell reported receiving the "baptism of the Spirit and speaking in other tongues." He immediately began preaching of his new experience in North and South Carolina, Alabama, Virginia, and Georgia.[11] On May 8, 1907, Cashwell opened a revival in Memphis. One participant wrote:

> We had been hearing of strange things happening in Wales and California how that people were being baptized with the Holy Ghost . . . We invited him to come to Memphis to tell us about this new thing . . . G. B. Cashwell [came] and we could scarcely wait for the message to end and the altar call given as we all sat with ears, eyes and heart wide open drinking in every word. We must have looked like a hungry bunch.[12]

It was at this meeting that H. G. Rodgers, guiding light in the founding of the Assemblies of God, received the "baptism of the Holy Spirit."

Rodgers was a popular fiddler in the barn dances of West Tennessee when the deaths of three of his children caused him to throw himself on their graves and confess his sins in 1894. Sensing a calling to ministry, he attended school briefly and then began a series of tent revivals. It was while traveling from revival to revival that Rodgers attended the Cashwell meeting that so changed his life. Rodgers teamed with Mack Pinson, who had received his baptism in the same meeting as Rodgers, and began establishing local congregations. Yearning for an organization to draw these new churches together, Rodgers called the 1909 conference in Dothan, Alabama, that ultimately led to the start of the Assemblies of God. By 1916 there were 118 Assemblies of God churches with 6,703 members in the United States, but none in Tennessee. The first Tennessee Assembly "set-in-order" met in Dyersburg, and by 1926 there were five churches with a combined membership of 364. The denomination grew rapidly, and by 1955 there were over 145 churches in the state.[13]

Cashwell's ministry led to the founding of a second denomination with roots in Tennessee. In 1902 A. J. Tomlinson, a salesman for the American Bible Society, joined the "Holiness Church at Camp Creek," the group that had experienced the gift of "tongues" at Shearer Schoolhouse in Cherokee, North Carolina. Within a year, Tomlinson became the church's pastor, which in 1907 moved to Cleveland, Tennessee, and took the name "Church of God." The new denomination was touched by the excitement of Azusa Street when Tomlinson attended one of Cashwell's meetings in 1908:

> On Sunday morning, January 12, while he was preaching, a peculiar sensation took hold of me, and almost unconsciously I slipped off my chair in a heap on the rostrum at Brother Cashwell's feet. I did not know what such an experience meant. My mind was clear, but a peculiar power so enveloped and thrilled my whole being that I concluded to yield myself up and await results. I was soon lost to

my surroundings as I lay there on the floor, occupied only with God and eternal things.[14]

Through experiences like this, the Church of God became involved in the broader Pentecostal movement and over the next fourteen years, Tomlinson traveled widely, holding revival meetings and organizing local churches. The church's official periodical, *The Church of God Evangel*, outlined the movement's doctrine and commended Azusa-like revival to its readers. In 1922 controversy forced Tomlinson out of the Church of God, and he started over with some two thousand followers. When Tomlinson died in 1943, the new group numbered nearly thirty-two thousand and later, in 1952, became legally designated the Church of God of Prophecy.[15]

Another denomination headquartered in Tennessee was begun when its founder went to Azusa Street for himself. Charles H. Mason, a black man born on a farm near Memphis, was dramatically converted in 1880 and baptized by his brother, Nelson, at nearby Mt. Olive Missionary Church. He was soon licensed by the Mt. Gale Missionary Baptist Church and shortly after experienced "sanctification" among Holiness believers in Arkansas. In 1895 Mason met Charles Price Jones, a black preacher from Jackson, Mississippi, and the two held a series of Holiness conventions that spawned a network of churches they called the "Church of God in Christ." When Mason heard of the Azusa revival, he made his way to California and was "Spirit baptized" during his five weeks "under Pentecost." He became convinced in Los Angeles that "tongues" speaking was the evidence of Spirit baptism. Upon returning to Memphis, Mason found that Jones disapproved of his Pentecostal views, and the two split, with Mason taking the majority of their followers and keeping the name Church of God in Christ. Mason's skillful leadership, which continued until his death in 1961, helped the denomination grow into the largest Pentecostal body in America. Headquartered in Memphis, the church has had tremendous impact on the black community in Tennessee, with its training centers, its preaching of biblical ethics, and its emphasis on "conservative living and avoidance of the dole."[16]

CURRENTS OF CHANGE

Pentecostalism was but one wave of change washing through Tennessee churches in the early twentieth century. Technology was another. So rapid was the pace of technological change in America that in the short span of fifty years the weaponry of the War between the States—rifles, sabers, canons, and hot-air balloons—were replaced by the technologies of the Great War—machine guns, mustard gas, tanks, submarines, and airplanes. Of course, the new technologies introduced many new comforts and conveniences as well, so they were a kind of double-edged sword.

If the new technologies were often mixed blessings, so were the processes that created them. Factories had to be located near cities in order to assure a sizable labor pool. In turn, the factories drew even more laborers from rural areas to the already ballooning cities. In time, immigrants joined their number, arriving as they did by the thousands in the late nineteenth and early twentieth centuries. These three forces—industrialization, urbanization, and immigration—transformed American society and left no state of the Union, including Tennessee, untouched. The challenge for the churches was to harness the new technologies to reach an increasingly urban, multicultural, and secular society.

The churches of Tennessee certainly had the numerical strength to meet the challenge. According to the religious census taken by the Census Bureau in 1906, 32 percent of the state's population were counted as church members. In fact, though the population had increased by 72 percent in the last quarter of the 1800s, church membership had increased 150 percent. The Baptists and the Methodists accounted for three-fourths of all church members, the Baptists numbering 241,396 and the Methodists trailing slightly at 227,170. Presbyterians ranked third and numbered 79,337, the Churches of Christ claimed 56,315, and the Christian

Church listed 17,784. Ninety-five percent of all Tennessee church members were found in these bodies—Pentecostalism's influence was still a few years off. The remaining five percent was comprised of seventeen thousand Roman Catholics, 7,800 Episcopalians, and approximately 3,200 Lutherans. There were also just under one thousand Jews in the state.[17]

Alas, despite their numerical strength, the denominations were too consumed with internal disputes and divisions to deal effectively with the challenges of the new century. Disputes over missionary societies and denominational structures resurfaced, and both were aggravated by Prohibition battles. Churches fought over the doctrine of the Second Coming, the definition of holiness, and, later of course, the Pentecostal experience. Cessationists, who believed that the gifts of the Spirit were no longer given after the apostolic age, found the stirring and confusion of Pentecost too much for them, and more than one "tongues-talker" was asked to leave his Tennessee church. Meanwhile, Christians who were suspicious of congregations who worked too closely with the state found much to fuel their fears during the Great War. The federal

7.1 *Alvin York.* The product of a poor community in east Tennesse, Alvin York became the greatest American hero in the First World War. Armed with only an infantry rifle and a pistol, he single-handedly defeated an entire German army machine gun unit, killing 25 and capturing 132. After the war, he turned down innumerable commercial opportunities to return to his family farm. Once home, he founded the Pall Mall Bible School and helped to establish the American Legion.

government issued sermon outlines to local churches, complete with stories of war atrocities, and some congregations supported the war with such fervor that their buildings became recruitment centers. Liberty Bonds and War Savings Stamps were sold in their sanctuaries, and war rallies were held in the largest churches of some cities.

All of these issues had the subtle effect of diverting the churches' attention from the high call of the gospel and needs of society. In Tennessee, the churches became together a "sub-culture that looked in upon itself," and though this may have kept them from some of the philosophical storms then tearing through the nation, it also made them focus their energies on preserving old wineskins rather than seeking the new wineskins so necessary for a society in upheaval.[18]

*M*ODERNISM AND *F*UNDAMENTALISM

One of the storms the churches in Tennessee could not avoid was the one over modernism. Throughout the nineteenth century, orthodox Christianity had come under unrelenting attack from the scholars and thinkers who followed in the wake of the Enlightenment. The writings of several of these intellectuals were like hammer blows to the edifice of Christian theology. In 1848 Karl Marx published his *Communist Manifesto*, which declared that religion is the "opiate" of the people, echoing Ludwig Feuerbach's contention that men created the idea of God for the psychological comfort the idea provided. In 1859 Charles Darwin's *The Origin of Species* suggested that man evolved from lower life forms and thus challenged the biblical teaching on creation. In 1885 Julius Wellhausen's *The History of Israel* subjected the Bible to the same techniques of literary criticism used on uninspired literature and thus brought into question biblical claims of authorship and inspiration. And in 1902 William James's *Varieties of Religious Experience* suggested that the power of religion is one of individual psychology rather than objective truth, that faith "works" only because a man wills it into being and not because his religion is necessarily "real." Each of these streams merged with other movements in the nineteenth century—Unitarianism, Transcendentalism, and even Theosophy—so that by the early twentieth century many ministers and university professors regarded the message of Jesus as one of a good man teaching men how to live rather than the Son of God showing men the way to a sovereign Creator. The battle between these two views was played out on seminary campuses, in denominational conventions, and even in local congregations. The words of conservative scholar J. Gresham Machen in his book of 1923, *Christianity and Liberalism*, expressed the thoughts of many Christians at the time:

> But one thing is perfectly plain—whether or not liberals are Christians, it is at any rate perfectly clear that liberalism is not Christianity. And that being the case, it is highly undesirable that liberalism and Christianity should continue to be propagated within the bounds of the same organization. A separation between the two parties in the Church is the crying need of the hour.[19]

To help combat the forces of modernism and liberalism, two wealthy Los Angeles businessmen, Lyman and Milton Stewart, started a fund of $250,000 to provide "every pastor, evangelist, minister, theological professor, theological student, Sunday school superintendent, YMCA and YWCA secretary in the English speaking world" with twelve booklets that explained the "fundamentals" of orthodox Christianity.[20] Written by eminent scholars like Princeton Seminary's Benjamin Warfield, the booklets expounded biblical doctrines like the virgin birth, the divinity of Jesus, miracles, the authority of Scripture, and the atonement. Between 1910 and 1915, more than 2,500,000 copies of *The Fundamentals: A Testimony* were sent to pastors and Christian workers throughout the world. A "fundamentalist" army came into existence, and in churches and lecture halls throughout the nation the errors of modernism were condemned and battle lines were drawn. In Tennessee, *The Fundamentals* were widely circulated, particularly among Baptists and Methodists. Organizations like the Anti-Evolution League and the Bible Crusaders ballooned in membership and drew many noted defenders of orthodoxy to the state.

Since most of the churches in Tennessee were already theologically conservative, they concerned themselves more with strengthening fundamentalism's hold on the state than with fighting modernism. Their specific concern was the doctrine of evolution. As early as 1878, a noted naturalist had been fired from Vanderbilt University—then still under Methodist control—for publishing a book entitled *Pre-Adamites*, which suggested that civilizations may have existed before the time of Adam. The issue resurfaced when William Riley, president of the World's Christian Fundamentals Association, toured the state in 1923 and was followed the next year by William Jennings Bryan. A former U.S. secretary of state and three-time Democratic presidential candidate, Bryan spoke in Nashville on the subject "Is the Bible True?" and "flayed" Darwin before a cheering crowd of thousands. The speech was so popular that it was reprinted in huge numbers and distributed to legislators when the 1925 General Assembly opened.

The speech hit its mark. On January 20, 1925, Senator John A. Shelton of Savannah delighted fundamentalists throughout the state when he proposed a bill to "prohibit the teaching of evolution in public schools." The next day, John Butler, a member of both the House of Representatives and the Primitive Baptist Church of Macon County, proposed a bill in that body designed to prohibit any public school teacher from teaching "any theory that denies the story of the Divine Creation of man as taught in the Bible, and to teach instead that man descended from a lower order of animals." The proposal became House Bill 185 and stipulated that conviction carried a fine of one hundred dollars to five hundred dollars.[21]

Passions were aroused on both sides of the issue. Richard Owensby, a Methodist pastor in Columbia, insisted that the legislators were "making monkeys of themselves" and suggested that "a state legislature could not possibly devise a more asinine performance." Legislators fired back in a House resolution that the minister's remarks were "unfair, unchristianlike and unpatri-

7.2 *Clarence Darrow.* The lead attorney for the American Civil Liberties Union in the infamous 1925 Scopes Trial in Dayton, Tennessee, Clarence Darrow was one of the most colorful characters of the early twentieth century. Though he ultimately lost his case in court, the issue of Darwinian evolution has reverberated throughout modern times.

otic."[22] They further suggested that "if the Protestant ministers in the state . . . would confine themselves . . . to preaching . . . the gospel . . . as found in the Bible . . . there would be no need for public demand for legislation on the teaching of evolution." Eastern journalists also joined the fray, as did university faculties and ministers of every denomination in the state. Despite the opposition, the measure passed, and nine days later, Governor Austin Peay—himself a Baptist who had stated, "It is the opinion of many that an abandonment of the old fashioned faith and belief in the Bible is our trouble to a large degree," and then affirmed that he agreed—signed the bill into law.[23]

Opponents of the law itched for an opportunity to challenge it in court, but none more than Roger Baldwin's American Civil Liberties Union. Planning to employ the "manipulated test case" strategy that would become its trademark, the ACLU searched for a teacher to act as plaintiff in a showcase trial. Baldwin found his mark in John T. Scopes of Dayton, Tennessee. On the last day of the school year, Scopes talked about evolution in the classroom, was reported, and later indicted by a grand jury. The trial that took place in July of 1925 captured worldwide attention, which was exactly what it was designed to do. Leading the prosecution was none other than William Jennings Bryan, and the champion for the defense was Clarence Darrow, the most famous attorney in the country.

The trial began on July 13, and for eight days Dayton felt like the center of the universe. More than two million words were telegraphed from the small town during the trial, and Dayton was a dateline for almost every major newspaper in the country. Scopes was found guilty and fined one hundred dollars, but the real victory of the trial came when Clarence Darrow played the role of "village atheist" in cross-examining a bumbling Bryan. Darrow succeeded in making Bryan appear like a reactionary hayseed, according to many observers, and the press suggested that the entire anti-evolution movement had become a laughingstock in the eyes of the nation.[24] A week after the trial, Bryan collapsed and died, many suspected, from the heat and stress of the trial. His admirers established Dayton's William Jennings Bryan University in his honor, a school dedicated to the "fundamentals" of Christianity. Amazingly, forty-two years after the trial, in 1967, the Tennessee evolution law was quietly repealed with little attention from the press or the public.

THE CRASH AND THE WAR

The ridicule engendered by the Scopes trial aside, the Roaring Twenties proved to be a decade of unprecedented prosperity and expansion for most churches. America experienced a postwar economic boom that made easy money available on a scale too tempting for most churches to pass up. Congregations initiated new building projects in huge numbers. In fact, more "beautiful and costly churches were built during the ten years after 1920 than at any time in our history." Nationwide, the value of church buildings doubled from 1916 to 1926. "In the year 1921, the amount spent for new church structures was $60,000,000; in 1926 the amount expended for the same purpose was $284,000,000."[25] The churches in Tennessee were not immune from the impulse to build. The Methodists built ten new churches in Hamilton County alone, one of which, Centenary Methodist, cost over three hundred thousand dollars. Chattanooga had as many new church buildings as Hamilton County but its Centenary Methodist required more than $425,000 to build. Churches ran up huge debts and all with the encouragement of local bankers. The Methodists alone showed an aggregate debt of $798,188.[26] Even before the unanticipated financial disaster of the Great Depression, Tennessee churches occasionally defaulted on excessive debts accumulated by unwise building committees and overly confident pastors.

When the "crash" of 1929 slammed into the nation, Tennessee churches entered a tragic period of decline. From just before the Great Depression until 1936, total church membership declined approximately 10 percent. The denominations bore this loss unevenly. The Christian Church lost only 4 percent while the Churches of Christ suffered a 31-percent reduction in membership. Baptists and Methodists, the two largest bodies in the state, lost 16 percent each. Reversing the trend was the Presbyterian Church, US with an increase of 11 percent, the only denomination to report a gain. Overall, there were two thousand fewer congregations in Tennessee at the end of the Depression than there were at the beginning.[27]

The loss of membership meant loss of income for most churches, and the repercussions were often heart-rending. Ministers' salaries were usually the first hit. Among Methodists, the average salary before the crash was a stellar $2,300. Afterwards, even the goal of $125 a month was unreachable. Baptists suffered the least because many of their pastors worked at nonreligious jobs and fulfilled their ministries after work hours. Still, when the wage-earning job was dissolved in the spiraling economy, hard times set in for both the minister's family and the congregation. Often parsonages had to be sold to pay off debts. Ministers were frequently released from their positions when congregations could no longer support them. Many churches closed as a result, and this so discouraged candidates for ministry that in the Tennessee Conference of the Methodist Church, for example, "only one person presented himself for candidacy in 1932; for each of the next two years, there was no one."[28]

Denominational ministries and institutions suffered as well. Support for missions dropped dramatically. The Baptists, who gave over $336,000 to world missions in 1927 could manage only $163,000 in 1933. Hampered not only by decreased support of the local church but also by the loss of funds in failed banks, denominational colleges and publishing houses suffered as well. Fundraisers found it "simply impossible to secure pledges when most people were finding it difficult to keep the wolf away from the door."[29] Schools closed as a result, most notably Centenary College in Cleveland and Burrit College at Spencer, the only Christian Church college in Tennessee. Publishing houses suffered from can-

7.3 *Christian Publishing.* Ever since the first half of the nineteenth century, Nashville had been a center for denominational printing and publishing. By the middle of the twentieth century the industry had grown to monumental proportions—the national publishing arms of the Methodists, the National Baptists, the Southern Baptists, the Churches of Christ, and the Nazarenes, as well as several large nondenominational companies, were by that time all located in Nashville. Today the city boasts the largest network of Christian suppliers, distributors, packagers, and promoters in the world.

7.4 *Mercy Ministry.* From the end of the nineteenth century to the middle of the twentieth century innumerable ministries to the poor and disenfranchised were established in Tennessee by the state's churches and private associations. Everything from rescue missions for the homeless and trade schools for the poor to development centers for underprivileged communities and crisis pregnancy centers thrust the historic care and compassion of the faith community into the modern world.

celed subscriptions and stayed afloat only by incurring debts that took years to pay off.

While the older denominations suffered horribly in the years after the crash, Pentecostal-Holiness churches thrived. Their model was Aimee Semple McPherson's Angelus Temple in California. McPherson's ministry astounded the church world during the Depression. While other churches foundered, the more than five thousand members of Angelus Temple met the physical needs of some 1.5 million poor, organized numerous community service projects, sponsored huge musical productions, led a movement against organized crime, and even joined the struggle for higher wages for police and firefighters. Meanwhile, McPherson started a denomination, founded a Bible college, sponsored numerous other women in ministry, and even traveled to Europe in the late thirties to confirm her concerns about Hitler, Mussolini, and Stalin. Her successes—and her bold preaching about Spirit baptism, tongues, and healing—raised the sights of Pentecostal-Holiness ministers throughout the nation. In Tennessee, the Pentecostal segment of the body of Christ grew dramatically. The Church of the Nazarene doubled its membership, one branch of the Assemblies of God increased threefold, and the Church of God grew to four times its size at the beginning of the Great Depression.[30]

On the morning of December 7, 1941, churchgoers throughout the state returned home to news of the Japanese bombing of Pearl Harbor. None of them could have imagined how much the resulting war would change their lives. Not only did some 9,613 Tennesseans give their lives in the war, but when military authorities examined the topography of Tennessee and found it similar to that of Germany, thousands of soldiers began flooding to the state to train for battle in Europe. Camps and airfields grew up almost overnight, towns struggled to accommodate the influx, and the bigger cities bulged with soldiers on leave. The culture of Tennessee spread with these soldiers first overseas and then throughout the nation, paving the way for the postwar popularity of country music. Tennessee was never the same again.

Oddly, the war years gave the churches a chance to recover from the devastations of the thirties. Increased attendance and wartime prosperity meant that churches could pay their debts. The number of candidates for ministry climbed, and Tennessee sent more than three hundred of its clergymen to serve as military chaplains. Missions came to a virtual halt, and travel restrictions hindered denominational activity, but overall the condition of the churches of Tennessee was vastly improved by war's end.[31] Decades later church leaders realized how strategic this time of strengthening was, for the world the churches of Tennessee were about to confront in the decades after the war was to be like nothing men had faced before in the history of American Christianity.

PROFILE 7 *A Pilgrim's Progress*

We are what we read, not merely what we eat.

Robert Penn Warrren

*T*he great Victorian preacher, Charles Spurgeon, read it more than a hundred times. E. M. Bounds kept a copy by his bedside and read from it every night before retiring. Stonewall Jackson kept a copy in his knapsack throughout his Southern campaigns. D. L. Moody and Ira Sankey shared favorite passages from it each night before beginning their evangelistic services. C. S. Lewis believed it was "a literary and spiritual masterpiece."[1] It is *A Pilgrim's Progress*, a fanciful allegory of the Christian life written primarily from a prison cell midway through the seventeenth century by John Bunyan.

The son of a poor brazier, born in 1628, Bunyan was a witness to some of the momentous events in English history: the civil war, the regicide of King Charles, the Cromwell protectorate, the great fire, the restoration of the monarchy, and the great Puritan purge. Those were tumultuous days that left an indelible mark of change upon the souls of both men and nations. Bunyan was no exception. After a dramatic adult conversion, he immersed himself in the life and work of a very small, nonconformist congregation.

After the demise of the protectorate and the subsequent restoration of the monarchy in 1660, persecutions were launched against all but established state churches. It was widely understood that religion was the primary influence on the nature and structure of culture. Preaching was considered to be a powerful force that had both eternal and temporal dimensions. Thus, they rightly predicted that a faithful exposition of the Bible would have immediate political as well as spiritual ramifications. Conservative Anglicans and Puritans thought that allowing unauthorized or unlearned men to preach would undermine the whole social fabric. They comprehended only too well the dynamic significance of worldviews.

7.5 *A Pilgrim's Progress*. The vivid imagery of *A Pilgrim's Progress*, the classic Christian allegory written by John Bunyan, left a deep impression on the faith communities of Tennessee—as it did in so many other places around the world. Many of Tennessee's greatest spiritual leaders have made its themes of redemption and hope against all odds their steadfast anchor in times of distress.

For nearly a decade, Bunyan had served as an unordained itinerant preacher and had frequently taken part in highly visible theological controversies. It was natural that the new governmental restrictions would focus on him. Thus, he was arrested for preaching to "unlawful assemblies and conventicles."[2]

The judges who were assigned to his case were all ex-royalists, most of whom had suffered fines, sequestrations, and even imprisonments during the Interregnum. They threatened and cajoled Bunyan, but he was unshakable. Finally, in frustration, they told him they would not release him from custody until he was willing to foreswear his illegal preaching. And so he was sent to the county *gaol*, where he spent twelve long years—recalcitrant to the end.

During his time in prison, he began writing the allegorical *A Pilgrim's Progress* as a sort of spiritual autobiography. It describes his temptations, trials, and frustrations as well as his determination to risk all for the sake of spiritual integrity and the quest for righteousness.

Like *The Canterbury Tales, Don Quixote, The Aeneid*, and even *The Inferno*, the story is written as a travelogue: the hero embarks on a great adventure and must face many perils along the way until at long last he arrives at his destination or meets his destiny. In this case, brave Christian leaves his secure home in search of the Celestial City. Along the way he meets a vast array of characters, both good and evil, in an alternating landscape of dizzying deprivation and dazzling debauchery.

Around the rough framework of Christian's salvation and early discipleship is an episodic series of fearsome and fast-paced battles, discoveries, and encounters. He guides us through Puritan England's fairs, fields, and foibles. And he uncovers its competing psychologies, passions, and perplexities. But perhaps the liveliest and the most stimulating scenes in the story are the characterizations of hypocrites and villains that Christian meets along the way. His loving, insightful, and exact observations of human nature are fiercely disarming and satirically precise. Bunyan's great universal appeal is this unerring genius in capturing the essence of everyday eccentricities.

Not surprisingly, A Pilgrim's Progress is the best-selling religious book in American history save the Bible,[3] and it recurs time and again in the documentary narratives of Tennessee's most influential religious leaders.[4] Much of that popularity has been manifested in the twentieth century when so many believers began to see themselves as pilgrims wandering in the wilderness of this poor, fallen world. Indeed, as Vanderbilt University professor John Crowe Ransom once asserted, "It may well be a more applicable parable for modernity than for any other period previous."[5] Indeed, it may.

8

The Changing Face of Faith

Modernism is in essence a provincialism, since it declines to look beyond the horizon of the moment. . . . The great mission of the wise is to take the longer view.

Richard Weaver

It was 1949, and the young preacher was caught in a crisis of the soul. He had preached the Bible, taught it as truth, and commended it to others as the Word of God. But now he was unsure. Doubt etched its way into his soul, and he was haunted by the distance of his own heart from what he preached to others. *Is the Bible really the word of God?* he wondered. *Can I be confident that the Scriptures are true?* The uncertainty gnawed at him. He told friends that he had lost his "peace," that he had "terrific pain at the base of his skull" that doctors could not explain and that was probably due to the tension of his agonizing battle with doubt.[1] What was he to do? What was his life, his ministry, if he couldn't reclaim his faith in the Bible?

One evening, hurt and confused, he wandered into the still August air, half in thought and half in prayer: "Lord, what shall I do? What shall be the direction of my life?" He knew he had reached a crossroads of faith, a defining moment in the path of his destiny. He walked, prayed, and anguished. Then, suddenly came the moment of resolve:

> I went back and I got my Bible, and I went out in the moonlight. And I got to a stump and put the Bible on the stump, and I knelt down, and I said, "Oh, God; I cannot prove certain things. I cannot

answer some of the questions . . . people are raising, but I accept this Book by faith as the Word of God."[2]

The dark clouds of disbelief parted. Later he remembered, "I had a tremendous sense of God's presence. I had a great peace that the decision I had made was right." The next morning he told a friend he had been "filled afresh with the Spirit of God." So it was that Billy Graham embraced again the message of his calling.[3]

It came just in time, too, for in a matter of days he was scheduled to begin the largest evangelistic crusade of his life, in the city of Los Angeles. Already he sensed the hand of God on the Los Angeles meetings, for he told friends "God had given him a vision that something unusual was going to happen." And it did. Thousands flocked to the "Canvas Cathedral" at the corner of Washington Boulevard and Hill Street, celebrities confessed Christ, and Graham preached in a "divine flow" he had never known

8.1 *Billy Graham.* Voice of faith and forgiveness, symbol of integrity and purity, friend of presidents and prime ministers, and bastion of strength and determination, Billy Graham is without a doubt the greatest evangelist of the twentieth century. His impact upon communities, churches, and nations has been and continues to be inestimable.

before. Then it happened, and just as the crusade seemed to be winding down: For reasons no one could explain, media magnate William Randolph Hearst telegraphed a two-word message to his newspapers throughout the country. It read simply, "Puff Graham." These two words changed Billy Graham's life. Media all over the world picked up the story of the Los Angeles meetings, and Graham's face soon graced the covers of *Time, Newsweek,* and *Life* magazines. His moment had come. The spiritually hungry souls of postwar America now looked to him and to the faith he had himself only recently recovered.[4]

*S*TREAMS OF *R*ENEWAL

Billy Graham's ministry arose at a time when the cause of Christ was hotly challenged by a uniquely American brand of postwar materialism. During the Great Depression and the Second World War, some sixteen years in all, Americans had suffered economic upheaval, the shortages and rationing of wartime, and all the sacrifices necessary to "help our boys overseas." When the war ended, though, America emerged as the richest and most powerful nation in the world, and her citizens wanted only to make up for the years of deprivation and lack. Almost overnight, the American dream ceased being a matter of making the world safe for democracy and became instead a pursuit of the good life—a quest for personal peace and affluence complete with a little house in the suburbs, a fast car with huge fins, and all the technology necessary for a life of comfort and diversion. The values of the age were symbolized by the film clips of a June Cleaver-type housewife proudly displaying her "modern, space-age" kitchen. The promise of a strong and noble society was somehow reflected in every shiny appliance.

But many in this age of triumphant materialism found themselves unable to answer the aching emptiness in their souls. They wanted something beyond the American vision of earthly success, something beyond the comfortable values of a secular democracy.

To the extent the churches reflected these values they offered no alternatives to the idols of the age, and the young, particularly, often found that the Christianity so loosely woven through their parents' lives was too inconsistently external to reach their deepening spiritual hunger.

This unfulfilling brand of cultural Christianity reached its zenith in what some called "The Age of Eisenhower." "Ike" was the kind of President who movingly proclaimed a national day of prayer and fasting, only to spend it playing golf. He had once inconsistently declared, "Our government makes no sense unless it is founded on a deeply felt religious faith—and I don't care what it is."[5] Though it was during the Eisenhower administration that the phrase "In God We Trust" became the national motto, the place for God in the American psyche was tragically small. Many Americans in the forties and fifties hungered for an invisible reality they could not define and to which many in their generation seemed completely oblivious. Already the discontent of the young was expressing itself in the writings of Allen Ginsberg and Jack Kerouac, in films like Marlon Brando's *The Wild One*, and in an innocuous philosophy of nonconformity called "Beat."

As though in anticipation of this spiritual desolation, revivals began on dozens of American college campuses in the late forties. But in 1949 Bethel Bible College in St. Paul, Northern Baptist Theological Seminary, and North Park College were each jolted by campus revivals. Then the floodgates broke, and in 1950 simultaneous revivals began all over the country: at Wheaton College near Chicago and throughout the Northwest—at Simpson Bible Institute, Pacific Northwest, the University of Washington, Seattle Pacific College, and Northwest Bible College. These were followed closely by awakenings at Baylor University in Texas and Houghton College in New York. Then, a particularly powerful revival took place on the campus of Asbury College in Wilmore, Kentucky. Students from the school took the message of a spiritual awakening to churches and campuses around the country, sparking still more stirrings. Soon it became obvious that this was not just an American phenomenon, for reports of revival were heard from as far away as Colegio Presbiteriana and São Paulo Theological Seminary in Brazil and South India Bible Institute.

All of these revivals were similar in style and impact to the extraordinary events that began at the little Pentecostal school, Lee College of Cleveland, Tennessee, on February 12. Students assembled in the College auditorium that Sunday evening expecting the usual weekly service. But before the evening speaker had a chance to read his text, "the Holy Ghost took charge." Spontaneous messages from the audience moved hearts, and the altar began to fill. "The service became a prayer meeting in which five or six were saved, and five or six received the Holy Ghost. It was wonderful to see the manifestations of the Spirit of God." The next day classes began as scheduled but when a 10 A.M. chapel started, the "glory" returned. The meeting lasted all day and continued almost unceasingly for eight days.[6] No one seemed concerned that classes weren't meeting. At one point the denomination's General Overseer tried to call the school, but the operator reported, "I cannot get Lee College. I have not been able to get them all afternoon." He was later told that the dormitories and academic buildings were empty, but the school's auditorium was full of students and faculty "tarrying before God all day and late into the night."[7]

The president of the college, J. Stewart Brinsfield, was caught up in the excitement as well: "I have been associated with the Church of God for more than 27 years and have witnessed many great revivals, but the meetings here have been the greatest in all my experience." The delighted president continued:

> The gifts of the Spirit have been manifested among faculty and students alike. To date practically every unsaved person has been brought to Christ. There were confessions of sin and disobedience. We had no way to count the numbers who received the Holy Ghost, because people from the outside were in our meetings. The whole auditorium was an altar. People sought God by the hundreds. This really was a mass revival.[8]

The faculty and the students gushed their enthusiasm. Nina Driggers, a teacher at the school, wrote, "This mighty power of the Holy Ghost was so great in the auditorium that it seemed to be a powerful magnet, pulling the people in. One could feel His divine presence as he entered the door.["]9 One of the many students whose lives were changed exclaimed, "There is no speech nor language that could fully describe it. It was the glory of God come down to earth."[10]

These college revivals had an impact far beyond the immediate experience of the students. Since many of the awakenings took place in denominational schools, renewal movements swept through churches and left in their wake not only revived believers but a new youthfulness that made the churches more relevant to their age. In addition, many students on the campuses during seasons of revival later entered the ministry themselves and continued to teach the values of prayer, repentance, sacrifice, and spiritual power in churches throughout the world. It was also significant that revivals, normally associated with the American frontier or the urban poor, took place on university campuses, the very centers of learning and sophistication. During these experiences, learned professors and award-winning scientists knelt next to kitchen help and students of every background to receive the grace of their God, and the very idea of revivals was forever changed. The breadth of the revivals contributed to a unity in the Christian community it had seldom known before. The renewal knew no barriers. Churches of every theological and cultural orientation were affected, and soon believers who would never have dreamed of crossing denominational lines found themselves singing choruses hand in hand with Christians of vastly different backgrounds from their own. It simply didn't matter any more.

Many observers at the time thought they saw the beginnings of a nationwide renewal. There was the ministry of Billy Graham, there were the campus revivals, and soon after there was the rise of the "healing evangelist." As historian David Edwin Harrell Jr. has written,

A generation grew up that would never forget the ecstatic years from 1947 to 1952, years filled with long nights of tense anticipation, a hypnotic yearning for the Holy Spirit, and stunning miracles for the believers performed by God's anointed revivalists.[11]

Standing firmly in the flow of the early Pentecostal revivals, ministers like William Branham, Oral Roberts, Jack Coe, A. A. Allen, and Gordon Lindsay began preaching crusades throughout the country, stressing miracles as a sign of God's love for men. Huge crowds flocked to the tents and meeting halls where these men spoke. Casting off the traditional Pentecostal suspicions of the media, this new generation of evangelists used magazines and television to reach the lost. Oral Roberts even made movies, and some ministers produced record albums of their services. This use of media crossed cultural and denominational lines, and raised even further "a vision of the unity of God's people."[12] Many saw this drawing together of Christians as a sign of the end times, as a preparation for the close of the age.

The early Pentecostal revivals, the campus revivals of the forties and fifties, and the ministries of the healing evangelists all appeared to merge in the astounding Charismatic movement that began in the early sixties. Before this time, the baptism of the Holy Spirit and the experience of tongues were largely enjoyed by Pentecostals, who were roundly criticized by the mainline denominations. The lines were clearly drawn, with those who claimed to have experienced the "blessings of Pentecost" perceived as extremists on the fringe of the body of Christ. This changed with the Charismatic movement, however. In 1960 Dennis Bennett, an Episcopalian priest in Van Nuys, California, claimed to have been "filled with the Holy Spirit" and to have "spoken in other tongues." Hundreds of his parishioners followed their priest in the experience. On April 3, 1960, Passion Sunday, Bennett shared his experience with his entire parish, but such opposition arose that by the third service of the day he felt obliged to announce his resignation. The story of Bennett's experience was carried in *Newsweek* and *Time* under such headlines as "Rector and a Rumpus" and "Speaking in Tongues."[13] This publicity generated the sense of a new movement, of an unusual combination of Pentecost with the historic churches, and soon what had been experienced largely in Pentecostal churches was occurring in nearly every denomination. The Charismatic movement would become one of the largest renewal movements in church history, jumping denominational lines, sweeping virtually every nation of the world, and prompting enormous change even in churches that rejected the "baptism of the Holy Spirit" as a feature of modern Christianity.

These streams of renewal wound their way through Tennessee as well as the rest of the country. Immediately following the war and building on the religious surge of the war years, Tennessee's churches joined the prayer breakfasts, revivals, and the "Back to God" campaigns then rushing through the rest of the country. The ministry of Billy Graham had tremendous influence among the conservative denominations of the state, particularly in Baptist churches, just as the college revivals reached onto the campuses of Tennessee colleges and universities. Beyond the revival at Lee College, for example, students from the Asbury awakening visited colleges farther south and launched entire movements of repentance, revival, and evangelism. The healing evangelists also found strong support from Tennessee's Pentecostal denominations and leaders, and the Charismatic movement washed through the state, simultaneously creating great joy and deep divisions. It was a time of growth and renewal for many Tennessee churches, for as Herman Norton observed, "Church attendance soared, membership increased, contributions mounted, and unprecedented sums were designated for new buildings, primarily in the suburban areas."[14]

*9*HE *6*HANGING *9*PIRITUAL *9*ANDSCAPE

But there were problems as well. Despite all the signs of blessing and increase, Christians who took stock of the treatment of blacks in the state found much that was inconsistent with the gospel of Jesus. Methodists and Southern Baptists spoke out against "the injustice and indignities against blacks" and pledged to "conquer all prejudice" and teach children that "prejudice is unchristian."[15] In 1965 the Ku Klux Klan celebrated the largest

8.2 *Martin Luther King Jr.* The articulate and courageous leader of the Civil Rights Movement, Dr. Matin Luther King Jr. utilized the Bible's emphasis on justice, freedom, and equality to utterly transform the political climate in the United States. His tragic 1968 assassination in Memphis only reinforced the magnitude of his contribution to the entire nation.

membership in its history, and not until a Remington 30.06 was fired at a black man standing on the balcony of Memphis's Lorraine Motel on April 4, 1968, did many Tennesseans wake up to how deep the problem of hatred really was. The man was Dr. Martin Luther King Jr., and the death of the Civil Rights movement's nonviolent leader was attended by the worst outburst of arson, looting, and criminal activity in the nation's history. The churches, confronted by the tragedy of their own silence, began to understand just how much their healing influence was needed and yet how much the problems of society had taken root in their own pews.

In fact, the entire decade of the sixties sounded a wake-up call for the churches of the nation. For many, the first indication of a crisis was when the U.S. Supreme Court ruled in the 1962 *Engel v. Vitale* case that thirty-nine million school children could not start their day with prayer. Tennessee pastors were outraged, and many warned that the ruling was a clear sign of the loss of Christian consensus in the nation. A second alarm sounded with the dramatic influx of non-Christian religions. Eastern religious influences, already on the rise since the experience of American soldiers in the Far East during the Second World War, were given a boost through the pop-music group, the Beatles, and their friendship with guru Maharishi Mahesh Yogi.[16] Hindu organizations in India sent "missionaries" to the west, and often eastern spiritual practices were repackaged for western consumption, as in the case of transcendental meditation, which was even permitted in public schools and universities. New and shocking religions arose, like Anton Szandor LaVey's Church of Satan, and while more mainstream groups looked on in horror, these alternative religions gained thousands of disciples. And the use of hallucinogenic drugs, encouraged by the Beatles and their friend, Timothy Leary,[17] left thousands open to the suggestion of a wide variety of religious influences, particularly those like Krishna Consciousness, which stressed mindlessness and a distancing of self from the material world. Tennessee's Christians were outraged when John Lennon claimed that the Beatles were "more popular than Jesus Christ,"[18] but by the end of the decade it seemed only too apparent that Lennon may have been right.

The decades following the sixties found the churches living in the spiritual wake of that tumultuous time. True, renewal movements continued, growing out of the Charismatic movement, the campus revivals, and the desire of noncharismatic denominations to keep pace. Churches put more power in the hands of the people, mimicked secular art in their presentations, and allowed alternative dress, music, and even language. Choruses often supplanted hymns, guitars replaced organs, and youth groups often listened to the nominally religious lyrics of "He Ain't Heavy, He's My Brother" and "Morning Has Broken." Musicals like *Jesus Christ Superstar* and *Godspell* tried to make the gospel fit a contemporary mold, and some sermons portrayed Jesus as something of a "flower child" from another era. But the fundamental issues the sixties raised had yet to be solved. Churches continued to wrestle

over birth control, abortion, and the many fruits of the sexual revolution. They found themselves battling in spiritual matters the
same apathy and cynicism that Watergate produced in politics.
And there was the nagging reality that despite the rhetoric, blacks
and minorities were no better off. Quite simply, the streams of
renewal coursing through the churches didn't seem to be having
much impact on society as a whole.

Some Christians were not surprised, then, to find a religion of
racial backlash moving into the black community. The popularity
of Malcolm X, whose murder in 1965 made him a martyr in the
black community, brought the teachings of the Nation of Islam to
national attention, and many blacks, convinced that Christianity
was a white man's religion, converted to the teachings of Malcolm
X's mentor, Elijah Muhammad. Nation of Islam doctrines include
the idea that white men are devils who were grafted from the black
man some 6,700 years ago by a scientist named Yakub. The black
man, who is "original man" according to the Nation of Islam,
should separate himself from the white man and take comfort in
the fact that God, who is also black, will seek "retribution" against
all whites for the way they have treated blacks. Elijah
Muhammad's teaching was first established in Tennessee in the
1960s when a man called Shabazz opened a storefront mosque on
Nashville's Jefferson Street. In time, Elijah Muhammad himself
sent Earl X. King to Nashville "with nothing but his teaching" to
establish the faith and draw together the black community. New
converts took "Fruit of Islam" classes and, like all Nation of Islam
devotees, attended three meetings a week, recited prayers five
times a day, ate one meal a day, abstained from drugs, alcohol,
tobacco, gambling, illicit sex, and "soul food," meaning primarily
pork.[19] The movement has grown slowly since then, but with the
recent popularity of Louis Farrakhan and his Million Man March
on Washington, D.C., the more than eight thousand members of
the Nation of Islam in Tennessee expect their numbers to increase
dramatically.[20]

The churches of Tennessee found it easy to see in movements
like the Nation of Islam a reflection of their own decline. Despite
the renewal movements that continued to inspire churches

throughout the state, new religions were unquestionably drawing adherents in increasing numbers. Part of the reason for this shift was the tide of immigrants and refugees that began entering the state in the seventies. Some were dislocated by wars and political upheavals in their homelands. Others simply came for the educational and work opportunities. But most of them brought their religions with them, and this produced an undeniable change in the spiritual complexion of the state.

Buddhism was bolstered in the state by Laotian, Vietnamese, Burmese, Thai, Cambodian, Korean, and Filipino immigrants, many of whom settled in Murfreesboro and built numerous temples around the state. Some of the temples were even built in former church buildings, as with the North Edgefield Baptist Church in Nashville, which became a Buddhist temple in 1981.

Christian churches often didn't know how to respond to the new religions. In 1982 a Nashville organization of congregations officially welcomed the new Buddhist Temple "in the name of God and country."[21] One Nashville Temple even shared a parking lot with the True Christian Pentecostal Witnesses, a black Pentecostal church whose style stood in stark contrast to the contemplative manner of the monks next door. The Buddhists in Tennessee today are encouraged and often represented by Win Myint, professor of mathematics at Tennessee State University. Born in Burma, Myint is the founder of several Buddhist temples and a member of the board of the Nashville chapter of the National Conference of Christians and Jews.

Traditional Islam has grown in Tennessee in the last three decades through similar patterns of immigration. Though some of those increasing Islamic numbers are native blacks who, like Malcolm X in his later years, embraced traditional Islam rather than the version taught by Elijah Muhammad, immigrants from the Middle East have accounted for most of the new strength of Islam in Tennessee. Among the largest Islamic groups in the state are the Kurds, who, after the Gulf War of the early nineties and Saddam Hussein's *Anfal* against them, flooded into Tennessee. Nashville now ranks with Dallas and San Diego as one of the three U.S. centers of Kurdish life. Together, Muslims in Tennessee outnumber Episcopalians and are part of a rapidly growing national movement. Several cities in the state have Islamic centers, and in 1991, Ilyas Muhammad became the first Muslim ever to pray at a daily session of the State Senate. Muhammad, whose appearance was meant to placate those who complained of "too much Jesus," first chanted his prayer in Arabic, and then repeated it in English.[22]

Hinduism has also made its appearance in Tennessee in recent years. In fact, one of the most unique buildings in all of Tennessee is the *Sri Ganesha Temple* that stands on Old Hickory Boulevard in the Bellevue section of Nashville. Built by master artisans brought specially from India for the project, the Temple displays three-thousand-pound idols and elephant gods quite foreign to the Christian churches in the surrounding area. When the Temple opened on Labor Day in 1991, more than a thousand Hindu families gathered from Middle Tennessee alone, with another two thousand joining them from surrounding areas. At a cost of $2.5 million, the twenty-one-thousand-square-foot building was clearly built in the belief that Hinduism will continue growing in Tennessee as it has throughout the United States.[23]

Still other movements and faiths have grown rapidly in recent decades and have challenged the hold of orthodox Christianity. Mormonism, which is the fastest growing religion in America, grew from 19,500 members statewide in 1986 to more than twenty-three thousand in 1991. This pace of growth has increased rapidly and new "stakes," or groups of congregations, have multiplied throughout the state. An average of nearly fifty Tennesseans now join the church each month with most of these converts coming from the pews of mainline Christian denominations.[24] The Jehovah's Witnesses have also spread their influence in recent years. In 1989, a series of conferences in Nashville drew more than eleven thousand Jehovah's Witnesses from throughout Tennessee, Kentucky, and northern Alabama. Most orthodox Christians regard the Witnesses as a cult since they use the Bible to defend their heterodox beliefs,[25] but the energetic evangelistic techniques of the faith pull many thousands of converts a year from churches throughout the nation. The New Age movement, with its unusual combination of eastern mysticism, liberal politics, and

8.3 *The Mega-Church.* A trend at the end of the twentieth century toward gargantuanism in almost everything—from shopping malls and office buildings to entertainment parks to hotel complexes—also affected the church. Huge congregations with memberships numbering in the thousands began to replace the little neighborhood parish. In Tennessee a number of these institutions—such as Belview Baptist in Memphis, Two Rivers Baptist in Nashville, and Christ Community Church in Franklin—began to dominate the leadership scene in extraordinary ways.

holistic medicine, has also taken firm root in Tennessee's cities and particularly near the universities and intellectual centers. In Nashville, where Athena stands in her replica Parthenon, it is not uncommon to see bumper stickers that proclaim "The Goddess is alive and magic is afoot," clearly a statement of what some scholars have called the "new paganism of the nineties."[26]

Despite their loss of monopoly on the state's spiritual life, though, the Christian churches have remained a vital force throughout the state. In recent years, while some denominations have suffered loss, many churches have achieved stunning growth. The lines have also become blurred between renewal and mainline churches, so that it is not uncommon to find churches from traditional denominations experimenting with entertainment-oriented "seeker services," contemporary music, and even many of the practices of healing, worship, and spontaneous prayer normally associated with the Pentecostal or Charismatic experience. A new unity among churches has also been evident in recent years. Marches for Jesus, city-wide prayer meetings, racial reconciliation events, pro-life rallies, and united worship meetings have spurred hopes for revival and the dissolving of cultural and religious barriers that often come with revival. Christians have also discovered a fresh unity in the midst of battle. As biblical values have increasingly come under attack in a variety of arenas, believers have unified to oppose abortion, to build alternative schools, to oppose a state lottery, to uphold zoning laws, to bolster conservative political coalitions, and even to fight age-old battles over evolution in the public schools and the public posting of the Ten Commandments once again.

8.4 *Contemporary Christian Music.* Beginning with the Jesus Movement in California during the sixties and seventies, contemporary Christian music quickly became one of the most popular forms of entertainment in the country. Combining contemporary musical styles—like rock, folk, pop, rap, soul, and country—with gospel-oriented lyrics, the new form of expression grew into a vast industry. And the industry found its home in Nashville: Music City.

Yet the heat generated by some of these debates and the rapidly expanding number of religions in the state only confirm what history reveals: that religion has become the main business of Tennessee. As Professor Paul Conkin of Vanderbilt has written, "If one tries to calculate the role of Tennesseans or Tennessee institutions upon American culture as a whole, one has to begin with this religious impact."[27] The denominations of Tennessee now have more than thirty-two million members in the United States and millions more abroad. They comprise one-third of the Protestant membership in the United States and half of all black church membership.[28] Aside from this, "Tennessee leads the world in religious publishing."[29] Clearly, the history of Tennessee—and some would say its destiny—is tied to the power of faith and to the business of proclaiming that faith throughout the nations of the world.

PROFILE 8   *The Agrarians*

---

*Every region has an indigenous literary voice; ours is a reflection of
both our conflicted past and our obfuscated future.*

M. E. Bradford

In 1930 an extraordinary group of Southern historians, poets,
political scientists, novelists, and journalists published a prophetic
collection of essays warning against the looming loss of the original vision of American life—a vision of both liberty and virtue.
Including contributions from such literary luminaries as Robert
Penn Warren, Donald Davidson, Allen Tate, Andrew Nelson Lytle,
Stark Young, and John Crowe Ransom, the symposium, entitled *I'll
Take My Stand*, poignantly voiced the complex intellectual, emotional, and spiritual consternation of men standing on the
precipice of catastrophic cultural change.

The men were alarmed by what they perceived to be a steady
erosion of the rule of law in modern American life. They feared
that, as was the case in the eighteenth century, our liberties were
facing a fearsome challenge from the almost omnipresent and
omnipotent forces of monolithic government. They said:

> When we remember the high expectations held universally by the
> founders of the American union for a more perfect order of society,
> and then consider the state of life in this country today, it is bound
> to appear to reasonable people that somehow the experiment has
> very nearly proved abortive, and that in some way a great com-
> monwealth has gone wrong.[1]

They were determined to warn against the creeping dehu-
manization of an ideological secularism that they believed was
already beginning to dominate American life:

> There is evidently a kind of thinking that rejoices in setting up a
> social objective which has no relation to the individual. Men are pre-
> pared to sacrifice their private dignity and happiness to an abstract

social ideal, and without asking whether the social ideal produces the welfare of any individual man whatsoever.[2]

They knew full well that they were essentially standing against the rising tide of industrial modernity, nevertheless they were convinced that ordinary Americans would ultimately hear and heed their warning—otherwise, the nation would collapse under the weight of corruption:

> If the republic is to live up to its ideals and be what it could be, then it had better look long and hard at what it is in danger of becoming and devote conscious effort to controlling its own destiny, rather than continuing to drift along on the tides of economic materialism.[3]

Clearly, the contributors were old-line conservatives in the tradition of Americans like John Adams, Fisher Ames, John Randolph, and John Calhoun. But they also drew on the rich European conservative tradition of men like Edmund Burke, Walter Bagehot, Robert Southey, and Thomas Macaulay. As political scientist Louis Rubin later commented:

> They were writing squarely out of an old American tradition, one that we find imbedded in American thought almost from the earliest days. The tradition was that of the pastorale; they were invoking the humane virtues of a simpler, more elemental, non-acquisitive existence, as a needed rebuke to the acquisitive, essentially materialistic compulsions of a society that from the outset was very much engaged in seeking wealth, power, and plenty on a continent whose prolific natural resources and vast acres of usable land, forests, and rivers were there for the taking.[4]

Short-term pessimists but long-term optimists, they believed that eventually a grassroots movement would restore the principles of the rule of law and that the American dream could be preserved for future generations. Though they were not economists or sociologists or activists, their vision was a comprehensive blueprint for a genuinely principle-based conservative renewal.

Thus, they believed in an extremely limited form of government and took a dim view of government intervention. They went so far as to assert that communities should "ask practically nothing of the federal government in domestic legislation." Further, they believed that this limited governmental structure should be predicated primarily on the tenets of "local self-government" and "decentralization."⁵

8.5 *The Agrarians.* In 1980 four of the surviving Agrarians met at a reunion at Vanderbilt University in Nashville. From left to right they are: Robert Penn Warren, Andrew Nelson Lytle, Lyle Lanier, and Cleanth Brooks. Though their impact was minimized by critics throughout their lives, their influence is actually stronger today than ever before.

They were not minimalists or libertarians. Instead they were realists who envisioned a society which called "only for enough government to prevent men from injuring one another." It was by its very nature, a "non-ideological" and "*laissez faire* society." It was an "individualistic society" that "only asked to be let alone."⁶

Not surprisingly then, the contributors to the symposium opposed the idea that "the government should set up an economic super organization, which in turn would become the government."[10] They regarded socialism, democratic liberalism, communism, and republican cooperationism with equal disdain. In fact, they professed an ingrained "suspicion of all schemes that propose to coerce our people to their alleged benefit."[7]

They believed that it was necessary "to employ a certain skepticism even at the expense of the Cult of Science, and to say it is an Americanism, which looks innocent and disinterested, but really is not either." They were not resistant to technological progress so much as they were resistant to the crass and inhuman humanism that often accompanies industrial advance. They believed that "a way of life that omits or de-emphasizes the more spiritual side of existence is necessarily disastrous to all phases of life."[8]

Clearly then, the men who contributed to *I'll Take My Stand* believed that society ought to be defined by its moral and cultural values. They yearned for return to that early American ethic of freedom and liberty that was "for the most part stable, religious, and agrarian; where the goodness of life was measured by a scale of values having little to do with material values."[9]

In essence, they believed in humanizing the scale of modern life: "restoring such practices as manners, conversation, hospitality, sympathy, family life, romantic love—the social exchanges which reveal and develop sensibility in human affairs." They believed in a "realistic, stable, and hereditable life." Thus, they favored continuity and tradition over change for the sake of change: "The past is always a rebuke to the present; it's a better rebuke than any dream of the future. It's a better rebuke because you can see what some of the costs were, what frail virtues were achieved in the past by frail men."[10]

After all, they said, "Affections, and long memories, attach to the ancient bowers of life in the provinces; but they will not attach to what is always changing."[11]

Although they believed that all of these foundational truths were "self-evident" in the sense that they are written on the fleshly tablet of every man's heart, they were not so idealistic as to believe that the truths would be universally accepted.[12] In fact, they knew that such reasoning would inevitably be a stumbling block to some and mere foolishness to others.[13] All too often men suppress reality in one way, shape, or form.

As a matter of fact, though *I'll Take My Stand* caused quite a stir when it was first released, very few critics gave it much chance of actually affecting the course of events or the destiny of the nation. It was assumed that "the wheels of progress could not possibly be redirected." The contributors were chided for their "naiveté," "impracticality," and "idealism." They were written off as "merely nostalgic," "hopelessly utopian," and "enthusiasts for an epochal past that can never again be recaptured."[14]

For some fifty years it looked as if the critics might be right. The course of the twentieth century appeared to be a stern rebuke to the basic principles of the symposium. Like the English Distributists and the Continental Christian Democrats, with whom they shared so many basic presuppositions, the contributors seemed tragically out of step with the times.

But now all that has changed. Recent turns of events have vindicated their emphasis on less government, lower taxes, family values, minimal regulation, and localism. Their innate distrust of professional politicians, propagandizing media, and commercial tomfoolery have suddenly been translated by a spontaneous grassroots advent into populist megatrends. The fulfillment of their improbable prophetic caveat is even now unfolding as we race toward the end of the century.

Appendix 1

Tennessee Historical Markers

*T*hroughout the state of Tennessee, there are a number of obvious reminders of the strategic role religion has played in the life and history of the state: the historical markers alongside our roadways and outside our most cherished monuments. The following is a selected list of those markers—bounteous evidence of our great spiritual legacy.[1]

1 A 51 Acuff Chapel, (US 11 W) Sullivan Co., 10 miles west of Bristol

Established in 1786, this was the first Methodist Episcopal Church to be erected on Tennessee soil. Bishop Francis Asbury preached here often. A ten-day revival held here by Reverend John A. Granade began the Great Revival of 1780-81. Reverend Francis Acuff was a convert at the Granade meeting.

1 A 35 Taylor's Meeting House, (US 11 W) Sullivan Co., 1.5 miles southwest of Blountville

The Presbyterian Church established here in 1773 is probably the first church of any denomination to be established within the borders of Tennessee. It was also used as a fort, and school was held here on Sundays, in pioneer times.

1 B 17 New Providence Church, (US 11 W) Hawkins Co., at road junction in Stony Point about 6.5 miles west of Church Hill

One half mile west is this Presbyterian Church, established in Carter's Valley in 1780 by Reverend Charles Cummings and Reverend Samuel Doak. It was moved to its present location in 1815. A cemetery is at the old site.

1 E 45 Washington Presbyterian Church, (US 11 W) Knox County at intersection with Ellistown Road (south of Skaggston)

This church was founded in 1802. In its cemetery are buried early settlers and Revolutionary War veterans, including Colonel

John Sawyers, William Roberts, Samuel Crawford, and Simon Harris. The last, a former fifer in the 2nd Virginia Regiment at the age of 12, came here in 1817 and built a log house, still standing, about .5 mile north of the church.

1 E 38 First Presbyterian Church, Knox Co., in Knoxville, in churchyard of 1st Pres. Church

Founded 1792, with James White, John Adair, and George McNutt as founding elders. White, who gave the ground for the church, is buried here, as are Samuel Carrick, first pastor and president of Blount College (now the University of Tennessee), William Blount, governor of the Southwest Territory, and many other prominent pioneers.

2 E 22 The Trail of Tears, (US 70 S) Cannon Co., about 100 yards east of junction with route 53

In the valley to the south, the part of the Cherokee Nation that took part in the enforced overland migration to Indian Territory rested for about three weeks in 1839. About 15,000 persons of various ages took part in the march. Several who died while here were buried in this area.

3 A 78 Downtown Presbyterian Church, Davidson Co., Nashville, at corner 5th Ave. and Church St.

From 1814 to 1955 this was the site of the First Presbyterian Church. President Andrew Jackson was received into the church in 1838. James K. Polk was inaugurated governor here in 1839. The building designed in the Egyptian style by William Strickland, architect of the state capitol, was dedicated in 1851. When the First Church moved, the Downtown Church was organized.

3 A 74 Holy Rosary Cathedral, Davidson Co., Nashville, on northeast slope of Capitol Hill

Near here in 1820 the first Catholic Church in Tennessee was built by Irish Catholic workers then building a bridge over the Cumberland River. In 1830 a brick structure known as Holy Rosary Cathedral succeeded the frame building. Here Bishop R. P. Miles, first bishop of Tennessee, was installed Oct. 15, 1838. When St.

Mary's Cathedral was built in 1847, Holy Rosary Church became St. John's Hospital and Orphanage. The site was sold to the state in 1857.

3 E 8 Birth of a Church, (US 70) Dickson Co., about 25 yards west of Montgomery Bell Park entrance

1.1 miles southwest is a restoration of the log cabin in which Finis Ewing, Samuel King, and Samuel McAdow organized the Cumberland Presbyterian Church on Feb. 4, 1810. The congregation was made up of secedent members of the Presbyterian Church and others in the area.

3 E 11 The Old Log House, Dickson Co., at site of birthplace of Cumberland Presbyterian Church (Montgomery Bell Park)

Replica of the home of Reverend Samuel McAdow where he, together with Reverend Finis Ewing and Reverend Samuel King, founded the Cumberland Presbyterian Church on Feb. 4, 1810. Outgrowth of the Great Revival of 1800, the new denomination rose to minister to the spiritual needs of a pioneer people who turned from the doctrine of predestination to embrace the "whosoever will" gospel of the new church. "Cumberland" was for this Cumberland region; "Presbyterian" described the form of government.

4 A 14 Hollowrock Church, (US 70) Carroll Co., near Bruceton

Founded in 1822, this Primitive Baptist Church has been in constant use. It holds an annual foot-washing ceremony the first Sunday in May, which is attended by communicants and witnesses from many parts of this and neighboring states.

4 D 31 Lane College, Madison Co., in Jackson, opposite main gate of college

Founded in 1882 by the Colored Methodist Episcopal Church of America as a high school under the direction of Bishop Isaac Lane, with his daughter as principal. It became Lane Institute in 1883. Its first president, Reverend T. F. Saunders, served from 1887 to 1903. It received its present name in 1895.

4 E 11 Trinity in the Fields, (US 70) Tipton Co., northeast of Mason 2.5 miles north

This chapel of the Protestant Episcopal Church was built on land given by Maj. William Taylor in 1847, replacing St. Andrews, established 1834, burned 1845. Trinity's first rector was the Reverend James W. Rogers. Descendants of the original communicants make an annual pilgrimage here each Trinity Sunday.

4 E 52 First Methodist Church, Shelby Co., in Memphis, corner of 2nd Ave. and Poplar St.

Organized in 1826, the first building was of frame, with split-log benches, built 1832. A new building was erected in 1845. During Federal occupation, a minister detailed by the Union commander occupied the pulpit. It was later closed temporarily by yellow fever; otherwise it has operated continuously since its foundation. The present building was completed in 1892.

1 A 57 Salem Church, Washington Co., Rt. 34 (US 11 E) at junction of road with Washington College Marker

Organized in 1780 by Reverend Samuel Doak. Here, the first Tuesday in August 1785, was formed Abington Presbytery with Doak as moderator. This first presbytery on Tennessee soil was taken from Hanover Presbytery; it included churches south of New River and west of the Appalachian Mountains. Members were Hezekiah Balch, Charles Cummings, Samuel Houston, Adam Rankin, and David Rice.

1 C 27 Ebenezer, (US 11 E) Greene Co., at crossroads in Chuckey

1.5 miles south an early Methodist society in Tennessee was organized in 1790. The family of Henry Earnest, who settled here in 1779, comprised four-fifths of the membership. The annual convention of the Western Conference was held here in 1795. Stone Dam Campground was nearby.

1 C 26 New Hope Meeting, (US 11 E) Greene Co., 1.5 miles west of crossroads in Chuckey

About 2 miles north, beside Ripley Creek, this Quaker Meeting was organized on Feb. 28, 1795, by settlers from Pennsylvania and North Carolina. Among its founders were

Samuel Ellis, clerk; Samuel Frazier, recorder; Benjamin Iddings, Ellis Ellis, Elihu Swain, and Joseph Thornburg, overseers; Daniel Bonine and George Haworth, overseers of the poor.

1 B 28 Bent Creek Church, (US 11 E) Hamblen Co., in Whitesburg, opposite present First Baptist Church

This Baptist church is successor to the church established about one mile southwest by Elder Tidence Lane and Elder William Murphy in 1785. A cemetery is near the original church site, which stood on the Old Stage Road from Abingdon to Knoxville. This road, made by immigrant pioneers, followed game and Indian trails.

1 A 24 Buffalo Ridge Church, (US 23) Washington Co., 3.15 miles north of junction with Route 34 (US 11 E) 5.0 miles

This pioneer Baptist Church, established in 1779 by the Reverend Tidence Lane, was the first Baptist Church on Tennessee soil. The church itself has been moved to Gray's Station; the cemetery remains. Here is buried the Reverend Jonathan Mulkey, 1752-1824, who was its second pastor.

1 A 55 Providence Church, (State 81) Washington Co., south of Fall Branch

4 miles southwest, this Presbyterian church was organized in 1780 by Reverend Samuel Doak. Hanover Presbytery met here Aug. 20, 1783, with Samuel Doak, Charles Cummings, and Hezekiah Balch present. On Aug. 21, Reverend Sam Houston was ordained with Doak as moderator. The first Presbyterian minister to be ordained in Tennessee, he later returned to Virginia.

1 A 59 Cherokee Church, Holston Baptist Association, Washington Co., Rt. 81, at road junction 4.5 miles south of Jonesboro

This Baptist church was organized the first Saturday in September, 1783. Here, the fourth Saturday in October, 1786, Holston Association was organized with Tidence Lane as moderator and William Murphy as clerk. Seven churches were represented. This was the first Baptist Association in Tennessee.

1 D 10 Big Spring Church, (US 25 E) Claiborne Co., about 8 miles southeast of Tazewell

This Baptist Church is one of the oldest church buildings in Tennessee. Drew Harrell hewed the logs and assisted the Reverend Tidence Lane in erecting the building in the winter of 1795-96. Lane is buried near Whitesburg, Tennessee.

1 C 4 Shiloh Church, (US 441) Sevier Co., 1 mile north of bridge over Pigeon River

In 1802 Methodist Bishop Francis Asbury preached in the home of Mitchel Porter, Revolutionary War veteran, who lived two miles north of here. In 1808 Asbury returned to Sevier County and preached in the newly built log chapel located 400 yards west of here. Shiloh Cemetery grew up around this chapel.

1 C 14 Forks of Little Pigeon Church, (US 441) Sevier Co., in Sevierville

100 yards northeast, this Baptist Church, established 1789, was reportedly the first of any denomination in Sevier Co. Spencer Clack, a Revolutionary War veteran, was the first church clerk; Richard Wood was the first pastor until his death in 1831. The church has moved to a new location; the old cemetery remains.

1 E 46 New Providence Church, Blount Co., in Maryville, at corner of Cates and Broadway

This Presbyterian Church was founded in 1786 by Reverend Archibald Scott of Virginia. In 1792 Reverend Gideon Blackburn built a log church here; the stones in the present wall are from a church that replaced it in 1829; the brick church replaced it in 1858. In its cemetery, which was closed to burials in 1905, are 13 known veterans of the Revolutionary War and War of 1812.

1 E 19 Eusebia Church, (US 411) Blount Co., 6.1 miles east of bridge over Little River

Early settlers coming down the Great War & Trading Path in 1784-85 camped here; it was the scene of their first death and burial. In 1786 the Reverend Archibald Scott of Virginia organized a Presbyterian congregation in the area; the church was built near where the cemetery had been started.

1 E 17 Baker's Creek Church, (US 129) Blount Co., 12 miles south of Maryville

This Presbyterian Church was established in 1796. Its first pastor was the Reverend Gideon Blackburn, who served an extensive circuit in the area. Elizabeth Paxton Houston, mother of Sam Houston, is buried here.

2 B 23 The Scopes Trial, (US 27) Rhea Co., in Dayton, in courthouse yard

Here, July 10-21, 1925, John Thomas Scopes, a county high school teacher, was tried for teaching that man descended from a lower order of animals, in violation of a lately passed state law. William Jennings Bryan assisted the prosecution; Clarence Darrow, Arthur Garfield Hayes, and Dudley Field Malone assisted the defense. Scopes was convicted.

2 A 60 Candy's Creek Cherokee Indian Mission, (State 60) Bradley Co., about 1,000 ft. south of where Rt. 60 crosses Candy's Creek

.4 mile east of this spot stood the Candy's Creek Cherokee Indian Mission school and church, organized by Dr. Samuel A. Worcester and other ministers from the Brainerd Mission and accepted by the Union Presbytery in 1824. The first church organized in what is now Bradley County, it was closed in 1838 when the Cherokees were removed to the west.

2 A 55 Brainerd Mission, Hamilton Co., Rt. 2 (US 11), near Brainerd Cemetery

Established 1817 by the American Board of Commissioners for Foreign Missions, it played an important part in the educational development and christianizing of the Cherokee. Brainerd Cemetery contains graves of whites and Indians who died at the Mission, which was discontinued in 1838, at the time of the Cherokee removal.

2 A 56 The University of the South, Hamilton Co., town of Lookout Mountain, on west side of East Brow Rd.

Founded here on July 4, 1857, when its first trustees, representing Episcopal dioceses in ten southern states, met to adopt the plan of Bishop (later Confederate General) Leonidas Polk for a university to be sponsored by the Episcopal Church. Following the colorful ceremony here, a second meeting of the board was held in Montgomery, Alabama, in November 1857, and Sewanee, Tennessee, was chosen as the site.

2 A 47 Spiritualist Camp Ground, Hamilton Co., in Lookout Mountain, at west end of Green St. Bridge

The Natural Bridge is nearby. Near here was also the Natural Bridge Hotel, acquired by the Southern Spiritualists' Association in 1885. Daily meetings, including lectures and private séances, were first held in the hotel, later in an octagonal pavilion, capacity about 500. The most renowned mediums in the country participated. The project was abandoned about 1890.

2 E 5 Old Stone Fort, (US 41) Coffee Co., 1 mile north of Manchester

About .5 mile southwest are remains of a stone fortification and moat of ancient and unknown origin. One theory is that it was built by a party of twelfth-century Welsh voyagers who entered the country via the Gulf of Mexico. Near here also was the capital of the Indian province of Chisca, to which De Soto sent scouts in 1540.

3 D 23 Harpeth Church, (US 431) Williamson Co., 200 yards south of Davidson Co. line

Ground for this Presbyterian church was donated by the five McCutchen brothers, sons of a Revolutionary War veteran to whom it was granted. A log cabin housed it from 1811 to 1836, when the present building was begun. O. B. Hayes was pastor, David Bell and Robert McCutchen were elders, and James McCutchen was secretary.

3 D 51 St. Paul's Episcopal Church, Williamson Co., in Franklin

This "Mother Church of the Diocese of Tennessee" was begun in 1831, four years after its congregation was organized in 1824. Here James H. Otey, its first rector, was elected the first bishop of Tennessee. It was so damaged through use as a Civil War barracks and hospital that it had to be rebuilt in 1869. It is the oldest Episcopal church and congregation in Tennessee, and the oldest

Episcopal church building in continual use west of the Appalachians.

3 D 45 Confederate Cemetery, (US 431) Williamson Co., about 1.5 miles south of Franklin

Following the Battle of Franklin on Nov. 30, 1864, John McGavock, owner of Carnton, collected and buried here the bodies of 1,496 Confederates. The four general officers killed there were interred elsewhere after being brought to the house. Other Confederates were later buried here.

3 D 40 McConnico Meeting House, (State 96) Williamson Co., about 3 miles east of Franklin, near junction with Clovercroft Road

About 100 yards southwest stood the church where Garner McConnico, a pioneer from Lunenburg Co., Virginia, organized a Primitive Baptist congregation about 1799. Destroyed by storm in 1909, the church was rebuilt at its present location on the Liberty Pike, about 3 miles northwest. The old cemetery remains.

3 B 15 Twelve Corner Church, (State 135) Jackson Co., .6 miles north of Putnam Co. line

On a hillock 300 yards from here stood this church, officially named Spring Creek Baptist Church. Organized July 7, 1802, with Samuel Meger and Jacob Cooms as first presbyters and Thomas McBride as moderator. Was the parent church for others established hereabouts. The church site has been moved. The old cemetery remains.

3 G 25 Bethbirei Church, Marshall Co., Rt. 11 (US 31 A) south of junction with Rt. 64

Founded 1810, its organizational sermon was preached by Reverend Samuel Finley on June 10. Descendants of its founders live in the vicinity. Its third pastor, Reverend Thomas Hall, organized in 1815 the Rock Creek Bible Society, which still distributes Scriptures without note or comment.

3 G 24 Church of the Redeemer, (US 41 A) Bedford Co., in Shelbyville, corner of N. Jefferson and E. Lane Streets

This was Lot 44 of the original town plan. A log church was built here in 1815. The Presbyterians used it and built the present church in 1817. In 1856 a Catholic congregation bought the building, selling to the Northern Methodists in 1894. The Methodists sold the building at auction in 1934. The Protestant Episcopal Diocese of Tennessee bought it in 1935 and consecrated it in 1936.

2 E 25 Beersheba Inn, (State 56) Grundy Co., in roadside park at Beersheba Springs .25 mile southeast

In 1837 several log structures were built and later joined together. Later buildings of handmade brick were added. Enlargement to present form was made by Col. John Armfield in 1857. In antebellum days the courtyard was the scene of varied diversions and activities, including missionary services by Episcopal Bishops Otey and Polk.

3 B 29 Beech Cumberland Presbyterian Church, Sumner County, at intersection of new road with 31 E at Jones Lumber Co. in Hendersonville

The first Synod of the Cumberland Presbyterian Church was constituted on Oct. 5, 1813, at the church located 6.4 miles northwest on Long Hollow Pike. The congregation was organized in 1798 by Thomas Craighead. In 1828 the stone building was erected with walls 3 feet thick. William Montgomery, pioneer surveyor for the Federal Government, and John McMurtry, soldier in the Revolutionary War, are buried in the churchyard.

3 D 38 Zion, (State 99) Maury Co., at road junction 3.4 miles west of junction with Route 50

About 1 mile south, in 1807, a Presbyterian colony from South Carolina built a log meeting house and established a community around it. A school soon followed. A brick church was built in 1815, the present structure in 1847. Many descendants of the founders are in the present congregation.

3 D 37 St. John's, (US 43) Maury Co., seven miles south of Columbia

Consecrated Sept. 4, 1842 by James Hervey Otey, first Episcopal Bishop of Tennessee, this church was built by Leonidas Polk, then Missionary Bishop of the Southwest, and his three brothers, George, Lucius, and Rufus, who divided a grant received from their father, Colonel William Polk, of North Carolina. Memorial services are held here on Whitsunday.

4 A 22 Bethel College, (US 79) Carroll Co., in McKenzie, opposite college entrance

Founded as Bethel Seminary at McLemoresville in 1842 by the West Tennessee Synod, Cumberland Presbyterian Church, with Reverend Reuben Burrow, principal. Incorporated in 1847, it became Bethel College in 1850 and moved here in 1872. It was presented to the General Assembly, Cumberland Presbyterian Church, in 1919.

3 C 26 Mount Zion, (State 49) Robertson Co., at junction with Washington Road

The Methodist church nearby was first organized by Jesse Walker in 1798. It first met at the home of Samuel Crockett, a veteran of the Revolutionary War. The first church was built in 1804 on land donated by Crockett and the Reverend Patrick Martin. It was replaced by a second building in 1844 and a third in 1883.

3 C 42 Saint Michael's Mission, Robertson Co., on State Hwy. 49, at intersection of Washington Road 5.3 mi. southwest of Springfield

About 3.5 miles northwest stands the oldest active Catholic church in Tennessee, on land from the Wessyngton estate, dedicated on May 8, 1842. Lumber for the rear addition, built in 1934, came from the Glenraven estate. The tower was added in 1942, the centennial year. During 1864-65 the missioner was the famous Father Abram Ryan, "poet-priest of the Confederacy."

4 A 18 Roan's Creek Church, (State 22) Carroll Co., about 12 miles south of Huntingdon

In July 1825 William Holmes and wife, Levi McWhirter and wife, and Polly Holmes, met in the grove of large oaks directly to the west and organized a Bible school. This was the beginning of this Church of Christ. In early days, camp meetings were held here during the first week in October.

4 E 25 Mt. Carmel Church, (State 59) Tipton Co., about 4 miles south of Covington

Founded in 1834 by James Holmes, a former missionary to the Chickasaw Indians, with the assistance of settlers from Bethany in Iredell County, North Carolina, the first church was built here in 1836, the congregation having previously met in a stable. Besides many prominent pioneers, several Confederate soldiers are buried here.

4 E 15 Immanuel Church, (State 57) Fayette Co., in La Grange

This Protestant Episcopal Church was first established as a mission in 1832, then consecrated in 1843. Reverend Samuel George Litton was its missionary and first rector. It was established by the efforts of Mrs. Mary Hayes Gloster, a widow from Warrenton, North Carolina. Her slaves built it in exact copy of the church of her former home.

Appendix 2

Internet Resources
for Further Study

Compiled by Phil Bennett

Associate Reformed Presbyterian Church
http://www.arpsynod.org/

Barton W. Stone (History of the Christian Church in the West)
http://www.mun.ca/rels/restmov/texts/bstone/
history.html

Center for the Advancement of Paleo-Orthodoxy (Conservative Presbyterianism)
http://capo.org/

Christian Church (Disciples of Christ)
http://www.disciples.org

Church of God (Reaching into the 21st Century)
http://www.mindspring.com/~cog/cog.html

Dissertations Pertaining to the American Restoration Movement
http://www.ag.uiuc.edu/~mcmillan/Restlit/Biblio/
dissert1.html

Great Christian Books (Published Educational and Historical Resources)
http://www.greatchristianbooks.com

Groen Van Prinsterer Institute for History
http://capo.org/vanprinsterer/

History of the Presbyterian Church (USA)
http://www.pcusa.org/pcusa/ch/220/572/00741/bpc3.htm

Judaism and Jewish Resources
hhtp://ursa-major.spdcc.com/home/trb/judaism.html

King's Meadow Study Center (Tennessee Religious Think Tank)
http://capo.org/kmsc/index.htm

Kuyper Institute (Christianity and Politics)
http://capo.org/kuyper/

Methodist Archives and Research Centre
http://rylibweb.man.ac.uk/data1/dg/text/method.html

Orthodox Presbyterianism
http://capo.org/premise/

Presbyterian Church in America
http://www.nol.net/~wqent/pca

Religions of the World
http://www.networx.on.ca/~eaf/religion.htm

Stone-Campbell Restoration Movement Resources
http://www.ag.uiuc.edu/~mcmillan/Restlit/rlindx.html

Tennessee Blue Book
http://www.state.tn.us/sos/blue.htm

Tennessee Tech History Web Site
http://www.tntech.edu/www/acad/hist/history.html

Theology from a Bunch of Dead Guys (Hall of Church History)
http://www.gty.org/~phil/hall.htm

United Methodist Church History
http://www.netins.net/showcase/umsource/umhist.html

Appendix 3

Selected Bibliography

Adair, James. *History of the American Indians.* Johnson City, Tenn.: Watauga Press, 1930.

Adams, Henry. *The United States in 1800.* Ithaca, N.Y.: Cornell University Press, 1960.

Ahlstrom, Sidney. *A Religious History of the American People.* New Haven, Conn.: Yale University Press, 1972.

Bartleman, Frank. *How Pentecost Came to Los Angeles.* Los Angeles, Calif.: Bartleman Press, 1925.

Bennett, Lerone, Jr. *Before the Mayflower: A History of Black America.* Chicago: Johnson Publishing, 1987.

Blassingame, John W. *The Slave Community: Plantation Life in the Antebellum South.* New York: Oxford University Press, 1979.

Brown, John P. *Old Frontiers.* Kingsport, Tenn.: Southern Publishers, 1938.

Brumback, Carl. *Suddenly . . . From Heaven: A History of the Assemblies of God.* Springfield, Mo.: Gospel Publishing House, 1961.

Burnett, J. J. *Sketches of Tennessee's Pioneer Baptist Preachers.* Nashville: Marshall & Bruce, 1919.

Burns, Frank. *Davidson County.* Memphis: Memphis State University Press, 1989.

Cairns, Earle E. *An Endless Line of Splendor.* Wheaton, Ill.: Tyndale House, 1986.

Calhoun, William Gunn. *Samuel Doak 1749-1830.* Washington, Tenn.: Washington College Academy, 1966.

Carter, Cullen T. *Methodism in the Wilderness, 1786-1836.* Nashville: Parthenon Press, 1960.

Cartwright, Peter. *Autobiography of Peter Cartwright.* Nashville, TN: Cokesbury, 1956.

Cleveland, Catherine C. *The Great Revival in the West, 1797-1805.* Chicago: University of Chicago Press, 1916.

Commager, Henry Steele, ed. *Documents of American History.* New York: Appleton Century-Crofts, 1948.

Conn, Charles W. *Like a Mighty River.* Cleveland, TN: Church of God Publishing, 1955.

Cord, Robert L. *Separation of Church and State: Historical Fact and Current Fiction.* New York: Lambeth Press, 1982.

Corlew, Robert E. *Tennessee: A Short History.* Knoxville, Tenn: University of Tennessee Press, 1981.

Davidson, Donald, et al. *I'll Take My Stand.* Baton Rouge, La.: Louisiana State University, 1930.

———. *The Tennessee.* Nashville: J. S. Sanders, 1991.

Dole, Don H. *Nashville in the New South, 1880-1930.* Knoxville, Tenn.: University of Tennessee Press, 1985.

Dorsett, Lyle Wesley. *E. M. Bounds, Man of Prayer.* Grand Rapids: Zondervan Publishing, 1991.

Drake, Benjamin. *Life of Tecumseh.* Salem, Mass.: Ayer Publishers, 1988.

Eckert, Allan W. *A Sorrow in Our Hearts.* New York: Bantam Books, 1992.

Eiland, William U. *Nashville's Mother Church: The History of the Ryman Auditorium.* Old Hickory, Tenn.: Thomas-Parris, 1992.

Fell, Barry. *American B. C.* New York: Pocket Books, 1989.

Fogel, Robert and Stanley Engerman. *Time on the Cross.* Boston: Little, Brown, 1974.

Fuson, Robert H., trans. *The Log of Christopher Columbus.* Camden, N.J.: International Marine Publishing, 1987.

Gee, Donald. *The Pentecostal Movement.* London: Elim Publishing, 1949.

Gibson, Arrell M. *The Chickasaws.* Norman, Okla.: University of Oklahoma Press, 1971.

Gilbert, Bill. *God Gave Us This Country.* New York: Atheneum, 1989.

Gledden, Jonathan. *The Winning of the Frontier.* New York: Barton and Steele, 1957.

Grant, George. *The Last Crusader.* Wheaton, Ill.: Crossway Books, 1992.

Hakluyt, Richard. *The Principal Navigations Voyages Traffiques and Discoveries of the English Nation.* New York: Macmillan, 1904.

Hardeman, Keith. *The Spiritual Awakeners: American Revivalists from Solomon Stoddard to D. L. Moody.* Chicago, Ill.: Moody Press, 1983.

Harrell, David Edwin, Jr. *All Things Are Possible: The Healing and Charismatic Revivals in Modern America.* Bloomington, Ind.: Indiana University Press, 1975.

Harris, Jack. *Freemasonry.* Springdale, Penn.: Whitaker House, 1983.

Jackson, Peter. *The Southern Agrarians.* Nashville: Franklin Publishing, 1955.

Jackson, Thomas Whitehall. *The Native Peoples of America.* New York: Horton and Ammon, 1966.

John, I. G. *Handbook of Methodist Missions.* Nashville: Board of Missions, Methodist Episcopal Church, South, 1893.

Johnson, Charles A. *The Frontier Camp Meeting.* Dallas, Tex.: Southern Methodist University Press, 1955.

Johnson, Mayme Hart. *A Treasury of Tennessee Churches.* Brentwood, Tenn.: JMP Productions, 1986.

Kendrick, Klaude. *The Promise Fulfilled: A History of the Modern Pentecostal Movement.* Springfield, Mo.: Gospel Publishing House, 1961.

Kendall, W. Fred. *A History of the Tennessee Baptist Convention.* Brentwood, Tenn.: Tennessee Baptist Convention, 1974.

Kennedy, Billy. *The Scots-Irish in the Hills of Tennessee.* Londonderry, Tenn.: Causeway Press, 1995.

Lacy, Benjamin Rice, Jr. *Revivals in the Midst of the Years.* Hopewell, Ky.: Royal Publishers, 1968.

Lamon, Lester C. *Blacks in Tennessee, 1791-1970.* Knoxville, Tenn.: University of Tennessee Press, 1981.

Liston, Robert. *Slavery in America: The History of Slavery, Black American Series.* New York: McGraw-Hill, 1970.

Loveland, Anne C. *Southern Evangelicals and the Social Order 1800-1860.* Indianapolis, Ind.: Bobbs-Merrill, 1967.

McDowell, Jason. *The South at War and Peace*. Atlanta: Battle Banner Press, 1978.

McFerrin, James B. *History of Methodism in Tennessee*. Nashville: Southern Methodist Publishing, 1872.

McLoughlin, William G. *Cherokees and Missionaries, 1789-1839*. Norman, Okla.: University of Oklahoma Press, 1995.

————. *The Cherokees and Christianity, 1794-1870*. Athens, Ga.: University of Georgia Press, 1994.

Malone, Bill. *Country Music USA*. Austin, Tex.: University of Texas Press, 1991.

Maury, Timothy. *Tennessee Memories*. Knoxville, Tenn.: Watauga Association Press, 1962.

Mooney, James. *Myths of the Cherokee and Sacred Formulas of the Cherokee*. Nashville: Charles and Randy Elder, 1982.

Murray, Iain H. *Revival and Revivalism*. Carlisle, Penn.: Banner of Truth Trust, 1994.

Nettels, Curtis P. *The Roots of American Civilization*. New York: F. S. Crofts, 1939.

Nickols, John Thomas. *The Pentecostals*. Plainfield, N.J.: Logos International, 1966.

Niebuhr, H. Richard. *The Social Sources of Denominationalism*. New York: Living Age Books, 1957.

Noll, Mark, ed. *Eerdmans Handbook to Christianity in America*. Grand Rapids: William B. Eerdmans, 1983.

Norton, Herman A. *Religion in Tennessee, 1777-1945*. Knoxville, Tenn.: University of Tennessee Press, 1981.

Orr, J. Edwin. *Good News in Bad Times.* Grand Rapids: Zondervan Publishing, 1953.

Pollock, John. *Billy Graham.* Grand Rapids: Zondervan Publishing, 1966.

Posey, Walter Brownlow. *The Presbyterian Church in the Old Southwest, 1778-1838.* Richmond, Va.: John Knox Press, 1952.

Rasnake, J. Samuel. *Stones by the River: A History of the Tennessee District of the Assemblies of God.* Bristol, Tenn.: Westhighlands Church, 1975.

Richardson, James D., ed. *A Compilation of the Messages and Papers of the Presidents, 1789-1897.* Washington, D.C.: Bureau of National Literature, 1897.

Davies-Rodgers, Ellen. *The Romance of the Episcopal Church in West Tennessee.* Memphis: Plantation Press, 1964.

Rogers, John. *The Biography of Elder Barton Warren Stone.* Joplin, Mo.: College Press, 1986.

Roosevelt, Theodore. *The Winning of the West.* New York: G. P. Putnam, 1895.

Ruchames, Louis. *The Abolitionists: A Collection of Their Writings.* New York: G. P. Putnam 1963.

Satz, Ronald N. *Tennessee's Indian Peoples.* Knoxville, Tenn.: University of Tennessee Press, 1979.

Scott, Otto. *The Secret Six: John Brown and the Abolitionist Movement.* Seattle: UncommonBooks, 1979.

Speer, William. *The Great Revival of 1800.* Philadelphia: Presbyterian Board of Publication, 1872.

Stritch, Thomas. *The Catholic Church in Tennessee.* Nashville: Catholic Center, 1987.

Sweet, William Warren. *The Story of Religion in America.* New York: Harper and Row, 1950.

Synan, Vinson. *The Holiness-Pentecostal Movement.* Grand Rapids: William B. Eerdmans, 1971.

Thompson, Ernest Trice. *Presbyterians in the South.* Richmond, Va.: John Knox Press, 1963.

Trelease, Allen W. *White Terror: The Ku Klux Klan Conspiracy and Southern Reconstruction.* Baton Rouge, La.: Louisiana State University Press, 1971.

Weaver, Richard. *Ideas Have Consequences.* Chicago: University of Chicago Press, 1948.

West, Earl Irvin. *The Search for the Ancient Order.* Nashville: Gospel Advocate, 1965.

Weisberger, Bernard A. *They Gathered at the River.* Boston: Little, Brown, 1958.

Wilberforce, William. *Real Christianity.* Portland, Ore.: Multnomah Press, 1982.

Wilkins, Joshua. *Independent Americas.* Nashville: Blamires and Son, 1891.

Williams, Samuel Cole. *Beginnings of West Tennessee.* Johnson City, Tenn.: Watauga Press, 1930.

———. *Dawn of Tennessee Valley and Tennessee History.* Johnson City, TN: Watauga Press, 1937.

Willis, J. Barton. *Pilgrim's Progress: A Literary Investigation.* London: Dillon Masters, 1988.

Wilson, Thomas A. *Church and State in American Jurisprudence.* Nashville: Scholastic Press, 1973.

Wish, Harvey, ed. *Confessions of Nat Turner.* New York: Farrar, Straus, 1964.

Woodward, Grace Steele. *The Cherokees.* Norman, Okla.: University of Oklahoma Press, 1963.

Notes

Illustrations
A. Courtesy of Cumberland Historical Society
B. Courtesy of Tennessee Cultural Library
C. Courtesy of Mt. Olive Christian Archives
D. Courtesy of Whitefield College Library
E. Courtesy of Asbury Center for Evangelism
F. Courtesy of Langston University Library

Acknowledgments
1 Philippians 1:2-6, NKJV

Introduction
1 John D. Williams, *The Theory and Practice of History* (New York: Harper, 1957), vi.
2 Ibid.
3 Ibid.
4 *Macbeth* 5.5
5 J. Williams, *History*, vi.
6 Alister McGrath, *The Christian Theology Reader* (Oxford: Blackwell, 1995), 27.
7 C. S. Lewis, *The Abolition of Man* (New York: Collier Books, 1955), 35.

Chapter 1
1 We use the arrival of the European pioneers as a point of departure for our discussion of Indian religions because until these settlers there was no written record of Indian culture. The Indians were a preliterate people who transmitted their traditions orally. This is not to imply, though, that the Indians had no meaningful history prior to the coming of the settlers—far from it.
2 John P. Brown, *Old Frontiers* (Kingsport, Tenn.: Southern Publishers, Inc., 1938), 14.
3 Donald Davidson, *The Tennessee*, vol. 1 (Nashville: J. S. Sanders & Company, 1991), 42.
4 Ibid.
5 Grace Steele Woodward, *The Cherokees* (Norman, Okla.: Univ. of Oklahoma Press, 1963), 36.
6 Ibid.
7 Ibid., 36-37.
8 Ibid.

9   Ibid., 34.

10   Ibid., 33.

11   Brown, *Old Frontiers*, 26.

12   Davidson, *The Tennessee*, 1:43.

13   Woodward, *The Cherokees*, 34.

14   Davidson, *The Tennessee*, 1:58.

15   Woodward, *The Cherokees*, 34.

16   Davidson, *The Tennessee*, 1:46.

17   Ibid., 1:49.

18   Ibid., 1:52.

19   Ibid., 1:51.

20   James Mooney, *Myths of the Cherokee and Sacred Formulas of the Cherokee* (Nashville: Charles & Randy Elder, Booksellers, 1982), 330-32.

21   William G. McLoughlin, *Cherokees and Missionaries, 1789-1830* (Norman, Okla.: Univ. of Oklahoma Press, 1995), 21.

22   Ibid.

23   Ibid., 22.

24   Ibid.

25   Ibid.

26   Ibid.

27   Ibid.

28   Bill Gilbert, *God Gave Us This Country* (New York: Atheneum, 1989), 39, 38.

29   Benjamin Drake, *Life of Tecumseh* (Salem, Mass.: Ayer Company Publishers, Inc., 1988), 21.

30   Ibid., 9.

31   Allan W. Eckert, *A Sorrow in Our Hearts* (New York: Bantam Books, 1992), 63.

32   Ibid.

33   Drake, *Tecumseh*, 14-15.

34   James Adair, *History of the American Indians* (Johnson City, Tenn.: The Watauga Press, 1930), 5-6.

35   Ibid.

36   Arrell M. Gibson, *The Chickasaws* (Norman, Okla.: University of Oklahoma Press, 1971), 7.

37   Ibid., 8.

38   Ibid., 10.

39   Ibid.

40   Ibid.

41   Ibid.

42   Adair, *American Indians*, 182-83.

43   Gibson, *The Chickasaws*, 11-12.

44 Ibid.
45 Ronald N. Satz, *Tennessee's Indian Peoples* (Knoxville, Tenn.: The Univ. of Tennessee Press, 1979), 56.
46 Curtis P. Nettels, *The Roots of American Civilization* (New York: F. S. Crofts & Co., 1939), 40.
47 Brown, *Old Frontiers*, 34, 46.
48 Ibid., 39.
49 Robert E. Corlew, *Tennessee: A Short History* (Knoxville, Tenn.: The Univ. of Tennessee Press, 1981), 26.
50 Mark Noll, ed., *Eerdmans' Handbook to Christianity in America* (Grand Rapids: William B. Eerdmans, 1983), 13.
51 James H. Landess, *Utopian Dreams* (Atlanta, Ga.: Karell Communications, 1968), 42.

Profile 1
1 Mark Arnold, *Work and Dreams* (New York: Hellicon Press, 1869), 48.
2 Walter Brueggemann, *The Land* (Philadelphia: Fortress Press, 1977), 5.
3 Ibid.

Chapter 2
1 C. S. Lewis, *George MacDonald: An Anthology* (New York: Macmillan, 1946), 16.
2 Barry Fell, *American B. C.* (New York: Pocket Books, 1989), 325.
3 Ibid., 329.
4 Ibid.
5 Ibid.
6 Ibid.
7 Ibid.
8 Richard Hakluyt, *The Principal Navigations Voyages, Traffiques and Discoveries of the English Nation*, vol. 7 (New York: Macmillan, 1904), 134, 135.
9 Davidson, *The Tennessee*, 1:21.
10 Ibid.
11 James Hunter, *A Dance Called America* (Edinburgh, UK: Mainstream, 1994), 42-44.
12 Ibid., 43.
13 Ibid.
14 Ibid.
15 Theodore Roosevelt, *The Winning of the West* (New York: G. P. Putnam's Sons, 1895), 1:139, 1:169.
16 Sidney Ahlstrom, *A Religion of the American People* (New Haven: Yale Univ. Press, 1972), 431.

17 Samuel Cole Williams, *Dawn of Tennessee Valley and Tennessee History* (Johnson City, Tenn.: The Watauga Press, 1937), 209.

18 Ibid.

19 Billy Kennedy, *The Scots-Irish in the Hills of Tennessee* (Londonderry, TN: Causeway Press, 1995), 38.

20 Roosevelt, *Winning of the West*, 1:193.

21 Walter Brownlow Posey, *The Presbyterian Church in the Old Southwest, 1778-1838* (Richmond, Va.: John Knox Press, 1952), 19.

22 Herman A. Norton, *Religion in Tennessee, 1777-1945* (Knoxville, TN: Univ. of Tennessee Press, 1981), 4.

23 John Wilkins, *Independent America* (Nashville, Tenn.: Blamires and Son, 1891), 74.

24 William Gunn Calhoun, comp., *Samuel Doak 1749-1830* (Washington, TN: Washington College Academy, 1966), 7.

25 Roosevelt, *Winning of the West*, 2:222.

26 Ibid.

27 Wilkins, *Independent America*, 12.

28 Kennedy, *Scots-Irish in Tennessee*, 139-40.

29 Ibid.

30 Ibid.

31 Ibid., 141.

32 Ibid.

33 *The Peabody Reflector and Alumni News*, #17.

34 Woodward, *The Cherokees*, 123.

35 Ibid., 125.

36 Norton, *Religion in Tennessee*, 8.

37 Kennedy, *Scots-Irish*, 29.

38 Norton, *Religion in Tennessee*, 9.

39 Wilkins, *Independent America*, 107.

40 Ibid., 109.

41 J. J. Burnett, *Sketches of Tennessee's Pioneer Baptist Preachers* (Nashville: Press of Marshall & Bruce Company, 1919), 319.

42 Norton, *Religion in Tennessee*, 13.

43 Burnett, *Pioneer Baptist Preachers*, 359-364.

44 Ibid., 390.

45 Ibid., 531.

46 Arthur Thomas, *Methodism* (London: Methodist Publishing Centre, 1966), xxi.

47 Ibid.

48 Walter B. Posey, "Bishop Asbury Visits Tennessee, Extracts from His Journal," *Tennessee Historical Quarterly* 15, no. 3 (1958): 258-59.

49 Henry Adams, *The United States in 1800* (Ithaca, N.Y.:Cornell Univ. Press, 1960), 127.

50 Norton, *Religion in Tennessee*, 16.

Profile 2
1 Herman Ruggles, *The Republic of Vermont* (Boston: New England Historical Society, 1966), 64.
2 James Breaux, *The West Florida Parishes* (Baton Rouge: Griffin, Lee, and Thibideaux, 1971), 91.
3 Noel Gerson, *Franklin: America's Lost State* (New York: Collier, 1968).
4 James Buchanan, *The Presbyterian Destiny* (Charlotte, N.C.: Certic Press, 1977), 183.

Chapter 3
1 William Speer, *The Great Revival of 1800* (Philadelphia: Presbyterian Board of Publications, 1872), 13-14.
2 William Warren Sweet, *The Story of Religion in America* (New York: Harper and Row, 1950), 223-25.
3 Ibid.
4 Ibid.
5 Bernard A. Weisberger, *They Gathered at the River* (Boston: Little, Brown & Co., 1958), 3.
6 Franklin Cole, *They Preached Liberty* (Indianapolis, Ind.: Liberty Press, 1951), 111.
7 Ibid., 142.
8 Keith Hardeman, *The Spiritual Awakeners: American Revivalists from Solomon Stoddard to D. L. Moody* (Chicago: Moody Press, 1983), 113.
9 Ibid., 112.
10 Proverbs 29:18, NIV.
11 Norton, *Religion in Tennessee*, 18.
12 John Rogers, *The Biography of Elder Barton Warren Stone* (Joplin, Mo.: College Press Publishing Co., Inc., 1986), 8.
13 Ibid.
14 Ibid.
15 Iain H. Murray, *Revival and Revivalism* (Carlisle, Penn.: The Banner of Truth Trust, 1994), 150.
16 Catherine C. Cleveland, *The Great Revival in the West, 1797-1805* (Chicago: Univ. of Chicago Press, 1916), 40.
17 Ibid.
18 Ibid.
19 Murray, *Revival and Revivalism*, 151.
20 Charles A. Johnson, *The Frontier Camp Meeting* (Dallas: Southern Methodist Univ. Press, 1955), 35.
21 Ibid.
22 Ibid.

23 Ibid.
24 Rogers, *Barton Warren Stone*, 34, 41-42.
25 Ibid.
26 Rogers, *Barton Warren Stone*, 41.
27 Ibid.
28 Ibid.
29 The "anxious bench" was a special seating area reserved for those "under conviction" or those in the throes of "spiritual turmoil."
30 Bill Malone, *Country Music USA* (Austin: Univ. of Texas Press, 1991).
31 Missionary Society of Connecticut, *The Connecticut Evangelical Magazine*, March 1802.
32 Norton, *Religion in Tennessee, 1777-1945*, 22.
33 Ibid.
34 Ibid.
35 Ibid., 25.
36 Ibid.
37 Ibid., 28.
38 Cullen T. Carter, *Methodism in the Wilderness, 1786-1836* (Nashville: The Parthenon Press, 1960), 27-28.
39 Ibid.
40 Norton, *Religion in Tennessee*, 32.
41 Corlew, *A Short History*, 244, 34.
42 Ibid.
43 Benjamin Rice Lacy, Jr., *Revivals in the Midst of the Years* (Hopewell: Royal Publishers, Inc., 1968), 79.
44 Ibid.
45 Norton, *Religion in Tennessee, 1777-1945*, 39.
46 Ibid.
47 Eckert, *A Sorrow in Our Hearts*, 673.
48 Walter Brownlow Posey, "The Earthquake of 1811 and its Influence on Evangelistic Methods in the Churches of the Old South," *Tennessee Historical Magazine* 16: 110.
49 James B. McFerrin, *History of Methodism in Tennessee* (Nashville: Southern Methodist Publishing House, 1872), 263.
50 Peter Cartwright, *Autobiography of Peter Cartwright* (Nashville: Cokesbury, 1956), 206.
51 McFerrin, *Methodism in Tennessee*, 263-64.
52 John W. Tolbert, *Earthquakes: An American Terror* (New York: Ballwine and Kallistos, 1971), 62.
53 McLoughlin, *Cherokees and Missionaries*, 86.

Profile 3

1 Arnold Dallimore, *George Whitefield* (Edinburgh, UK: Banner of Truth, 1980), xxxvii.
2 Carl Vrestead, *Whitefield* (London: Empire Bible Association, 1936), 44.
3 Ibid., 90.
4 Ibid.
5 Dallimore, *George Whitefield*, 136.
6 Vrestead, *Whitefield*, 91.
7 *Christian History*, XII:2.

Chapter 4

1 John 17:21-22, NIV.
2 H. Richard Niebuhr, *The Social Sources of Denominationalism* (New York: Living Age Books, 1957), 187.
3 Norton, *Religion in Tennessee*, 31.
4 Ibid.
5 Ibid.
6 Ibid.
7 Ibid., 32.
8 Ibid.
9 Martin Lewis, *Denominational Statistics, 1805-1975* (Cincinnati: Lewis Research Assoc., 1978), 281.
10 McFerrin, *Methodism in Tennessee*, 260.
11 M. Lewis, *Statistics*, 282.
12 Corlew, *A Short History*, 245.
13 M. Lewis, *Statistics*, 283.
14 Norton, *Religion in Tennessee*, 42.
15 M. Lewis, *Statistics*, 314.
16 Ibid.
17 Ibid.
18 Norton, *Religion in Tennessee*, 53.
19 Ibid.
20 Ellen Davies-Rodgers, *The Romance of the Episcopal Church in West Tennessee* (Memphis: The Plantation Press, 1964), 41.
21 M. Lewis, *Statistics*, 410.
22 Corlew, *A Short History*, 248.
23 Norton, *Religion in Tennessee*, 47-48.
24 Corlew, *A Short History*, 248.
25 Norton, *Religion in Tennessee*, 48.
26 M. Lewis, *Statistics*, 119.
27 Mayme Hart Johnson, *A Treasury of Tennessee Churches* (Brentwood, Tenn.: JMP Productions, 1986), vi.

28 Frank Burns, *Davidson County* (Memphis: Memphis State Univ. Press, 1989), 17-18.

29 Earle E. Cairns, *An Endless Line of Splendor* (Wheaton, Ill.: Tyndale House, 1986), 136.

30 Jack Harris, *Freemasonry* (Springdale, Penn.: Whitaker House, 1983), 126.

31 Norton, *Religion in Tennessee*, 57.

32 William Bradford, *Of Plymouth Plantation* (New York: Alfred Knopf, 1979), 99.

33 Christopher Columbus, *The Log of Christopher Columbus*, trans. by Robert H. Fuson (Camden, N.J.: International Marine Publishing Company, 1987), 120.

34 George Grant, *The Last Crusader* (Wheaton, Ill.: Crossway Books, 1992), 121.

35 Robert L. Cord, *Separation of Church and State: Historical Fact and Current Fiction* (New York: Lambeth Press, 1982), 36-47.

36 James D. Richardson, ed., *A Compilation of the Messages and Papers of the Presidents, 1789-1897*, 2 (Washington, D.C.: Bureau of National Literature, 1897), 981.

37 William G. McLoughlin, *The Cherokees and Christianity, 1794-1870* (Athens: The University of Georgia Press, 1994), 38.

38 McLoughlin, *Cherokees & Missionaries, 1789-1839*, 64-65.

39 McLoughlin, *The Cherokees and Christianity, 1794-1870*, 16.

40 Ibid.

41 Ibid., 28.

42 Ibid., 30.

43 Ibid.

44 Davidson, *The Tennessee*, 1:261.

45 Brown, *Old Frontiers*, 495.

46 Satz, *Tennessee's Indian Peoples*, 85.

47 Davidson, *The Tennessee*, 1:264.

48 Ibid.

49 Ibid.

50 John Ehle, *Trail of Tears* (New York: Anchor Books, 1988), 53.

51 Ibid., 211.

52 McLoughlin, *The Cherokees and Christianity*, 100.

53 Ibid.

54 Ibid.

55 Davidson, *The Tennessee*, 1:274.

56 McLoughlin, *The Cherokees and Christianity*, 104.

57 Ehle, *Trail of Tears*, 291.

58 Brown, *Old Frontiers*, 495.

Profile 4

1   G. K. Chesterton, *Omnibus* (New York: Doran, 1953), 121.

Chapter 5

1   Harvey Wish, ed., "Confessions of Nat Turner," *Slavery in the South* (New York: Farrar, Strauss & Co., 1964), 8-10.

2   William Styron, "Nat Turner," *Encyclopedia Britannica* (New York: Britannica, 1970), 22:413.

3   Thomas Forbes, *Abolitionism* (New York: Portent Press, 1966), 82.

4   Louis Ruchames, *The Abolitionists: A Collection of Their Writings* (New York: G. P. Putnam's Sons, 1963), 31.

5   Lester C. Lamon, *Blacks in Tennessee, 1791-1970* (Knoxville, Tenn.: Univ. of Tennessee Press, 1981), 14.

6   Ernest Trice Thompson, *Presbyterianism in the South, Volume 1: 1607-1861* (Richmond, Va.: John Knox Press, 1963), 535.

7   William Wilberforce, *Real Christianity* (Portland, Ore.: Multnomah Press, 1982).

8   Otto Scott, *The Secret Six: John Brown and the Abolitionist Movement* (Murphrys, Calif.: Uncommon Books, 1979).

9   Chester Forrester Dunham, "The Attitude of the Northern Clergy Toward the South, 1860-1865" (Ph.D. diss., Univ. of Chicago, 1939), 2.

10 Ibid.

11 Thompson, *Presbyterianism in the South*, 1:545.

12 W. Fred Kendall, *A History of the Tennessee Baptist Convention* (Brentwood, Tenn.: Tennessee Baptist Convention, 1974), 101.

13 Garth T. Holden, *The Peculiar Institution* (Los Angeles: Scholastic Press, 1968), 91.

14 Thomas Stritch, *The Catholic Church in Tennessee* (Nashville: The Catholic Center, 1987), 138-39.

15 George Grant, ed., *The Patriot's Handbook* (Nashville: Cumberland House, 1996), 168.

16 Lamon, *Blacks in Tennessee*, 4, 6, 9-10, 16.

17 Corlew, *A Short History*, 209.

18 Robert Fogel and Stanley Engerman, *Time on the Cross* (Boston: Little Brown, 1974).

19 Robert Liston, *Slavery in America: The History of Slavery*, Black American Series (New York: McGraw-Hill, 1970), 70, 35-36, 38.

20 Samuel Cole Williams, *Beginning of West Tennessee* (Johnson City, Tenn.: Watauga Press, 1930), 258.

21 M. Lewis, *Statistics*, 542.

22 John W. Blassingame, *The Slave Community: Plantation Life in the Antebellum South* (New York: Oxford Univ. Press, 1979), 79-80.

23 Anne C. Loveland, *Southern Evangelicals and the Social Order 1800-1860* (Indianapolis, Ind.: Bobbs-Merril Co., 1967), 186-87.
24 Ibid.
25 Alexander MacDonald, *The Uncivil War* (Richmond, Va.: St. Andrews Press, 1953), 19.
26 Ibid.
27 Lleland Marshall, ed., *American Fact Book* (Albany, N.Y.: Fact Factory, 1989), 501.
28 MacDonald, *The Uncivil War*, viii.
29 Herman Norton, *Tennessee Christians* (Nashville: Reed and Co., 1971), 88.
30 Corlew, *A Short History*, 325.
31 Burns, *Davidson County*, 46.
32 Corlew, *A Short History*, 325.
33 MacDonald, *The Uncivil War*, 191-92.
34 G. Clinton Prim, Jr., "Born Again in the Trenches: Revivals in the Army of Tennessee," *Tennessee Historical Quarterly* (fall 1967): 250-272.
35 Ibid.
36 Ibid.
37 Ibid.
38 Ibid.
39 Ibid.
40 Sweet, *Religion in America*, 318.
41 Lyle Wesley Dorsett, *E. M. Bounds, Man of Prayer* (Grand Rapids: Zondervan, 1991), 20-21.
42 Ibid.
43 Ibid.
44 Grant, *Patriot's Handbook*, 331.
45 Cole Bannister, *Lincoln* (Chicago: Lincoln Historical Association, 1964), 142.
46 Henry Steele Commanger, ed., *Documents of American History* (New York: Appleton-Century-Crofts, Inc., 1948), 442-43.

Chapter 6

1   Lerone Bennett, Jr., *Before the Mayflower: A History of Black America* (Chicago: Johnson Publishing, 1987), 211.
2   Louis Washington, *The Black Soldier* (Powder Springs, Ga.: Grotto Press, 1991), 88.
3   Bennett, *Before the Mayflower*, 211-12.
4   I. G. John, *Handbook of Methodist Missions* (Nashville: Board of Missions, Methodist Episcopal Church, South, 1893), 81.
5   M. Lewis, *Statistics*, 427.

6 Antoinette Holsom, *Fighting Prejudice* (Powder Springs, Ga.: Grotto Press, 1989), 4.

7 Allan W. Trelease, *White Terror: The Ku Klux Klan Conspiracy and Southern Reconstruction* (Baton Rouge: Louisiana State Univ. Press, 1971), 3.

8 Bennett, *Before the Mayflower*, 231.

9 Ibid.

10 Corlew, *A Short History*, 338, 419.

11 M. Lewis, *Statistics*, 248.

12 Norton, *Religion in Tennessee*, 76.

13 Murray, *Revival and Revivalism*, 407.

14 Norton, *Religion in Tennessee*, 69.

15 Ibid., 70.

16 Ibid.

17 Earl Irvin West, *The Search for the Ancient Order*, vol. 1 (Nashville: Gospel Advocate Company, 1965), 114-15.

18 Corlew, *A Short History*, 402.

19 Daniel Reid, Robert Linder, Bruce Shelley, Harry Stout, eds., *Dictionary of Christianity in America* (Downers Grove, Ill.: Intervarsity Press, 1990), 1163.

20 Ibid.

21 Don H. Dole, *Nashville in the New South, 1880-1930* (Knoxville: Univ. of Tennessee Press, 1985), 80.

22 Corlew, *A Short History*, 405.

23 Norton, *Religion in Tennessee*, 91.

24 Melvin E. Deiter, "Wesleyan-Holiness Aspects of Pentecostal Origins," Vinson Synan, ed., *Aspects of Pentecostal-Charismatic Origins* (Plainfield, N.J.: Logos International, 1975), 98.

25 Norton, *Religion in Tennessee*, 82.

26 M. Lewis, *Statistics*, 201.

27 Ibid., 202.

28 Kathleen Minnix, "That Memorable Meeting: Sam Jones and the Nashville Revival of 1885," *Tennessee Historical Quarterly* (fall 1989): 151-61.

29 Ibid., 153.

30 Ibid., 152.

31 Ibid.

32 Ibid., 154, 155.

33 Ibid., 156.

34 William U. Eiland, *Nashville's Mother Church: The History of the Ryman Auditorium* (Old Hickory, Tenn.: Thomas-Parris Printing, 1992), 13.

35 Cairns, *Line of Splendor*, 165.

36 Minnix, "That Memorable Meeting," 153.

37 Ibid.

Profile 6
1 Harold Tribble Cole, *The Coming Terror* (New York: Languine, 1936), 23.

Chapter 7
1 Klaude Kendrick, *The Promise Fulfilled: A History of the Modern Pentecostal Movement* (Springfield, Mo.: Gospel Publishing House, 1961), 47.
2 Charles Parham, "The Latter Rain," *The Apostolic Faith* 28 (April 1951): 3.
3 Kendrick, *The Promise Fulfilled*, 55-56.
4 John Thomas Nickols, *The Pentecostals* (Plainfield, N.J.: Logos International, 1966), 31.
5 Kendrick, *The Promise Fulfilled*, 65.
6 Carl Brumback, *Suddenly . . . From Heaven: A History of the Assemblies of God* (Springfield, Ill.: Gospel Publishing House, 1961), 39.
7 "Weird Babel of Tongues," *Los Angeles Times*, 18 April 1906, 1.
8 Donald Gee, *The Pentecostal Movement* (London: Elim Publishing Co, Ltd., 1949), 12.
9 Tolbert, *Earthquakes*, 44-49.
10 Frank Bartleman, *How Pentecost Came to Los Angeles* (Los Angeles: By the author, 1925), 47.
11 Vinson Synan, *The Holiness-Pentecostal Movement* (Grand Rapids: William B. Eerdmans, 1971), 123.
12 J. Samuel Rasnake, *Stones by the River: A History of the Tennessee District of the Assemblies of God* (Bristol, Tenn.: Westhighlands Church, 1975), 38.
13 M. Lewis, *Statistics*, 42.
14 Charles W. Conn, *Like a Mighty River* (Cleveland: Church of God Publishing House, 1955), 42.
15 M. Lewis, *Statistics*, 126.
16 Lamon, *Blacks in Tennessee*, 96.
17 Norton, *Religion in Tennessee*, 81.
18 Ibid., 87.
19 Noll, *Christianity in America*, 378.
20 Ibid.
21 Corlew, *A Short History*, 541.
22 Ibid.
23 Norton, *Religion in Tennessee*, 102.
24 Bryant Colbert, *The Creation Debate* (Dallas, TX: Ex Nihilo Press, 1987), 62.

25 Sweet, *Religion in America*, 413.
26 Ibid.
27 Ibid.
28 Norton, *Religion in Tennessee*, 110.
29 Ibid., 111.
30 M. Lewis, *Statistics*, vi.
31 Norton, *Religion in Tennessee*, 111.

Profile 7
1 J. Barton Willis, *Pilgrim's Progress: A Literary Investigation*, (London: Dillon Masters, 1988), 92.
2 Ibid., 19.
3 Ibid., 3.
4 Ibid., 4-7.
5 Willis, *Pilgrim's Progress: A Literary Investigation*, 92.

Chapter 8
1 John Pollock, *Billy Graham* (Grand Rapids: Zondervan, 1966), 59.
2 Ibid., 53.
3 Ibid., 30.
4 J. Edwin Orr, *Good News in Bad Times* (Grand Rapids: Zondervan, 1953), 154.
5 Ibid.
6 *The Church of God Evangel*, 41:2 (11 March 1950): 16.
7 "Zeno C. Tharp, Assistant General Overseer, Writes," *Church of God Evangel* (4 March 1950): 10.
8 J. Stewart Brinsfield, "Heart Thrilling," *Church of God Evangel* (4 March 1950): 8.
9 "Mrs. Nina Driggers, Teacher, Writes," *Church of God Evangel* (4 March 1950): 10.
10 J. B. Orcutt (of Virginia), "Students Speak," *Church of God Evangel* (4 March 1950): 8, 9.
11 David Edwin Harrell, Jr., *All Things Are Possible: The Healing and Charismatic Revivals in Modern America* (Bloomington: Indiana Univ. Press, 1975), 21.
12 Ibid., 95.
13 Michael Bellisocci, *The Charismatics* (Grand Rapids: Theologos, 1981), 9.
14 Norton, *Religion in Tennessee*, 117.
15 Ibid.
16 James Talbot, *The Beatles: A Generational Fulcrum* (New York: Thomas Eppworth and Sons, 1974), 214-19.
17 Ibid., 221-22.

18 Ibid., 189-90.
19 *The Tennessean Magazine,* 9 July 1972, 6.
20 Norton, *Religion in Tennessee,* 118.
21 *The Nashville Banner,* 16 February 1982.
22 *The Tennessean,* 6 March 1991.
23 *Antithesis Report,* 4 December 1991.
24 Ibid.
25 Ibid.
26 Ibid.
27 Paul Conkin, "Evangelicals, Fugitives, and Hillbillies," *Tennessee Historical Quarterly* 54, no. 3 (fall 1995): 225.
28 M. Lewis, *Statistics,* xi.
29 Conkin, "Evangelicals, Fugitives, and Hillbillies," 225.

Profile 8
1   Donald Davidson, ed., *I'll Take My Stand* (Baton Rouge, La.: Lousiana State Univ., 1930), 201.
2   Ibid., xlvi.
3   Ibid., xx.
4   Ibid., xv.
5   Ibid., 75, 88.
6   Ibid.
7   Ibid., xli, 115.
8   Ibid., xl, xxxiii.
9   Ibid., 29.
10 Ibid., xliii, 5, xxx-xxxi.
11 Ibid.
12 See Romans 1:19-22.
13 See 1 Corinthians 1:23.
14 Peter Jackson, *The Southern Agrarians* (Nashville: Franklin Publishing, 1955), 126, 184, 212.

Appendix 1
1   Reprinted with permission from the Tennessee Historical Commission.

Index

About the Authors

Stephen Mansfield is a Christian leader known for his passionate teaching, strategic vision, and sense of humor. He is currently the senior pastor at Nashville's Belmont Church and has written a number of books on history and leadership, including *Never Give In: The Extraordinary Character of Winston Churchill*. He has just completed a doctorate in literature and philosophy to the great relief of his wife, Patricia, and their two children, Jonathan and Elizabeth.

George Grant is the director of the King's Meadow Study Center, the editor of the *Arx Axiom* newsletter, a regular columnist for *World* and *Table Talk* magazines, the editorial director for Highland Books, and a teaching fellow at the Franklin Classical School. He is the author of more than two dozen books in the areas of history, biography, politics, literature, and social criticisms, as well as hundreds of essays, articles, and columns. He lives on a small farm in Tennessee with his wife, Karen, and their three children, Joel, Joanna, and Jesse.

Printed in the USA
CPSIA information can be obtained
at www.ICGtesting.com
JSHW012037250324
59897JS00013B/91

9 781888 952148